How Silicon Valley Unleashed Techno-feudalism

How Silicon Valley Unleashed Techno-feudalism

The Making of the Digital Economy

Cédric Durand
Translated by David Broder

VERSO
London • New York

This work was published with the help of the French
Ministry of Culture – Centre national du livre
Ouvrage publié avec le concours du Ministère français
chargé de la culture – Centre national du livre

FONDS GÉNÉRAL
DE L'UNIVERSITÉ DE GENÈVE

This English-language edition first published by Verso 2024
Translation © David Broder 2024
First published as *Technoféodalisme: Critique de l'économie numérique*
© Éditions La Découverte 2020

1 3 5 7 9 10 8 6 4 2

Verso
UK: 6 Meard Street, London W1F 0EG
US: 388 Atlantic Avenue, Brooklyn, NY 11217
versobooks.com

Verso is the imprint of New Left Books

ISBN-13: 978-1-80429-438-3
ISBN-13: 978-1-83929-440-6 (UK EBK)
ISBN-13: 978-1-83929-441-3 (US EBK)

British Library Cataloguing in Publication Data
A catalogue record for this book is available from the British Library

Library of Congress Cataloging-in-Publication Data

ANames: Durand, Cédric, author. | Broder, David, translator.
Title: How silicon valley unleashed techno-feudalism : the making of the
    digital economy / Cédric Durand, David Broder.
Other titles: Techno-féodalisme. English
Description: Brooklyn : Verso, 2024. | Includes bibliographical references
    and index.
Identifiers: LCCN 2024016823 (print) | LCCN 2024016824 (ebook) | ISBN
    9781804294383 (hardback) | ISBN 9781804294413 (ebook)
Subjects: LCSH: Electronic commerce. | Capitalism—History—21st century.
Classification: LCC HC79.I55 D87418 2024 (print) | LCC HC79.I55 (ebook) |
    DDC 381/.142—dc23/eng/20240514
LC record available at https://lccn.loc.gov/2024016823
LC ebook record available at https://lccn.loc.gov/2024016824

Typeset in Minion Pro by Hewer Text UK Ltd, Edinburgh
Printed and bound by CPI Group (UK) Ltd, Croydon CR0 4YY

MIX
Paper | Supporting
responsible forestry
FSC
www.fsc.org   FSC® C171272

Contents

Preface to the English-Language Edition

Since the publication of this book in French in 2020, the forces unleashed by the digital world have pursued their transformative work without let-up. This is producing anthropological, semiotic, sociological, economic, and political changes, and – if we think of the ever-denser artificial layer of satellites that surround planet Earth – even geological ones. No dimension of human social being is left unscathed by this powerful reworking of the circulation of information and of the production of knowledge. The mass rollout of ready-made AI tools is the latest frontier in this powerful movement of dis-embedding, re-articulating, and re-embedding knowledge.

How should we make sense of this epochal shift? That is the fundamental question which we here explore from the perspective of critical political economy, following two intertwined lines of argument.

The first is, I suppose, not ever so controversial. Through a genealogical inquiry into this technological revolution, I explore the macrosocio-political aspects of how it is unfolding. Analysing the emergence and deployment of socio-economic discourses on digital technology, I show how political mobilisation has shaped an institutional landscape favourable to businesses and financial investors engaged in the IT sector.

Over recent decades, intellectual enclosures, the deregulation of service and labour markets, and decreasing taxes on capital have given rise to a specific form of digital economy. Driven by the logic of profit-making, it is oriented towards the commodification of traces of life, the replacement of old forms of cultural sociability, and the provision of new anthropogenetic services. As a result, it nurtures a concentration of the gains at the top of the distribution and fuels Big Tech's historically unprecedented concentration of capacities for social control.

In the meantime, behind a puerile enthusiasm for modern gadgetry, the general public and, to a large extent, policymakers are kept in the dark about the origins of this transformative process and the pervasiveness of the changes it brings. Instead of the much-needed democratic debate about the desirable parameters of such technological change, we get a childish flattering of consumer sovereignty, condemning atomised individuals to political inertia while a hurricane is casting asunder the basic parameters of social interaction.

The second thesis is more disputed. Opposing the zealots of the Silicon Valley consensus, which promised a rejuvenation of capitalism through digital capabilities, I explore further the insights of cyberpunk popular culture and of the media theorist McKenzie Wark concerning the regressive tendencies accompanying the new forces of information in late capitalism. The hypothesis is that they contain the potential to alter meaningfully the inner logic of the system itself. This is the significance of *techno-feudalism*, a concept which has flourished in recent years, as critically assessed in a series of articles published in *New Left Review* in 2022. In 2023, the eponymous title of a popular book by Yanis Varoufakis paid an implicit homage to this discussion.

My proposition is based on a twofold reminiscence of *feudal* traits in the age of algorithms that derives from the fact that the rollout of digital technology above all concerns economic coordination – that is, the generic modes of organising social and economic interdependences. From this, it follows that the imperfect but foundational distinction between the economic and the political realms in capitalism is increasingly blurred, a blurriness that was the norm in feudal times. The for-profit curation of news, social relations, and, more generally, scientific and operational knowledge cannot be regarded as a purely economic issue; it entails a political dimension that is increasingly scrutinised but whose inner logic is not necessarily understood. For instance, antitrust attempts to revive competition miss the inherently socio-political dimension of digital coordination and the need for political intervention to deliberately shape the quality of the coordination mechanism. For now, at least in Western countries, public authorities increasingly depend on big tech's infrastructural power in order to fulfil government tasks, in turn further increasing tech giants' political competencies and eroding governments' capacities to rein them in.

Along with this growing overlap of economic and political power in the hands of knowledge operators, investment behaviour is also evolving. The tendency identified here is a slippage: from a logic of investment for production, capable of generating positive economic gains through increased operational efficiency, towards a logic of investment for control dominated by a zero-sum dynamic. The unfolding of predatory relations through a growing disjunction between value production and appropriation would be a second feature reminiscent of feudalism. But here we are ultimately faced with an empirical question of what the threshold is. When appropriation exceeds capitalist exploitation, we will be able to say that the system has mutated – that is, if it has not already done so.

December 2023

Introduction

On 1 March 1990, US Secret Service agents armed with a search warrant broke into Steve Jackson Games – a small company based in Austin, Texas, which designs and publishes role-playing games (RPGs). The officials seized three computers, two laser printers, some floppy disks, and various papers. But their haul also included a manuscript. This was the latest 'GURPS' – Generic Universal RolePlaying System – a product that the company had made its speciality. Entitled 'Cyberpunk', this was a genre toolkit made up of rules, characters, and scenarios that form the building blocks of the universe that players are encouraged to bring to life. Its editor, Loyd Blankenship, had been arrested shortly beforehand for alleged hacking offences. He was also the author of a hacker manifesto published in 1986, and investigators were coming after him. The Bell telecommunications company had noticed that a file mapping the organisation of the 911 emergency system had been copied onto a server named 'Illuminati' that was administered by Blankenship. The judicial proceedings were soon dropped. But the book in question – which authorities described, with no little overstatement, as a 'manual of computer crime' – reaped huge publicity from this episode.[1]

---

1 Jon Peterson, 'Your Cyberpunk Games Are Dangerous/Offworld', boing-boing. net, 8 May 2015; Peter H. Lewis, 'The Executive Computer: Can Invaders Be Stopped

In the 'Economics' section of this text, the idea of techno-feudalism is introduced under the heading 'Corporations':

> As the world becomes tougher, the corporations adapt by becoming tougher themselves, out of necessity. This 'we protect our own' attitude is sometimes called techno-feudalism. Like feudalism, it is a reaction to a chaotic environment, a promise of service and loyalty from the workers in exchange for a promise of support and protection from the corporation ... In an unregulated world, corporations can band together, forming quasi-monopolies where all can maximize profit by reducing consumer choice, and by taking over or eliminating competition that tries to defy their pacts.[2]

Blankenship offers players a cyberpunk dystopia in which there is no counterweight to big business's power. Giant corporations, more powerful than the state, become the dominant forces in society. As a result, the role of the citizen is marginalised in favour of various stakeholders (shareholders, workers, customers, creditors) tied in to these companies. So, the predominant social relationship outlined here is defined by attachment – that is, individuals' dependence upon private companies. Firms have become protectors, islands of stability in a chaotic world. These powerful private monopolies have risen above governments to the point of becoming fiefdoms. The managements of the big firms enjoy a combined political and economic power over the social spaces that they control, and over the individuals who inhabit them.

Of course, this cyberpunk projection from the 1980s did not claim to have any kind of predictive powers. This was just a playful fantasy that might be able to provide us with the keys to understanding the contemporary world. And yet ... just a few decades on, it's hard to avoid

---

but Civil Liberties Upheld?', *New York Times*, 9 September 1990; 'The Top Ten Media Errors about the SJ Games Raid', sjgames.com, 12 October 1994.

2 Loyd Blankenship, *Gurps Cyberpunk: High-Tech Low-Life Roleplaying*, Austin: Steve Jackson Games, 1990, p. 104.

noticing that some of the inklings expressed in this fantasy are highly relevant to our own present.

Firstly, it is undeniable that multinationals have considerably extended their grip over contemporary societies. And it's not just a question of size. With telematics, intellectual property rights, and the centralisation of data, much tighter control is being exerted over territories and individuals.

Secondly, while governments are not retreating from this position per se, there are signs that their hold is weakening relative to large corporations. For example, the effective tax rate for multinationals fell from over 35 per cent in the 1990s to less than 25 per cent in the second half of the 2010s.[3] At the same time, business circles have considerably increased their ability to hold sway over politics, as they have stepped up spending on lobbying and expanded their ever-less-subtle bids for influence, far removed from formal democratic procedures.[4] Democracy, exhausted by its loss of substance, is running out of steam, and the reconfiguration of the electoral field in high-income countries points to the weakening of the liberal political order. Today, this auxiliary of the modern state is faltering under the pressure of yawning inequalities.

As for the world becoming more chaotic, there are various signs that lend credence to this idea. The mounting discussion of ecological collapse brings the cyberpunk dystopia into the present. And one of the possible responses to systemic vulnerabilities is a securitarian agenda designed to contain the threat of social chaos.[5]

3 Rochelle Toplensky, 'Multinationals Pay Lower Taxes Than a Decade Ago', *Financial Times*, 11 March 2018. Various studies focusing on US firms confirm this trend. See Scott D. Dyreng, Michelle Hanlon, Edward L. Maydew, and Jacob R. Thornock, 'Changes in Corporate Effective Tax Rates over the Past 25 Years', *Journal of Financial Economics* 124, no. 3, 2017, pp. 441–63; Thomas Wright and Gabriel Zucman, 'The Exorbitant Tax Privilege', NBER Working Paper, w24983, 2018.

4 Data on official lobbying spending in the United States can be found on opensecrets.org; for the European level, see the website lobbyfacts.eu. Pepper D. Culpepper, *Quiet Politics and Business Power: Corporate Control in Europe and Japan*, Cambridge: Cambridge University Press, 2012.

5 Nick Bostrom, 'The Vulnerable World Hypothesis', *Global Policy* 10, no. 4, 2019.

These considerations do not prove anything. They are mere pointers, echoing the hunch that we are faced with a techno-feudal regression. This offers us a thread to pull on, a lead to delve into, a possible starting point. Nothing more. But a start is already something, if we want to tackle one of the key questions of political economy of our time: What do capitalism and digital technology have to do with each other? How do the profit motive and the fluidity of the digital world interact? Could it be that a change of systemic logic is taking place – but that our vision is so clouded by capitalism's overlapping crises that we haven't seen it clearly yet?

That is the hypothesis explored in this book. It is divided into four chapters. The first chapter is focused on deconstruction. It looks at the genealogy of the narrative that heralds a new golden age of capitalism thanks to digital technology and reveals its aporias. We are truly living in a fantasy world. Since the last years of the twentieth century, Silicon Valley and its start-ups have exerted a magnetic attraction on the political imagination, giving late capitalism the lustre of a mythical youth. But where does this ideology come from? What are its theoretical underpinnings? What are its flaws?

The second chapter looks at the new forms of domination associated with digital technology. How are individual behaviours rooted in virtual territories? How do the logics of algorithmic surveillance relate to the logics of politics and the economy? From the big Californian firms to the Chinese social credit system, we need to take stock of an entirely new social and political substrate.

The third chapter is devoted to the economic consequences of the rise of what economists call intangible assets – immaterial products (software, databases, trademarks, etc.) that are being rolled out far beyond the tech sector. The process of globalisation is reflected in the international dispersal of production processes, which leads to a worldwide competition between territories and workers. Yet there is a counterpoint to this intensification of competition among the subaltern: namely, the powerful dynamics of monopolisation, favouring the multinationals which control the information infrastructure crucial to global value chains. As the tightening of intellectual property rights restricts the use of knowledge to these firms' benefit, the industrialisation of IT processes is fuelling rentier logics of unprecedented power, heralding a new age of monopolies.

Recognising the importance of the socio-economic changes that are at work today, our final chapter considers their implications for capitalism's future. The focus, here, is on the logic of the mode of production as a whole – that is, the political and economic constraints on agents and the dynamics that result. An in-depth discussion of the concept of feudalism brings out the singularities of capitalism and highlights the paradoxical resurgence in contemporary societies of a medieval-style social metabolism: what I call the techno-feudal hypothesis.

1

The Poverty of the Californian Ideology

Unprocedural and prompt to manoeuvre/
Destined to perish like an adventurer

Charles Péguy[1]

Silicon Valley is the nickname for the area south of San Francisco Bay, around the city of San José. It was granted this moniker in the early 1970s, as it became home to a large number of firms manufacturing electronic components from semiconductor materials including silicon. It was here that Intel developed the first microprocessor, and it was here that Steve Wozniak and Steve Jobs created and marketed their first personal computer, Apple I, in 1976. With Stanford University, the venture capital firms on Sand Hill Road, and the Ames Research Center where NASA engineers run their supercomputers, Silicon Valley is also an ecosystem of remarkable synergies between state-of-the-art research, public investment, and private entrepreneurship – for decades attracting researchers and engineers from around the world. This exceptional dynamism has made this small corner of California, with a population of

---

1 Charles Péguy, 'La tapisserie de sainte Geneviève et de Jeanne d'Arc', in *Morceaux choisis de poésie*, Paris: Gallimard, 1962, p. 91.

under 4 million, the headquarters of an impressive array of tech giants including Alphabet, Facebook, Hewlett Packard, Netflix, and Tesla. The area also has the highest concentration of millionaires and billionaires anywhere in the United States.[2]

This singular location is a paradise for start-ups. Truly a hero of our time, the start-up's success lies in its direct combination of two powerful aspirations: on the one hand, full professional autonomy, promising the satisfaction of a working life that is both intense and fun; and on the other, a collective adventure, which though bearing a high chance of failure also offers the distant lustre of invention and fortune that makes this risk-taking worthwhile. Hail those who arrive at the magic formula: the right idea, at the right time, able to spread like wildfire! The saga of the US West Coast start-ups that have become tech giants feeds this all-conquering imaginary of audacity, open-mindedness, and opportunity.

These were the signifiers that the freshly elected French president Emmanuel Macron sought to mobilise on 15 June 2017, when he posted an English-language tweet proclaiming, 'I want France to be a start-up nation. A nation that thinks and moves like a start-up.' Taken literally, the president's tweet is rather odd: for the concept of a start-up nation is an oxymoron.[3] Don't nine out of ten start-ups end up in failure? Indeed, this is their very principle: launching an innovative company requires accepting a high probability of failure in exchange for the possibility of a huge return on investment. While such risks can be taken on by individual rich entrepreneurs, large wealth funds, big companies via their subsidiaries, or indeed states via special programmes, it would be economically foolish to commit an entire country to this path. But now it would seem that

---

2 Elizabeth Eaves, 'America's Greediest Cities', *Forbes*, 3 December 2007.

3 The concept 'start-up nation' is borrowed from the book of the same name dedicated to the Israeli tech sector, which seeks to explain why this young country of only 7.1 million inhabitants had sixty-three companies listed on the NASDAQ (the main US stock exchange for the high-tech sector) at the beginning of 2009, more than any other foreign country. The authors, close to neo-con circles, argue that compulsory military service and immigration are the two major reasons for Israel's success, on account of the risk-taking spirit they instil. See Dan Senor and Saul Singer, *Start-Up Nation: The Story of Israel's Economic Miracle*, New York: Twelve, 2009; Gal Beckerman, 'Senor Decides against Running for Senate, Citing Family and Business', *The Forward*, 24 March 2010.

spawning a handful of unicorns – start-ups that achieve a $1 billion valuation within ten years – has become the ultimate in ambitious policy.

This new way of casting economic policy issues in entrepreneurial terms is the result of changing doctrines in policy-making circles. The post–World War II Keynesian consensus emphasised the role of fiscal policy in achieving full employment. The Washington consensus of the late twentieth century was obsessed with using deregulation, privatisation, and austerity to make markets work optimally. Since the 2000s, the Silicon Valley consensus has focused on the aims of innovation and entrepreneurship in the knowledge economy.[4] It takes the Californian experience as its model and mobilises the powerful imaginary which this model brings with it. Yet the socio-economic changes which this experience has prompted are leading to a series of paradoxical results – undermining the fundamental postulates of this consensus and pointing towards its eventual overcoming.

The Silicon Valley Consensus

> Ideological expressions have never been pure fictions; they represent a distorted consciousness of realities, and as such they have been real factors that have in turn produced real distorting effects.
>
> Guy Debord[5]

By the early 2000s, the global capitalist project into which the United States had enlisted the world's political and economic elites stood alone.

4 The term 'Silicon Valley consensus' was coined by MIT's Michael Piore, who has used it in a series of papers and presentations. See Michael Piore and David Skinner, 'Economic Policy in the Time of Reactionary Populism', International Conference on Globalization: Regional Growth and the 4th Industrial Revolution, Bologna, 2017; Michael Piore and Cauam Ferreira Cardoso, 'SENAI + ISIS: The Silicon Valley Consensus Meets Organizational Challenges in Brazil', MIT-IPC Working Paper, 17-005, 2017. Nevertheless, the idea was already present in other authors, including Mariana Mazzucato, who speaks of the 'Silicon Valley myth'. See Mariana Mazzucato, *The Entrepreneurial State: Debunking Public vs. Private Sector Myths*, London: Anthem Press, 2014.

5 Guy Debord, *Society of the Spectacle*, trans. Ken Knabb, Berkeley, CA: Bureau of Public Secrets, 2014, p. 114.

Having won a knockout victory over the Soviet bloc, its principles – free trade, free movement of capital, and equal treatment of investors regardless of nationality – were being implemented in most countries.[6] This project was, however, weakened by both the calamitous record of the policies stemming from the Washington consensus, and the resistance to which these same policies gave rise.

The various forms of structural adjustment plans implemented in Latin America and Africa over the past two decades had not helped these regions' development. In most of the ex-socialist countries of eastern Europe, the shock therapy so triumphantly implemented by Western experts succeeded in producing an economic collapse from which – with few exceptions – these societies are yet to recover even decades later.[7] Finally, in the wake of the Asian crisis of 1997, brutal interventions by the International Monetary Fund (IMF) went on the offensive against the unorthodox policies which had allowed some industrial catch-up in previous decades. Not only did the directly affected populations rise up across the region, but a section of the elites in developing countries openly sought to rid themselves of Western experts' influence. Seeking to free themselves of the IMF's grip in the event of a fresh crisis, many governments turned to neo-mercantilist policies in order to build up foreign exchange reserves. Among economists, criticism intensified even within international institutions,[8] echoing the growing street protests. In this period, there was not a single major international summit that was not disrupted by demonstrations and blockades, for instance the ones that marked the World Trade Organization (WTO) conference in Seattle in 1999 or the Genoa G8 summit in 2001. Broadcast in spectacular TV images, these protests buried

---

6 Sam Gindin and Leo Panitch, *The Making of Global Capitalism: The Political Economy of American Empire*, London: Verso, 2012.

7 Branko Milanović, 'For Whom the Wall Fell? A Balance Sheet of the Transition to Capitalism', *The Globalist* (blog), 7 November 2014.

8 Joseph E. Stiglitz, *Globalization and Its Discontents*, New York: Norton, 2002; Dani Rodrik, 'Goodbye Washington Consensus, Hello Washington Confusion? A Review of the World Bank's Economic Growth in the 1990s: Learning from a Decade of Reform', *Journal of Economic Literature* 44, no. 4, 2006, pp. 973–87; Ben Fine, Costas Lapavitsas and Jonathan Pincus, *Development Policy in the Twenty-First Century: Beyond the Post-Washington Consensus*, London: Routledge, 2003.

the idea of a 'happy globalisation' and caused cracks in the hegemony of the doctrine that stood behind it. By the year 2000, the market euphoria that had greeted the fall of the former Soviet bloc had completely faded.

As Louis Althusser famously put it, 'ideology represents the imaginary relationship of individuals to their real conditions of existence'.[9] As another philosopher, Fredric Jameson, writes, ideology forms a 'cognitive map' that allows individuals to envisage their situation in relation to a wider totality.[10] So, if a putatively dominant ideology is to aggregate wills and become operational, it must offer a perspective that is both general and practical – that is, it must propose a vision of the world that, in producing meaning, allows for the deployment of actions at the local level. In the new situation that marked the turn of the millennium, pointing out the failure of the socialist economies and *dirigiste* development models was no longer enough. Now that capitalism no longer had any rivals, what had served as its central ideological resource over previous decades had become outdated. It was no longer enough to propose a return to the natural market order under the motto 'stabilisation-liberalisation-privatisation'. Rather, capitalism's fragility was now, first and foremost, internal; it stemmed from the opposition that neoliberal policies produced, and the repeated crises to which these same policies gave rise.

The doctrine that took shape at the turn of the millennium sought its legitimating principle in the very dynamics of capitalism. The positive discursive regime that was now put in place sought to ground governments' economic practices in the intrinsic virtues of what Marx called the 'permanent revolution' carried forth by capital.[11] Seeking to consolidate the legitimacy of a capitalism that was now fragile as well as triumphant, the chosen ideological path foregrounded its Promethean development – that is, the revolutionary energy which was now being exhibited by the meteoric spread of the internet and the boom in the 'new economy' in

---

9 Louis Althusser, 'Ideology and Ideological State Apparatuses (Notes Towards an Investigation)', trans. Ben Brewster, 1970, text from marxists.org.

10 Fredric Jameson, 'Postmodernism, or the Cultural Logic of Late Capitalism', *New Left Review* 1, no. 146, 1984, p. 90.

11 See Karl Marx, *Grundrisse: Foundations of the Critique of Political Economy*, London: Penguin Books, 1993, pp. 276–8.

the United States. But, unlike the mass consumerism that W. W. Rostow promised in *The Stages of Economic Growth* in his day, this process now stands as an end in itself, as a principle of social and economic regeneration.[12] A narrative was spun glorifying a great capitalist epic, of which the Silicon Valley experience offered an edifying illustration. Its heroes: the entrepreneurs, able against all odds to transform human creativity into a salvational technological progress.

Since the turn of the millennium, economic policy's new ideological horizon has been the concern to stimulate this technological force propelling capitalism forward. Yet, such a *doxa* could not be written overnight. Before examining how it became widespread and how it ultimately crystallised, at the turn of the millennium, in the grey literature of the Organisation for Economic Co-operation and Development (OECD), we must first trace its Californian origins. It was there, in the San Francisco region, that the elementary particles of the doctrinal nucleus were assembled, allowing this new consensus to propagate itself across the planet and to maintain its inertial force through good times and bad until the end of the 2010s, even despite the bursting of the dotcom bubble in 2001 and the great crisis of 2008.

The Californian Ideology

At the end of the twentieth century, the advent of the internet created a new social space at the crossroads of IT, telecommunications, and the media. Suddenly, everyday practices were transformed, new competitive advantages emerged, and information travelled down unprecedented channels. Amid such great upheavals, whoever had an interpretation to offer had a good chance of a hearing. This mood explains the worldwide spread of what Richard Barbrook and Andy Cameron have called the 'Californian ideology'.[13] This ideology is the product of the hybridisation of the hippie

---

12 Walt Whitman Rostow, *The Stages of Economic Growth: A Non-Communist Manifesto*, Cambridge: Cambridge University Press, 1971.

13 Richard Barbrook and Andy Cameron, 'The Californian Ideology', *Science as Culture* 6, no. 1, 1996, pp. 44–72.

counterculture of the 1960s – itself rooted in a rich soil of political radical-
ism – and the enthusiastic embrace of free-market principles by the new
Californian entrepreneurs.[14] If, at first glance, everything would seem to set
these two cultures at odds with one another, they would find common
ground in the seemingly liberating potential of the new technologies.

The Last Utopias. Published in 1975, Ernest Callenbach's *Ecotopia* was
the last great utopian text of the twentieth century.[15] Inspired by the
alternatives that were then flourishing in various locations along the US
West Coast, the book describes a new country comprising northern
California, Oregon, and Washington state. Having seceded from the rest
of the United States, this is a carless territory where power is decentralised, consumption is essentially local, self-management generally
prevails, and sexual relations are not exclusive. Daily life is organised in
autonomous communities, built around extended families. Well
informed about the contemporary state of techno-scientific knowledge,
Callenbach meticulously described an ecologically sustainable production system, based on the local production of renewable energy and the
use of state-of-the-art military equipment to guarantee this radical political experiment's security. The story reflects the aspirations of an entire
generation which abhorred the productivism, consumerism, authoritarianism, and conservatism of US society. It also anticipated the rising
influence of environmental concerns on consumer behaviour.

If some of the hippies were deeply hostile to advances in science and
technology and called for a return to nature, this attitude was far from a

---

14 Mike Davis, 'The Year 1960', *New Left Review* 108, 2017. A more extensive
socio-political history of California is provided by Jeannette Estruth's doctoral
dissertation, 'A Political History of the Silicon Valley: Structural Change, Urban
Transformation, and Local Movements, 1945–1995', New York University, 2017.

15 Ernest Callenbach, *Ecotopia: The Notebooks and Reports of William Weston*,
Berkeley, CA: Banyan Tree Books/Heyday Books, 2004. This is, at least, the viewpoint expressed in 2012 by philosopher Fredric Jameson, a great specialist in the
archaeology of the future (*New Left Review* 75). Jameson has since published his own
utopia, *An American Utopia* (London: Verso, 2017). Here, we will not discuss the
various problematic propositions raised in *Ecotopia*, starting with its reference to a
form of mutually agreed racial segregation.

general rule. Although computers are practically absent from *Ecotopia*, technological issues are ubiquitous throughout its pages. We also find this techno-philosophy in other elements of Californian counterculture, which were more sensitive to the first beginnings of the digital revolution and saw the new information technologies as tools for realising their libertarian ideal. Highly influential, in this era, were the visionary works of the Canadian media theorist Marshall McLuhan. In the mid-1960s, he coined the metaphor of the global village, combining the idea of a worldwide network of horizontal communications with the flattening of hierarchical structures. For McLuhan, 'we everywhere resume person-to-person relations as if on the smallest village scale. It is a relation in depth, and without delegation of functions or powers.'[16] From this perspective, it is technological change that determines the emergence of a form of collective consciousness, at the scale of human society itself:

> Today, after more than a century of electric technology, we have extended our central nervous system itself in a global embrace, abolishing both space and time as far as our planet is concerned. Rapidly, we approach the final phase of the extensions of man – the technological simulation of consciousness, when the creative process of knowing will be collectively and corporately extended to the whole of human society, much as we have already extended our senses and our nerves by the various media.[17]

McLuhan combines prophesying about the impact of technology, rising individual power, and the rejection of authority – stating, for example, that 'the mark of our time is its revulsion against imposed patterns.'[18] This combination offered the more technophile hippies a vision of a world where the radical aspiration to individual autonomy could coexist with the sharing of each person's creativity, on a global

---

16 Marshall McLuhan, *Understanding Media: The Extensions of Man*, New York: McGraw-Hill, 1966, p. 255.

17 Ibid., p. 3.

18 Ibid., p. 5.

scale and without any form of delegation of power or subordination. This tour de force explains why for many, involvement in alternative community media and in computer clubs were each experienced as part of the same fight for an authentic democracy. This prism also allows us to understand why the Californian infatuation with information and communication technologies (ICTs) from the 1970s onwards seemed to be an extension of the social movements which masses of students had engaged in over the previous decade. This meant projecting the communitarian and anti-authoritarian aspirations of the counterculture onto a global scale, giving technologically augmented individuals the means to emancipate themselves from big business and big government.

Stewart Brand: From the *Whole Earth* Saga to Global Business. By the mid-2010s, reminders of the techno-libertarian aspiration of the 1960s still existed here and there, but only as fossils. When Google executives claim that digital technology will 'help reallocate the concentration of power away from states and institutions and transfer it to individuals', they are merely reiterating the promises that McLuhan made fifty years earlier.[19] But the world in which they are speaking no longer has much to do with the emancipatory impulse of that past era. Technological optimism is now often associated with right-wing political themes.

There were various channels which allowed some of the winds of 1960s Californian counterculture to breathe life into the renewal of conservative thought that began in the 1990s. Stewart Brand's trajectory is an emblematic case in point.[20] Born in 1938, he graduated from Stanford University with a biology degree in 1960, left to do his military service, then returned to study design and photography in San Francisco where, among other adventures, he organised the memorable Trips Festival in January 1966. Thousands of people flocked to the festival to

---

19 Eric Schmidt and Jared Cohen, *The New Digital Age: Reshaping the Future of People, Nations and Business*, London: Murray, 2014, p. 6.

20 Stewart Brand, 'Bio . . ', sb.longnow.org (personal site); Fred Turner, *From Counterculture to Cyberculture: Stewart Brand, the Whole Earth Network, and the Rise of Digital Utopianism*, Chicago: University of Chicago Press, 2010.

take part in the acid tests and to witness a great multimedia show featuring rock performances by acts like the Grateful Dead and the screening of psychedelic films. In 1968, Brand took part in what has since been called the 'mother of all demos', a demonstration of information technology led by Douglas Engelbart from the Stanford Research Institute. The demo saw the display of the main tools that were to make up the personal computers of the future: the mouse, the word processor, browser windows, hypertext links . . .

Brand also launched a campaign demanding that NASA publicly release its photographs of the whole Earth as seen from space, in order to accelerate ecological awareness. Then, through a road trip to hippie communities, he began circulating his *Whole Earth Catalogue*, which listed all the objects deemed useful and the means of obtaining them. The book enjoyed phenomenal success and became an emblem of the do-it-yourself spirit of the times. After issuing various other publications, in 1985 he cofounded WELL (Whole Earth 'Lectronic Link – one of the very first online discussion forums), became a visiting researcher at the MIT Media Lab, and gave a series of lectures to large multinationals like Shell and AT&T. In 1987, he was one of the founders of the Global Business Network, a Berkeley-based consulting firm which promised to help organisations seize the opportunities that technological and social change offered in achieving 'sustainable growth for a better future'.[21] Since then, Brand has devoted himself to lectures and publications on long-term thinking, in which he popularises the case for geoengineering and nuclear power.

Stewart Brand's biography thus provides a striking illustration of a certain kind of journey: one that began in the hippie community and ended with Brand coaching the dominant economic and political forces on how to drive change. Indeed, this shift took on an organic character in the early 1990s, in a context marked by a swing to the Right in the structuring terms of Californian politics.[22] It was in this period, between

---

21 Global Business Network, 'Where We Started', gbn.com.
22 Richard Walker, 'California Rages against the Dying of the Light', *New Left Review* 209, 1995, p. 42.

1993 and 1995, that a real alliance was established between, on the one hand, the technophile networks of the counterculture and, on the other hand, the business community and the New Right of the Republican Party around *Wired* magazine, the Progress & Freedom Foundation, and Republican politician Newt Gingrich.[23] A conservative reading of the potential of the new IT culture was now coming into shape.

Becoming Conservatives

The economic situation in the United States in the early 1990s was gloomy. Paul Krugman published a book entitled *The Age of Diminished Expectations*, in which he drew this disillusioned assessment: the country's economy no longer offered the kind of progress that previous generations had been able to take for granted. For most of the population, stagnant living standards had become the norm, and declining purchasing power was often the reality.[24] To most people's minds, the main cause of this grim state of affairs was low productivity. And indeed, as Robert Solow famously said, 'You can see the computer age everywhere but in the productivity statistics.'

Yet, things were stirring on the capital markets. From 1992, the number of IPOs and the funds raised by new start-ups increased massively.[25] This investor optimism formed the backdrop to the ideological transformation that was now set underway.

From its inception in 1993 to its dissolution in 2010, the Progress & Freedom Foundation (PFF) was a key player in the crystallisation of a right-wing ideology associated with the digital revolution. Funded by major IT, communications, and media companies such as Microsoft, AT&T, Walt Disney, Sony, Oracle, Vivendi, Google, and Yahoo!, the organisation's mission was to influence policymakers and public opinion on technological issues by combining a classic conservative

---

23 Turner, *From Counterculture to Cyberculture*, chapter 7.

24 Paul R. Krugman, *The Age of Diminished Expectations: US Economic Policy in the 1990s*, Cambridge, MA: MIT Press, 1990.

25 Benedict Evans, 'US Tech Funding', *Benedict Evans* (blog), 15 June 2015, fig. 19.

perspective with an enthusiastic appreciation of the digital revolution.[26] Over 23–24 August 1994, the PFF organised a conference in Atlanta entitled 'Cyberspace and the American Dream' which resulted in a book subtitled *A Magna Carta for the Knowledge Age*. Esther Dyson, George Gilder, Alvin Toffler, and George Keyworth were the volume's co-authors. The first three had the particularity of being both essayists/commentators and investors; they circulated between techno-scientific and business circles and occasionally appeared in the columns of *Wired*. Like the PFF, this magazine was born in 1993, and discussed the new technologies from economic, cultural, and political points of view; it soon became the main press organ popularising the Californian ideology. The fourth author, George Keyworth, was a former science advisor to Ronald Reagan and worked for the foundation. Together, they produced a document that was conceived as an outright manifesto, and which would bear major influence. Here, we can summarise the essence of its argument.[27]

The Magna Carta begins by taking up the idea, in vogue for some decades, that the ages of agriculture and industry were now to be succeeded by the information age.[28] In this account, the main event of the twentieth century was the 'overthrow of matter': 'In technology, economics, and the politics of nations, wealth – in the form of physical resources – has been losing value and significance. The powers of mind are everywhere ascendant over the brute force of things.'

---

26 'Our Mission', Progress & Freedom Foundation, pff.org.

27 Subsequent citations from the Magna Carta are taken from the online version, Esther Dyson, George Gilder, George Keyworth and Alvin Toffler, *Cyberspace and the American Dream: A Magna Carta for the Knowledge Age*, Progress & Freedom Foundation, August 1994, pff.org.

28 Since the 1970s, various authors had heralded the imminent advent of a new information age: Alain Touraine, *La Société post-industrielle*, Paris: Denoël, 1969; Zbigniew Brzezinski, *Between Two Ages: America's Role in the Technetronic Era*, New York: Viking Press, 1970; Daniel Bell, *The Coming of the Post-Industrial Society: A Venture in Social Forecasting*, New York: Basic Books, 1973; Alvin Toffler, *The Third Wave*, London: William Morrow & Company, 1980; Simon Nora and Alain Minc, *The Computerisation of Society*, Cambridge, MA: MIT Press, 1980; Ithiel de Sola Pool, *Technologies of Freedom*, Cambridge, MA: Harvard University Press, 1983.

The potential upheavals are enormous – for 'cyberspace is a bioelectronic environment that is literally universal'. A space occupied by ideas, which are navigated using software, it opens up a new frontier – the 'land of knowledge' which everyone must be able to explore. However, if this new age of knowledge was to deliver on its promise, the attitudes of the past would have to be abandoned. As the document puts it, this change 'also gives to leaders of the advanced democracies a special responsibility – to facilitate, hasten, and explain the transition'. And as luck would have it, the Magna Carta's purpose is to provide them with guidelines for fulfilling this very mission. Throughout, the text plays on an ambivalence between the descriptive and the prescriptive; it analyses and simultaneously demands the retreat of the state, an intensification of competition, and a great entrepreneurial cavalcade to bring technological solutions to humanity's most pressing problems and, more immediately, the difficulties facing the United States. All this recalls the words spoken by Jean-Pierre Léaud in Philippe Garrel's film *The Birth of Love*:

> In reality, you never know what is happening, you just know what you want to happen and that's how things happen. In '17, Lenin and his comrades didn't say, 'We're going to make the revolution because we want the revolution.' They said, 'All the conditions for revolution are ready, revolution is inevitable.' They made the revolution that would never have taken place if they had not made it, and that they would not have made if they had not thought it was inevitable simply because they wanted it.[29]

Like the Bolsheviks, the authors of the Magna Carta both forecasted the future and prescribed it, in one fell swoop. Their first decree was the death of the central institutional paradigm of modern life: bureaucratic organisation. If, for nearly a century, freedom-lovers had suffered the hegemony of the conformist values associated with mass industrial society, now they were getting their revenge: 'New information technologies are driving the financial costs of diversity – both product and personal

---

29 Philippe Garrel, *La Naissance de l'amour*, 1983.

– down towards zero, "demassifying" our institutions and our culture.' For it now had to be acknowledged that the complexity of the new social world 'is too great for any centrally planned bureaucracy to manage'. This meant not only consigning socialist projects to the scrap-heap, but also a massive retreat of the state. The Magna Carta thus predicted that 'a Third Wave government will be vastly smaller (perhaps by 50 per cent or more) than the current one – this is an inevitable implication of the transition from the centralized power structures of the industrial age to the dispersed, decentralized institutions of the Third'.

Here, the four authors play on a rather rudimentary technical determinism. Back at the end of the nineteenth century, many thought that the advent of electricity would allow for the revival of artisan trades, for access to distributed electrical energy would allow them to again become competitive with large industrial units able to draw on their own energy sources.[30] In 1993, in an interview for *Wired*, George Gilder deemed the internet a 'kind of metaphor for [Friedrich Hayek's] spontaneous order'. According to Gilder, the web showed 'that in order to have a very rich fabric of services you don't need a regimented system of control. When there's a lot of intelligence at the fringes everywhere, the actual network itself can be fairly simple.'[31]

The Magna Carta combined this intuition with the idea that cyberspace consists of markets undergoing constant transformation. In this account, the effects of technological progress generate a dynamic of Schumpeterian 'creative destruction' on a global scale, as competition makes everyone into winners and losers. The IT industry in the United States provides a prime example of this. In 1980, the industry was dominated by a handful of large firms. A decade later, there was a spectacular collapse in their market share, starting with IBM's. Initially interpreted as a symptom of American decline, this upheaval actually heralded the opposite. For the advent of the personal computer brought a renaissance in American technological leadership over its Asian and European competitors:

---

30 Philippe Dockès and Bernard Rosier, *L'Histoire ambiguë. Croissance et développement en question*, Paris: PUF, 1988.
31 Kevin Kelly, 'George Gilder: When Bandwidth Is Free', *Wired*, 1 April 1993.

In the transition from mainframes to PCs, a vast new market was created. This market was characterized by dynamic competition consisting of easy access and low barriers to entry. Start-ups by the dozens took on the larger established companies – and won.

The lesson was clear: the predominance of the United States' IT industry over the rest of the world was owed to the dynamic competition it had been able to preserve in its domestic market. Hence 'if there is to be an "industrial policy for the knowledge age", it should focus on removing barriers to competition and massively deregulating the fast-growing telecommunications and computing industries'. So, governments' main objective should be to let this dynamic competition flourish, or even stimulate it.

This did not mean that governments should remain inert. In developing this third layer of their argument, the authors invoked the libertarian icon Ayn Rand.[32] Governments' responsibility was to create clear and enforceable property rights – an essential aid to markets' proper functioning. As the authors put it, 'to create the new cyberspace environment is to create new property – that is, new means of creating goods (including ideas) that serve people'. Intellectual property rights, electromagnetic frequencies and infrastructure networks were the new objects that needed to be caught in the nets of property. The bottom line, they explained, is that 'the key principle of ownership by the people – private

---

32 The quotation from Rand is interesting because, even though it dates from 1964 – before the main contributions to new theories of the firm – it anticipates the proprietary ideology that these theories helped to establish and with which the Magna Carta identified. According to Rand, 'It is the proper task of the government to protect individual rights and, as part of it, to formulate the laws by which these rights are to be implemented and adjudicated. It is the government's responsibility to define the application of individual rights to a given sphere of activity – to define (i.e., to identify), not to create, invent, donate, or expropriate. The question of defining the application of property rights has arisen frequently, in the wake of major scientific discoveries or inventions, such as the question of oil rights, vertical space rights, etc. In most cases, the American government was guided by the proper principle: it sought to protect all the individual rights involved, not to abrogate them', in 'The Property Status of Airwaves', *Objectivist Newsletter*, April 1964.

ownership – should govern every deliberation. Government does not own cyberspace, the people do.' In other words, private property alone had the right to lay its hands on cyberspace, but this itself required positive government intervention to define these new rights.

The reference to Ayn Rand here is very telling. The author of allegorical novels with a circulation of tens of millions of copies, her ideas remain extremely influential in the United States, even after her death in 1982. Her works are built around the central opposition between 'prime movers' – 'men of the mind' – and 'second handers' – 'mass men'.[33] When the authors of the Magna Carta speak of new property rights that need to be established, they are referring to the 'men of the mind' of the new Eldorado – cyberspace. Silicon Valley entrepreneurs revel in the mirror held up to them by Rand's heroes.[34] For, in it, they see an exciting and glorious image of their own superiority. The concept of disruption that they so cherish is closely associated with all that Rand celebrates: the ability to take risks, to push ahead of everyone else, and to shape the future relying on one's own intuition alone. The destructive side of the concept of disruption is fully embraced; for this means overthrowing the established rules in the name of innovation, in a Schumpeterian spirit. From Google to Uber and Facebook, Silicon Valley companies have not been shy about operating outside of any legal framework, or even defying the rules that do exist, in order to impose their innovations by fait accompli.[35]

---

33 Slavoj Žižek, 'The Actuality of Ayn Rand', *Journal of Ayn Rand Studies* 3, no. 2, 2002, p. 215.

34 In 2015, Uber's then CEO Travis Kalanick used the cover of *The Fountainhead*, one of Ayn Rand's bestsellers, as his Twitter avatar; Peter Thiel publicly professes his admiration for Rand; and according to Apple co-founder Steve Wozniak, Steve Jobs considered *Atlas Shrugged* to be one of the books that had guided him in life. See Jonathan Freedland, 'The New Age of Ayn Rand: How She Won Over Trump and Silicon Valley', *Guardian*, 10 April 2017. In Adam Curtis's documentary *All Watched Over by Machines of Loving Grace*, John McCaskey says of his experience as an IT entrepreneur in 1990s California, 'I really did feel like an Ayn Rand hero. I didn't just feel like one, I was one. I was building the products. I was thinking independently. I was being rational. I was taking pride in what I did.' See also Diane Anderson, 'Tech Titans Turn to "The Fountainhead" for Comfort', CNN.com, 13 June 2000.

35 The thrust of the argument is that the new digital universe has no need for statutory regulation of services (e.g., hotels, food safety, cabs . . .) since competition

George Monbiot gets to the heart of the matter when he writes that Ayn Rand devised 'the ugliest philosophy the postwar world has produced. Selfishness, it contends, is good, altruism evil, empathy and compassion are irrational and destructive. The poor deserve to die; the rich deserve unmediated power.'[36] It is precisely this philosophy that inspires the ideology of many Californian entrepreneurs, who consider themselves bearers of the historic mission outlined in the Magna Carta – nothing less than the creation of a new civilisation, based on the eternal truths of the 'American idea'.

International Projection

One of the attendees at the Atlanta conference that gave rise to the Magna Carta was Newt Gingrich. He is a key figure on the American right, from his battles to radicalise the Republican Party in the 1980s to his support for Donald Trump's victorious presidential campaign in 2016. In 1995, a year after the Atlanta conference, he was at the height of his powers: having become Speaker of the House of Representatives, he was named Man of the Year by *Time* magazine. That same year, he gave an interview to *Wired* magazine in which he claimed that 'if we establish an information-age, economically decisive, exciting America, the rest of the world will imitate us'.[37] This statement reflected a moment in which the Californian ideology was becoming globally dominant, providing much of the narrative underpinnings for the new economic policies that were about to be enacted. Indeed, it was also in 1995 that Ira Magaziner, a consultant for various high-tech firms, was commissioned by President Bill Clinton to define a growth strategy – a mission that led to a framework document for global electronic commerce, published in 1997.[38]

---

will take care of weeding out the bad actors; the only protection the public needs is a free market. See Paul Bradley Carr, 'Travis Shrugged: The Creepy, Dangerous Ideology behind Silicon Valley's Cult of Disruption', pando.com, 24 October 2012.

36 George Monbiot, 'How Ayn Rand Became the New Right's Version of Marx', *Guardian*, 5 March 2012.

37 Esther Dyson, 'Friend and Foe', *Wired*, 1 August 1995.

38 Clinton Administration, 'The Framework for Electronic Commerce', July 1997, clintonwhitehouse4.archives.gov.

This text marked a real turning point for the Clinton administration. Whereas its initial position had approached information technologies from a sectoral perspective of building up technological advantages, there now prevailed the idea of a growth regime appropriate to the digital age, radically different from that which had characterised the age of manufacturing industries.

Already during the 1992 presidential campaign, Bill Clinton had won the support of a large number of IT and electronics executives, luring them with promise of a traditional-type industrial policy that would serve their interests. The *New York Times* explained that 'at the heart of Mr. Clinton's national technology policy, forged with the help of industry leaders, is the belief that the Federal Government must play a larger role in shaping industries and markets'.[39] The proposed measures included targeted tax cuts, subsidies for specific technology programmes, government investment in infrastructure – but also a tightening of US foreign trade policy. Indeed, in the early 1990s, IT companies accused their international competitors of unfair competition, and they expected the future Clinton administration to take the anti-dumping measures that the Bush administration had denied them.

Five years later, with Clinton now in his second term, his administration's principles regarding electronic commerce had fully swung in the direction suggested by the Magna Carta. Now, the aim was no longer the defence of American technological leadership, but rather the creation of a suitable environment for a new industrial revolution that would forge a 'global community' and radically transform commerce by slashing transaction costs. The strategy set out in the 1997 framework document sought to guide this revolution and, above all, to prevent excessive regulation from hampering the dynamism of the global electronic market that was now taking form. The very idea of industrial policy was abandoned in favour of a series of now-familiar precepts. The framework document insisted that 'the private sector should lead'; that 'governments should avoid undue restrictions'; that 'where

---

39 Calvin Sims, 'Silicon Valley Takes a Partisan Leap of Faith', *New York Times*, 29 October 1992.

government intervention is necessary to facilitate electronic commerce, its goal should be to ensure competition, protect intellectual property'; and that 'governments should recognize the unique qualities of the internet', namely its 'decentralized nature' and 'tradition of bottom-up governance'.

Added to this was an internationalist touch – emphasising how important it was to provide the global electronic market with a coherent, cross-border legal framework. This last element is highly significant: for given the United States' leadership in international affairs, a truly global action programme was now being set in motion. Among other things, this included the Singapore Information Technology Agreement, which from March 1997 stipulated the elimination of customs duties on software and on manufacturing equipment associated with information technology.

On 24 August 1998, Ira Magaziner spoke at another edition of the Cyberspace and the American Dream conference organised by the Progress & Freedom Foundation.[40] Here, he ran through his role in the Clinton administration concerning issues related to electronic commerce and spoke of the work being done at the international level to bring about a common institutional architecture for the internet and global commerce. Consistent with the Randian orientation of the Magna Carta, he concluded asserting the need to rely 'first and foremost on the marketplace'. This 'involve[d] governments agreeing to do something that is very difficult for governments to do, which is to agree not to act'. This techno-liberal motif would now provide the framework within which economic policy addressed questions of innovation.

The Causes of Economic Growth

The importance attached to innovation issues in the OECD and in government circles has not dwindled over the past two decades. Neither the bursting of the dotcom bubble, nor the accounting scandals that

---

40 Ira Magaziner, 'Creating a Framework for Global Electronic Commerce', *Future Insight* 6, no. 1, 1999.

came to light afterward, nor the great crisis of 2008, had any real impact on this agenda, which was still at work up to the late 2010s. In a 2015 report, *The Innovation Imperative*, the OECD explained why:

> Innovation provides the foundation for new businesses, new jobs and productivity growth and is thus an important driver of economic growth and development. Innovation can help address pressing social and global challenges including demographic shifts, resource scarcity and the changing climate.[41]

There was not much new in these platitudes about the benefits of technological progress, entrusted with both invigorating economic development and solving the planet's major problems.[42] Indeed, this vision is hardly novel: already in the 1990s, it was the focus of thought-provoking studies focused on national innovation systems.[43] This approach concerned itself with the institutional and historical configurations that stood behind different countries' economic and technological performances. It explored the strategies of the major players (firms, universities, research laboratories) in each country, their public policies, and their socio-political balance, all with the aim of explaining the different courses that these nations had followed. For example, it examined

---

41 OECD, *The Innovation Imperative: Contributing to Productivity, Growth and Well-Being*, Paris, OECD Publishing, 2015, p. 11.

42 The case for public intervention to support scientific and technological production had been clearly advanced already in *The Endless Frontier*, the report written for President Roosevelt in 1945. Its author, Vannevar Bush, was the architect of the Manhattan Project, which gave the United States the atomic bomb. Military issues are therefore a common theme throughout his argument. But he also emphasises the economic stakes in terms of employment levels, citizens' standard of living, and the United States' international competitiveness. As he writes: 'There must be a stream of new scientific knowledge to turn the wheels of private and public enterprise.' See Vannevar Bush, *Science, the Endless Frontier: A Report to the President*, Washington, DC: United States Government Printing Office, 1945, p. 13.

43 Bruno Amable, 'Institutional Complementarity and Diversity of Social Systems of Innovation and Production', *Review of International Political Economy* 7, no. 4, 2000, pp. 645–87; Richard R. Nelson, *National Innovation Systems: A Comparative Analysis*, Oxford: Oxford University Press, 1993.

the underpinnings of US technological advance, Japan's spectacular postwar catch-up story, or Germany's long-term specialisation in mechanical engineering industries. Such an analytical framework is thus utterly at odds with neoliberal precepts that celebrate the autonomy of market mechanisms.

The new orthodoxy adopted by the OECD breaks entirely with this systemic perspective on the dynamics of innovation. In all its publications on this subject, it reminds us that a robust innovation policy requires sound macroeconomic management, competitive markets, and openness to international trade and investment. Its doctrine thus proceeds from the Washington consensus, but it adds a qualitative supplement in the form of a certain techno-optimism. While the OECD has no manifesto, properly speaking, we can find a substitute in the minutes of an informal workshop held at the OECD headquarters in Paris on 6 and 7 July 2000.[44] At this meeting, participants exchanged views on the causes of growth, in the context of the spread of information and communication technologies. The aim, here, was to understand the dynamism displayed by the US economy since 1995, which contrasted with the generalised instability in the countries of the Global South and the sluggishness of the rest of the rich world. The participants concluded that the US's success was to be attributed to its innovation. Although there was some reference to the importance of research and education, the discussion focused on three other elements, which became the pillars of the doctrine which was now taking form.

First, the report notes that 'Schumpeter's idea of creative destruction ... allow[s] a clear view of how developments at the firm and

---

44 The thirteen economists – all men – invited to the meeting came from leading universities in the English-speaking world (Dale Jorgenson from Harvard, Xavier Sala-i-Martin from Columbia, Jonathan Temple from Oxford, and Luigi Zingales from Chicago) and from public research institutions in Europe (Bruno Creepon from INSEE, Paul Butzen from the National Bank of Belgium) and Asia (Chin Hee Hahn from the Korea Development Institute and Kiyohiko Nishimura from the Tokyo Centre for Economic Research). Jonathan Temple, 'Summary of an Informal Workshop on the Causes of Economic Growth', OECD Economics Department Working Paper, 33, 260, 2000.

establishment level translate into aggregate productivity improvements'.[45] In other words, the authors attribute most of the improvement in productive efficiency to the replacement of worse-performing firms by innovative ones. This is a key point, connecting the question of innovation to the issue of entrepreneurship. It reinforces the belief that the innovation process is primarily driven by the market entry of new firms, free of organisational baggage and thus agile enough to bring disruption into the heart of established industries. It also echoes a new generation of theoretical works, initiated by Philippe Aghion and Peter Howitt among others, which model growth trajectories based on the mechanisms of creative destruction associated with the spread of innovation.[46]

Second, the authors conclude that 'the relatively strong performance of the United States may be associated with institutions that promote resource shifts across and within sectors, in response to innovation'. In doing so, they emphasise the flexibility of economies – meaning, the role of institutions that promote not only market competition between products, but also the mobility of labour and capital. The labour market has to be as flexible as possible, in order to allow for more responsive resource allocation and accelerate the spread of innovation. The argument also applies to capital, weighing in favour of an increased development of the financial system. In particular, it is stressed that 'if access to finance is made easier for young firms, this tends to undermine the position of industry incumbents'. The success of the United States is thus attributed to financial liberalisation, since 'the rapid reallocation towards "new economy" sectors . . . might not have been possible with a less developed financial sector'.

Third, the paper highlights 'the patent system, and the definition and protection of property rights more generally'. The underlying issue, here, is the appropriation of rents from innovation, and the role that these play as an incentive. Following in the footsteps of the aforementioned neo-Schumpeterian works on growth, the document points to the risk that

---

45 Ibid., p. 8.
46 Philippe Aghion and Peter Howitt, 'A Model of Growth through Creative Destruction', *NBER Working Paper*, w3223, 1990.

the rate of destruction will be too fast, to the point of discouraging inno-vation.[47] It is thus necessary to ensure that any gains associated with the success of creative activity are sufficiently high.

The originality of this new doctrine of innovation thus lies in its emphasis on the notion of creative destruction. Beyond the need for market flexibility, what the economists convened by the OECD in the summer of 2000 had learned from the US 'new economy' boom was the beneficial effect of competition tempered by incentives on innovation. This – highly partisan – credo would quickly spread across the various countries, via the groups of experts tasked with implementing structural reforms.[48]

Let us sum up what we have seen thus far. Since the turn of the millennium, a new doctrine has inspired economic policies. The Silicon Valley consensus goes beyond the Washington consensus. It places more emphasis on the dynamic efficiency of capitalism, as a movement of creative destruction, than on the static efficiency of resource allocation by the market. In so doing, this doctrine has extended its prescriptions beyond the stabilisation-liberalisation-privatisation triptych and put incentives centre stage. Henceforth, the public policies characteristic of the Silicon Valley consensus have been guided by the principles of sparing public intervention; freeing up entrepreneurial energies; flexibility of product, labour, and capital markets; and protection of innovators' property rights.

---

47 Philippe Aghion and Jean Tirole, 'The Management of Innovation', *Quarterly Journal of Economics* 109, no. 4, 1994, pp. 1185–209.

48 In the French case: Jacques Attali, *Rapport de la Commission pour la libération de la croissance française: 300 décisions pour changer la France*, Paris: La Documentation française, 2008. A series of other examples are given by Bruno Amable and Ivan Ledezma, *Libéralisation, innovation et croissance. Faut-il vraiment les associer?*, Paris: Éditions Rue d'Ulm, 2015.

Five Paradoxes of the New Capitalism

> Persistent and striking lack of success may be sufficient to ruin any government.
>
> Max Weber[49]

The propulsive force of the Silicon Valley consensus derives from its claim to make sense of the advance of digital technologies while also summoning the evocative power of the Californian experience. Silicon Valley, or, rather, the myth built around it, is the showcase of the new capitalism: a land of opportunity where, thanks to start-ups and venture capitalists, ideas flourish, jobs abound, and high-tech developments benefit the many. In light of this presumably happy experience, individual risk-taking and the lure of profit are celebrated in the name of the higher principle of innovation. This myth can be broken down into five basic elements: 1) the continuous reinvigoration of economic structures thanks to start-uppers' thirst for adventure; 2) the pinnacle of workplace autonomy and creativity; 3) a culture of openness and mobility; 4) the promise of shared prosperity; and finally, 5) the ideal of the state becoming obsolete. But, as we shall see, the actual development of the new capitalism is the exact opposite of each of these myths. Five paradoxes emerge, revealing just as many aporias which the Silicon Valley consensus ultimately runs into.

The Return of the Monopolies: The Paradox of the Start-Up

Summer 2017 saw a major controversy when a critic of Google was ousted from a foundation working on adaptation to the digital age that was partially funded by the Mountain View firm. Barry Lynn, an analyst long committed to the antitrust battle, was dismissed by the director of the New America Foundation shortly after he published an article praising the record €2.4 billion fine which the European Commission had

---

49 Max Weber, *Economy and Society: An Outline of Interpretive Sociology*, Berkeley: University of California Press, 1978, p. 263.

imposed on the search engine that July, punishing its abuse of its dominant market position. This was no isolated case: rather, it was an illustration of Google's discreet but largely successful effort to silence critics by
generously funding think tanks and other pressure groups.[50] Barry Lynn
and the Open Market Institute team he heads have since gone independent and continue to document the ongoing monopolisation process via
their online platform, drawing parallels between the new Silicon Valley
moguls and the John Rockefellers, Andrew Carnegies, and other 'robber
barons' of the turn of the twentieth century. They are thus actively
contributing to the emergence of an anti-monopoly political space that
is no longer confined to the left wing of the Democratic Party.[51] At the
2018 edition of the World Economic Forum in Davos, George Soros
issued an implacable indictment of the monopolies of the internet era:
while they provide crucial services of general interest, they hinder innovation and the proper functioning of markets, and constitute a threat to
individual freedoms and democracy; according to the billionaire, it is
inevitable that new regulation and new fiscal principles will soon put an
end to this situation.[52] On a more tongue-in-cheek note, the *Economist*
– acknowledging that these platforms are decidedly 'too BAADD' (that
is, Big, Anti-competitive, Addictive and Destructive to Democracy) –
published a mock memo for the CEOs of Facebook, Google, and
Amazon, detailing the strategic options open to them when faced with
the inevitable backlash.[53]

---

50 Kenneth P. Vogel, 'Google Critic Ousted from Think Tank Funded by the
Tech Giant', *New York Times*, 30 August 2017; Rachel M. Cohen, 'Has the New
America Foundation Lost Its Way?', *Washingtonian* (blog), 24 June 2018.

51 On the one hand, far-right conservative groups are speaking out against what
they see as attacks on free speech, in connection with digital platforms' user clauses
banning incitement to hatred. On the other hand, the establishment is worried about
the risks of public opinion being manipulated through fake news. See Elizabeth
Dwoskin and Hamza Shaban, 'In Silicon Valley, the Right Sounds a Surprising Battle
Cry: Regulate Tech Giants', *Washington Post*, 24 August 2017.

52 George Soros, 'Remarks Delivered at the World Economic Forum', george-
soros.com, 25 January 2018.

53 Eve Smith, 'The Techlash against Amazon, Facebook and Google – and What
They Can Do: A Memo to Big Tech', *Economist*, 20 January 2018.

The Aporia of the Start-Up. It is a fact: yesterday's friendly start-ups have become cut-throat monopolies. This reversal has created a brutal ideological dissonance in the Silicon Valley consensus and left the political image of the start-up rather fragile. For if this latter is supposed to embody an ideal of professional and economic achievement – enthusiastic commitment to one's work, the possibility of individual wealth – the start-up, like youth itself, is never more than a passing moment. Successful start-ups quickly move on from the status of young green shoots and become old branches. Their success deprives them of the qualities of agility and flexibility attributed to small structures and leads them instead to acquire other qualities specific to large economic units, such as resilience. So, if start-ups do not disappear, they soon become caught up in the process of the concentration and centralisation of capital – that is, the need to grow, either through internal investment or through mergers with other economic units. A start-up is nothing like a small company that can prosper in its own modest, sustainable way by serving a local market and providing a reasonable income to its owner. This kind of project, based on advances in research, can only be sustained if the initial technical or scientific impetus is transmuted into an economic force that can develop on a large scale. This operation is mounted under pressure from venture capitalists or business angels who have committed part of their personal fortune. They only accept the high risk of failure in exchange for an ambitious profit strategy, whose success will lead to the start-up becoming a large, traditional firm or else being absorbed by a larger company at a high price.

What happens when a start-up goes big? The imperative of capital valorisation, which at first serves to accelerate growth, is no less demanding even after this happens. As its momentum slows, the initial audacity turns into a voracious appetite to eat up other people's projects. YouTube was bought by Google in 2006; WhatsApp was snapped up by Facebook; Apple has already taken over around a hundred companies, including the music-identification app Shazam; Microsoft took over Skype in 2011; and Amazon counts AbeBooks, an online bookshop specialising in antiquarian books, and Whole Foods, a chain of upmarket organic supermarkets, among its many acquisitions. The long list of new services absorbed by the internet giants points to a change in the economic climate. It's not just that yesterday's start-ups have become large companies. Research into the evolution of industrial structures also points to a general trend towards consolidation.

A Revival of the Competitive Dynamic in the Last Quarter of the Twentieth Century. Until the 1980s, the dominant trend was towards integration. The paradigm of this period was the large, vertically integrated, multi-divisional firm as studied by Alfred Chandler, Jr. in his *The Visible Hand: The Managerial Revolution in American Business*.[54] This phase was characterised by a certain stability in terms of organisations: for instance, in the United States most of the companies that dominated their industrial sector in 1919 were still leading forces in 1969.[55] Of course, this stability is not absolute: there was a certain amount of turnover, with some firms disappearing or being absorbed, while new entrants found themselves a place, especially due to the growing might of certain sectors. But this internal mobility, linked to qualitative changes in production activities, accelerated sharply from the late 1970s onward. In several OECD countries, the size of companies began to shrink. There were also more firms starting up and disappearing, signalling major turbulence in the fabric of the economy. Lastly, globalisation has been accompanied by a certain deconcentration of the major multinationals, in terms of their market share.[56]

Five kinds of explanations have been put forward to account for the upturn in the competitive dynamic in the 1980s and 1990s. The first two are general in nature, pointing (i) to the specific nature of information and communication technologies, and (ii) to a phase in the long waves of

54 Alfred D. Chandler, Jr., *The Visible Hand: The Managerial Revolution in American Business*, Cambridge, MA: Belknap Press, 1977.

55 Naomi R. Lamoreaux, Daniel M. G. Raff and Peter Temin, 'Beyond Markets and Hierarchies: Toward a New Synthesis of American Business History', *NBER Working Paper*, 9029, 2002.

56 Giovanni Dosi et al., 'Technological Revolutions and the Evolution of Industrial Structures: Assessing the Impact of New Technologies upon the Size and Boundaries of Firms', *Capitalism and Society* 3, no. 1, 2008.

capitalism; the other three refer to features of the last quarter of the twentieth century, or more particularly (iii) the industrial catch-up by first Europe and then part of Asia, (iv) the restoration of financial hegemony, and (v) the effects of neoliberal policies.

The first explanation is in line with the Silicon Valley consensus, which associates such factors as the rise of ICTs, the disintegration of old concentrated economic structures, and the enduring vitality of small and diversified units. On this reading, the intensification of entrepreneurial activity should be attributed to the lesser advantages of integration and easier access to market exchange, thanks to falling communication costs and improvements in logistical processes. Added to this is a diversification of demand – the result of higher incomes, but also reflecting a certain demassification, linked to a greater variation in individual preferences.[57] According to this model, ICTs' intrinsic characteristics encourage production structures to favour small-scale capital, product diversification, and the mobility of production factors – and all this over the long term.

Yet, in fact, this phase of intensifying competition and restructuring through innovation proved short-lived. What the proponents of the Silicon Valley consensus had taken for a new and permanent principle of change in economic structures was no more than a passing fad. The idea that ICTs are the source of an absolutely unique entrepreneurial form led to a dead end, unable to account for what has been seen since then: that is, economic structures becoming increasingly rigid.

More than a century ago, Rosa Luxemburg observed that 'small capitalists play in the general course of capitalist development the role of pioneers of technical change'.[58] These words would suggest that technological change in general – and not just this or that technology specifically – undermines established industrial structures. Yet, even if we accept this hypothesis, we still need to clarify the reasons for the sheer pace of this renewal and, in particular, the temporary nature of the

---

57 Lamoreaux, Raff and Temin, 'Beyond Markets and Hierarchies'.

58 Rosa Luxemburg, 'Reform or Revolution', 1898, in *Reform or Revolution and Other Writings*, New York: Dover, 2006, p. 18.

upheavals in industrial structures in the final decades of the twentieth century. The 'long-wave' approach takes the view that such moments of turbulence in structures of production are temporary, but also recurrent, corresponding to intense phases of creative destruction: clusters of innovations appear, spread through the economy, destroying old structures before then establishing themselves and deploying their potential in new forms of economic organisation, before they lose their dynamism and are, in turn, destabilised by a new cluster of innovations.[59] The last quarter of the twentieth century would seem to correspond to such a phase of creative destruction, typical of the establishment of a new technological paradigm. One of the symptoms of these moments of upheaval is that the cognitive frameworks that determine businessmen's decisions become blurred, leading to errors of judgement whose enormity only becomes apparent in retrospect. This is how, for example, seventeen different companies, including Xerox, IBM, and Hewlett Packard, refused Steve Jobs's proposal to build a personal computer, thus prompting him to found Apple; or how, in 1986, IBM refused the offer to acquire a 10 per cent stake in Microsoft.[60]

The interpretation based on long waves can be combined with three other factors. The first is heightened international competition. Through a gradual industrial catch-up, European countries, Japan, and later other parts of Asia, gained a foothold in key industries where the United States had in 1945 enjoyed an uncontested domination. The dynamism of the

---

59 The long-wave approach was theorised by the Soviet economist Nicolai Kondratieff, who was executed in one of Stalin's jails in 1938. Christopher Freeman and Francisco Louçã, *As Time Goes By: From the Industrial Revolutions to the Information Revolution*, Oxford: Oxford University Press, 2001; Ernest Mandel, *Long Waves of Capitalist Development: A Marxist Interpretation*, London: Verso, 1980; Carlota Perez, 'Technological Revolutions and Techno-economic Paradigms', *Cambridge Journal of Economics* 34, no. 1, 2009. On the specific question of the changing industrial fabric, see Francisco Louçã and Sandro Mendonça, 'Steady Change: The 200 Largest US Manufacturing Firms throughout the 20th Century', *Industrial and Corporate Change* 11, no. 4, 2002, pp. 817–45.

60 David B. Audretsch, 'Technological Regimes, Industrial Demography and the Evolution of Industrial Structures', *Industrial and Corporate Change* 6, no. 1, 1997, p. 68.

catch-up phase, in which the various industrial stages were completed relatively harmoniously, was replaced by a new situation in which rivalries sharpened, with different countries occupying the same sectors.[61]

Another reading complementary to this one emphasises the restoration of the power of finance. From 1979 onwards, rising interest rates forced firms to cut back on their least profitable activities, and hastened the demise of the least competitive companies. This financial pressure was exacerbated by the growing importance of shareholder value in decision-making processes generally. Managers, who became ever more subject to the short-term value imperatives imposed by shareholders, had to give up on independently pursuing their internal growth policy, and rein in non-essential activities.[62]

The final factor is the implementation of neoliberal policies. Measures to deregulate and abandon industrial programmes at a domestic level, and to liberalise trade and investment at an international level, turned the competitive landscape upside down, undermining a series of institutional protections that had been enjoyed by large monopolistic firms at the national level.[63]

The Historical Trend towards Socialisation. The thesis that ICTs are a persistent factor in deconcentrating economic structures has come against the reality of consolidation which has been observed over the

61 Robert Brenner, *The Economics of Global Turbulence*, London: Verso, 2004; Jacques Mazier, Maurice Baslé, and Jean-François Vidal, *Quand les crises durent . . .*, Paris: Economica, 1984, p. 387; James Crotty, 'The Neoliberal Paradox: The Impact of Destructive Product Market Competition and Impatient Finance on Nonfinancial Corporations in the Neoliberal Era', *Review of Radical Political Economics* 35, no. 3, 2003, pp. 271–9.

62 William Lazonick and Mary O'Sullivan, 'Maximizing Shareholder Value: A New Ideology for Corporate Governance', *Economy and Society* 29, no. 1, 2000, pp. 13–35; Gérard Duménil and Dominique Lévy, 'Neo-liberal Dynamics: Toward a New Phase?', in Kees van der Pijl, Libby Assassi, and Duncan Wigan, eds, *Global Regulation: Managing Crises after the Imperial Turn*, Basingstoke: Houndsmills, 2004, pp. 41–63; Michel Aglietta and Antoine Rebérioux, *Dérives du capitalisme financier*, Paris: Albin Michel, 2004.

63 Pascal Petit, 'Structural Forms and Growth Regimes of the Post-Fordist Era', *Review of Social Economy* 57, no. 2, 1999, pp. 220–43.

past twenty years or so. Yet, there are other factors to account for the turbulence that affected the fabric of production at the end of the twentieth century. The 'long-wave' creative-destruction phase, the intensification of international competition, the rise of finance, and deregulation are all features of the period from the mid-1970s to the turn of the 2000s. What the proponents of the Silicon Valley consensus took for intrinsic features of the new techno-economic regime – start-ups' ability to overtake the leaders of yesteryear, the liberation of entrepreneurial energies through lower transaction costs, the correspondence between product diversification and small economic units – were merely the transient features of a settling-in period. Indeed, since the turn of the millennium, these realities have become much less conspicuous, and they have instead given way to new monopolies.

Evidently, some new platforms have emerged in recent years, with Airbnb and Uber as leading cases in point. Yet this ought not delude us: for the entrepreneurial dynamic of the 1990s really has run its course. There is a strong trend towards consolidation, starting in the United States. There has been a sharp decline in the number of firms entering and exiting the markets, a halving of the number of companies listed on the stock exchange, a rise in average company size, and an increased concentration of sales across most sectors.[64] This means that all indicators point to a remonopolisation of economic structures. An IMF study shows that across most sectors in the advanced economies, companies' market power has increased.[65] It highlights a 39 per cent increase in the

64 Ryan A. Decker et al., 'Where Has All the Skewness Gone? The Decline in High-Growth (Young) Firms in the US', *European Economic Review* 86c, 2016, pp. 4–23; Ryan A. Decker et al., 'Declining Business Dynamism: What We Know and the Way Forward', *American Economic Review* 106, no. 5, 2016, pp. 203–7; Gustavo Grullon, Yelena Larkin and Roni Michaely, 'The Disappearance of Public Firms and the Changing Nature of US Industries: Are US Industries Becoming More Concentrated?', *Swiss Finance Institute Research Paper*, 19–41, 2015; Kathleen Kahle and René M. Stulz, 'Is the US Public Corporation in Trouble?', *NBER Working Paper*, w2285J, 2016; T. Auvray et al., 'Corporate Financialization's Conservation and Transformation: From Mark I to Mark II', *Review of Evolutionary Political Economy* 2, 2021, pp. 431–57.

65 Federico Diez, Daniel Leigh, and Suchanan Tambunlertchai, *Global Market Power and Its Macroeconomic Implications*, IMF, 2018.

margin rate between 1980 and 2016, most of which has occurred since 2000 and which is associated with an improvement in profitability and concentration; this confirms that the rise in margins reflects an increase in corporate market power. Another lesson is that this general trend is mainly driven by a few companies whose revenues, margins, and profitability have increased considerably. The hypothesis of the rise of superstar firms, first documented in the United States, ultimately appears to be a widespread phenomenon across rich countries.[66]

To go a little further in understanding this dual movement – intensifying competition followed by a process of remonopolisation – we can draw on what Marx called the 'historical tendency of capitalist accumulation'. For him, its movement is linked to the socialisation of production, or in other words, the fact that labour and the use of the means of production are increasingly collective in nature. With the rollout of machines, for example, individual room for manoeuvre in the organisation of work tends to be reduced. As productive activity becomes less and less isolated, it takes on an immediately socialised or communal character: 'The co-operative character of the labour process is in this case a technical necessity dictated by the very nature of the instrument of labour.'[67]

Each person's work increasingly draws on the work of others, whether in terms of the methods learned, the standards adhered to, or the technical means used. What is more, the rhythm and quality of the work themselves become more collective. This is the counterpart of the deepening division of labour, the spread of technologies, and the intensified coordination that this growing complexity requires. The result is that the size of production units increases, at the same time as their interrelationships in 'networks' of companies become denser at both the domestic and international levels.[68]

---

66 David Autor et al., 'The Fall of the Labor Share and the Rise of Superstar Firms', *Quarterly Journal of Economics* 135, no. 2, May 2020, pp. 645–709.

67 Karl Marx, *Capital*, vol. 1, London: Penguin, 1990, p. 508.

68 For the purposes of setting out our argument here, we have greatly simplified the difficulties posed by Marx's discussion of socialisation. For a discussion of recent theoretical developments on this theme, see Riccardo Bellofiore, 'The Adventures of *Vergesellschaftung*', *Consecutio Rerum* 3, no. 5, 2018. For a summary of the argument, see Gérard Duménil and Dominique Lévy, 'Dynamiques des modes de production et des ordres sociaux', *Actuel Marx* 52, no. 2, 2012, p. 132.

Figure 1. The 'S'-curve of the socialisation of production

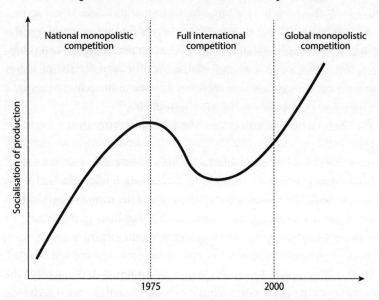

However, this historical movement towards the socialisation of production, which accompanies capital accumulation itself, is not continuous.
Figure 1 depicts it in the stylised form of an S-shaped curve, showing both
this historical tendency towards socialisation and its temporary retreat in
the last quarter of the twentieth century. Indeed, in phases of transition
from one techno-economic paradigm to another, this socialisation levels
off; thanks to the Schumpeterian process of creative destruction, certain
links dissolve while others only begin to emerge from the niches in which
they have formed. Obsolete work processes are scrapped by firm bank-
ruptcies; other, more individualised, more fragmented, not yet standardised ones develop in smaller social spaces. Many attempts fail – many of
these alternatives will be refused social validation when it comes to finding
funders or buyers. These dynamics, whether destructive or creative,
explain the interruption of the socialisation of production. On the other
hand, once they have become established, innovations enable socialisation
to be relaunched on an even larger scale, leading to an interpenetration of

labour processes at an even more granular level. Major innovations such as the steam engine, electricity, chemistry, mechanical engineering, and, of course, ICT, have each in their own way produced more fragmented production methods. But they have also been deployed on a larger scale, helping to give common features and rhythms to the most diverse productive activities across an ever-wider space. In this respect, the transition from national monopolistic competition to global monopolistic competition represents a step forward in socialisation.

The liberal theorist Ludwig Von Mises wrote in 1922 that

> most cartels and trusts would never have been set up had not the governments created the necessary conditions by protectionist measures. Manufacturing and commercial monopolies owe their origin not to a tendency immanent in capitalist economy but to governmental interventionist policy directed against free trade and *laisser-faire*.[69]

The trend in recent years towards the reconstitution of monopolies on a global scale runs exactly counter to this hypothesis and confirms Marx's idea of a tendency towards socialisation.

As we have seen, competition intensified in the last quarter of the twentieth century. This was, in part, a result of the gradual dismantling of protectionist barriers, but it was also an effect of industrial catch-up by several major countries, progress in the field of transport, and the ever-wider use of ICTs. However, after a phase of restructuring, these developments did not lead to the stabilisation of a new competitive order. Rather, they have led to a densification of techno-economic links between organisations, and to a bigger international, if not global, projection for large firms and the production networks which they dominate. Work processes have become more socialised and more internationalised. All this is the exact opposite of the idea – heralded by the conservative proponents of the Californian ideology – of the renewed spread of individualised labour processes.

---

69 Ludwig von Mises, *Socialism: An Economic and Sociological Analysis*, New Haven, CT: Yale University Press, 1951, pp. 390–1.

Preferring Control: The Paradox of the New Spirit of Capitalism

If the 'new spirit of capitalism' analysed by Luc Boltanski and Ève Chiapello had to be embodied in any one location, an obvious candidate would be the bright, modern buildings reserved for creatives at Silicon Valley's tech giants.[70] Google's HQ sells us the dream with its yoga sessions, free restaurants, and twenty-four-hour gyms. It showcases the innocent and open world that the company aims to bring to fruition.[71] This type of workspace is a masterly illustration of the reorganisation of subjectivities initiated by the 'neoliberal *epithumogenesis*' identified by Frédéric Lordon[72]:

> The desire to find employment should no longer be merely a mediated desire for the goods that wages circuitously permit buying, but an intrinsic desire for the activity for its own sake . . . desires for happy labour, or, to borrow directly from its own vocabulary, desires for 'fulfilment' and 'self-realisation' in and through work.[73]

Promising that their 'innovative Silicon Valley spirit is stronger than ever', Google proposes 'an environment where each individual can share their ideas with colleagues at any time, and seek their input'. And indeed, 'taking care of Googlers' seems like an effective way of sparking innovation.[74] Leaving plenty of room for virtuous cycles and the free play of complementarity and collaboration encourages the emergence of what, by definition, is still yet to be discovered. Xavier Niel attempts to drive

---

70 Luc Boltanski and Ève Chiapello, *The New Spirit of Capitalism*, trans. Gregory Elliott, London: Verso, 2007.

71 Émilien Dubrasier and Alexis Dubrasier, 'Dans la Google du loup', *Revue Z* 9, 2015–2016.

72 From the ancient Greek *epithumía* (desire, lust, wish) and the Latin *genere* (to produce, to engender), the concept of *epithumogenesis* means a 'desire-producing work, a deliberate engineering of affects'. See Frédéric Lordon, *Willing Slaves of Capital: Spinoza and Marx on Desire*, London: Verso, 2014, p. 51.

73 Ibid, p. 52.

74 Quotes from Google's 'Mountain View (Global HQ)' career page, google .com.

this same spirit of innovation-through-fun in the flexible offices and the chill zone of Station F, his Paris start-up campus.

The flexibility that facilitates creative work seems reminiscent of the anti-authoritarian revolt of the 1960s, and it would certainly be nice to believe for a second that this could really be the new face of work. Unfortunately, this is not the case. For all the fine rhetoric cooked up in relaxed West Coast offices, the organisational changes that they are actually promoting fuel exactly the opposite dynamic. Marx pointed to the possibility of an increase in the expenditure of labour, in a time that remains the same, thanks to 'a heightened tension of labour-power, and a closer filling-up of the pores of the working day, i.e. a condensation of labour'.[75] Philippe Askenazy now describes the same phenomenon as neo-Stakhanovism. In the warehouses of Amazon or Lidl, in call centres, in the cabs of lorry drivers, or at supermarket checkouts, information technologies are making it possible to smoke out all idle time, to impose new demands on workers and introduce means of surveillance that reach far into their private lives.[76]

The rollout of voice-direction systems is an extreme illustration of the increased constraints that logistics employees have to cope with. Using voice recognition software to communicate directly with the central computer unit, Amazon's order pickers follow step-by-step instructions given over their headphones by a digital voice. Each time that a worker

75 Marx, *Capital*, vol. 1, p. 534.

76 Jean-Robert Viallet's documentary series *La Mise à mort du travail* and the reports broadcast on Élise Lucet's TV programme *Cash Investigation* show the dynamics of work intensification associated with ICTs and the effects that these have on employees. The principle of the hunt for idle time has been pinpointed by sociologists and labour economists since the turn of the millennium, although they place greater emphasis on the *combination* of autonomy and control than on the *polarisation* between these two trends. See 'Travail, ton univers impitoyable', *Cash Investigation*, 19 September 2017; Jean-Robert Viallet, *La Mise à mort du travail*, France 2 and France 3, Yami 2 Productions, 2009; Jean-Pierre Durand, *La Chaîne invisible. Travailler aujourd'hui, flux tendu et servitude volontaire*, Paris: Seuil, 2004; Philippe Askenazy, *La Croissance moderne. Organisations innovantes du travail*, Paris: Economica, 'Approfondissement de la connaissance économique', 2002. See also Ifeoma Ajunwa, Kate Crawford, and Jason Schultz, 'Limitless Worker Surveillance', *California Law Review* 105, no. 3, 2017, p. 735.

picks a parcel, she validates it by reading into the microphone the numbers corresponding to the quantities concerned – thus producing the data that will inform her assessment and decide whether she will be awarded a productivity bonus. This is a brutal system. One worker, Arthur, remembers his first time working with it:

> I nearly got the hell out of there right away! I thought it was really creepy. Honestly, it's kind of spooky ... The voice and everything, which goes 'repeat, this word is not understood'. Especially at the start, when you aren't doing it properly, it happens all the time, you go nuts.

Sociologist David Gaboriau, who gathered this testimony, observes that this voice direction drastically narrows the worker's ability to reappropriate time.[77] While playful subversion strategies and small acts of resistance make it possible to keep a certain distance from such a violent dispossession of one's own self, the margins of individual and collective autonomy are limited in the extreme.

Developments in the organisation of call centre work provide another example of the effects of present-day technological innovations on work organisation. Since the early 2000s, management have gained a much greater control over call centre employees' activity, as a result of the combination of the computer and the telephone. Firstly, automation means that working hours can be controlled much more closely. Workers log in when they start their working day and log out when they stop. Their breaks are automatically timed. As with lateness, any excessive breaks are reported directly to the supervisor. What is more, computerisation makes it possible to record and process a whole range of data on individual performance, putting quantitative, decontextualised information in the hands of managers that is difficult for employees to

---

77 David Gaboriau, 'Quand l'ouvrier devient robot. Représentations et pratiques ouvrières face au stigmate de la déqualification', *L'Homme et la société* 3, no. 205, 2017, pp. 245–68; David Gaboriau, 'Le nez dans le micro. Répercussions du travail sous commande vocale dans les entrepôts de la grande distribution alimentaire', *La Nouvelle Revue du travail*, no. 1, 2012.

challenge.[78] And secondly, the introduction of artificial intelligence programmes in call centres is leading to a further intensification of this control. We are all familiar with the messages from customer service departments telling us that a conversation may be recorded for quality control purposes. This is the case for 1 per cent to 2 per cent of calls. But Microsoft partner Sayint is now offering much more than just checks via sampling: it has developed a technology with which 'you can be sure that your employees are meeting your requirements 100 per cent of the time'. The software records and analyses all conversations in full. The algorithms deal with making sure that the rules have been followed, monitor the sentiment that the two parties convey in their diction and intonation, and give a score to each performance. If a problem is detected, it is immediately reported to the supervisor. The machines are thus tasked with monitoring, evaluation, and, indirectly, decisions affecting workers' pay. This development opens up a deep well of questions for trade unions, and presents traps that human resources departments risk falling into.[79] In any case, it takes us a long way from the Californian dream of newly convivial workspaces.

These two examples illustrate a deterioration in the quality of work; and while this may take widely varying forms depending on the sector and the type of job, it is corroborated by large-scale statistical data. Between 1995 and 2015, European countries saw both an increase in the level of managerial demands and a reduction in the room for employee decision-making across almost all occupations.[80] Each of these two factors is associated with lower job satisfaction. This toxic mix is pushing an increasing proportion of employees into situations of work-related stress, and this has harmful effects both for their health and for society as

78 Jamie Woodcock, *Working the Phones: Control and Resistance in Call Centres*, London: Pluto Press, 2017, pp. 50, 65–6.

79 On the issues raised by algorithmic supervision, see Sarah O'Connor, 'Algorithms at Work Signal a Shift to Management by Numbers', *Financial Times*, 6 February 2018; UNI Global Union, 'Top 10 Principles for Ethical Artificial Intelligence', thefutureworldofwork.com, 2017.

80 Philippe Askenazy, *Share the Wealth: How to End Rentier Capitalism*, London: Verso, 2021, chapters 4 and 5. In May 2018 the author reported that the developments that the book observed in the EU15 countries had continued at least as far as 2015.

a whole. One part of this picture worth noting is that senior managers are the only ones spared. While they, like everyone else, are loaded with increased demands, this extra burden goes hand in hand with a greater autonomy, which offsets the negative effects. The media's preoccupation with 'stressed-out managers' is rather more a reflection of these social layers' capacity to gain visibility, than of them being especially subject to pressure. In truth, this category is relatively *less* affected.

Studies of the United States also show a downward trend since the 1970s.[81] While, on average, work has become richer in terms of the variety of skills used, or with regard to employee autonomy and interdependence, these apparently positive developments are not reflected in any increase in job satisfaction. This is owed to a lack of progress in terms of the meaning of the work performed – scattered amid the fragmentation of tasks – and of the interest to be had in it. This stagnation is the consequence of a reorganisation of work imposed on employees, in which autonomy is conceded to teams only for the sake of achieving an intensification of their activity. It is quite a symptom of disillusionment with the prospect of professional fulfilment that younger generations now value the intrinsic qualities of work less than their elders.[82]

As the psychologist Yves Clot has shown, job satisfaction is inextricably linked to people's power to act, and it is the hobbling of this power to act that degrades work itself:

> To *live* in the workplace is . . . to be able to develop one's activity there, its objectives, its tools, its addressees, by having initiative in shaping the organisation of one's work. Conversely, subjects' activity becomes disaffected when the connections between different aspects of the workplace come to operate independently of this potential initiative. Paradoxically, we will then act without feeling active. But this

---

81 Lauren A. Wegman et al., 'Placing Job Characteristics in Context: Cross-Temporal Meta-analysis of Changes in Job Characteristics since 1975', *Journal of Management* 44, no. 1, 2016, pp. 352–86.

82 Jean M. Twenge, 'A Review of the Empirical Evidence on Generational Differences in Work Attitudes', *Journal of Business and Psychology* 25, no. 2, 2010, pp. 204–5.

disaffection belittles the subject, leaving them derealised, and this also has some bearing on the effectiveness of their working activity, even apart from its effects on their health. This is because the circle of mental processes closes in on him and they become impossible to transform. In this movement, the emotions experienced, which range from resentment towards others to a loss of self-esteem, are no longer motivating or able to fuel dynamism. They no longer develop individual and collective subjective energy. On the contrary, they envelop this energy, protecting it while sterilising it. Psychological activity no longer passes through the emotions. It stops there. The aborted development of activity is lost in emotions which degenerate into 'sad passions', new obstacles to development, indeed into psychic defences – including collective ones – the stoking of which can become an outright fictitious job.[83]

Individual and collective subjective energies must be able to flourish, for good-quality work to be had. Only if individuals can influence the organisation of their professional activity and identify with its aims can they experience satisfaction in their work. Indeed, if the spread of ICT use has translated into a degradation of professional activity, this is because digital tools do not allow most employees to define the purpose and the form of their work. As a result, overactivity and feelings of insignificance often go hand in hand, creating a toxic brew.

This directly contradicts Californian ideology's promise that digital technology will increase individual powers of action. Still, there is no reason to believe that this is an intrinsic effect of these technologies themselves. The problem lies rather more in the use of technology in the capitalist labour process, and the determinants that shape it. The introduction of new technologies is a response to both economic and political pressures. On the one hand, it is driven by a logic of reducing costs, for the sake of companies' survival and, more immediately, their profitability. On the other hand, the organisation of work is also the site in which the wage relation is reproduced, as the political subordination of labour

---

83 Yves Clot, *Travail et pouvoir d'agir*, Paris: PUF, 2014, chapter I.

to capital; and its reproduction is all the more guaranteed, the fewer resources are left in the hands of subordinates.

Competitive pressures have made it necessary for work to become more complex and require more skilled employees. Thus, contrary to the hypothesis that capital is driving a tendency towards the deskilling of work, there is no linear evolution towards a deepening of Taylorisation.[84] Rising levels of education are linked to the sophistication of professional practices. However, this is not synonymous with the liberation of work. This is, firstly, because there can be a simultaneous rise in skills in some sectors of the economy while others are deskilled. In this respect, the example of voice-directed warehouse workers illustrates the persistence and even radicalisation of a dispossession of work that is every bit the contemporary of a relaxation of authority in the creative segments of the digital economy. Secondly, work can be both more complex and more oppressive, because it is more controlled. For example, the stepped-up surveillance of call centre work often goes hand in hand with an increase in the complexity of the worker's tasks, whether in terms of the precision and technical nature of the topics dealt with, their ability to analyse the given situation, or the emotional labour involved in the conversation with customers.

If competitiveness is an imperative, this cannot alone explain why more democratic forms of work organisation are not being developed further. There has been a flowering of so-called 'liberated company' initiatives, in which managers set out to relax hierarchical constraints, the better to unleash employees' initiative and increase their productivity. But even when they are not mere publicity stunts, these experiments are rarely extended – even when they do find success in terms of making

---

84 Harry Braverman, *Labor and Monopoly Capital: The Degradation of Work in the Twentieth Century*, New York: NYU Press, 1998. From the 1980s onwards, it was thus possible to identify a correlated rise in the abstraction and complexity of manual work. In the 1980s and 1990s, the Toyotist model, which allowed a degree of feedback from the point of production to the supervisory-managerial level, gradually took precedence over a strictly Taylorian concept of top-down vertical organisation of industrial work. See Benjamin Coriat, *L'Atelier et le robot. Essai sur le fordisme et la production de masse à l'âge de l'électronique*, Paris: Christian Bourgois, 1994, pp. 218–30.

production more efficient, as with the case of the Volvo plant in Uddevalla, which was shuttered in the early 1990s, or General Motors' Saturn project, definitively abandoned in 2009.[85]

In short, while the introduction of new ICT-related systems in the organisation of work responds to the economic need for competitiveness, and tends to require more skilled employees, it must also be analysed in terms of its effects in changing power relations.[86] The power relationship between capital and labour will shift in employees' favour only if they are given greater latitude in the use of the means of production and the organisation of operations. Conversely, the position of employers – or management – will be improved by the information they have on their employees' actions. This explains why, by and large, they prefer instruments of control that allow them to supervise the execution of employees' tasks as closely as possible.

So, this is not just a question of efficiency or performance. What is at stake, here, is also political. As the Polish economist Michal Kalecki pointed out in his day, '"discipline in the factories" and "political stability" are more appreciated than profits by business leaders'.[87] Managers and directors make decisions on the forms of ICT use in the workplace with the knowledge that to organise production democratically would be incompatible with reproducing their own dominant position.

The zealots for the Californian ideology got one thing right: ICTs have indeed gone hand in hand with a process of increasing skill levels and task complexity. However, the prospects of emancipation have been bartered for increased demands on employees and control over the work process, in turn creating situations of stress and deep dissatisfaction.

---

85 Thomas Coutrot, *Libérer le travail. Pourquoi la gauche s'en moque et pourquoi ça doit changer*, Paris: Seuil, 2018, chapters 6–7. The Saturn experiment is discussed in more detail by Mary O'Sullivan, *Contests for Corporate Control: Corporate Governance and Economic Performance in the United States and Germany*, Oxford: Oxford University Press, 2001, pp. 213–19.

86 Frederick Guy and Peter Skott, 'Power-Biased Technological Change and the Rise in Earnings Inequality', John Roemer Lecture, University of Massachusetts, 2005.

87 Michal Kalecki, 'Political Aspects of Full Employment', *Political Quarterly* 14, no. 4, 1943, p. 326.

Most employees have found that capital's preference for control has outweighed the promises of the 'new spirit of capitalism'.

Increased Spatial Polarisation: The Paradox of Intangibles

Those seeking to explain why Silicon Valley's innovation dynamic has been such a success often point to the culture of freedom and openness said to reign in this region. In the late 1980s, French scholars returning from a research visit to California thus highlighted 'the ease and speed of transfers of knowledge, ideas and technologies from one company to another and from one field to another'. More than 'the conditions of knowledge production', they concluded, it was 'the conditions of its circulation, dissemination and incorporation that appear to have played a decisive role, and this is closely connected to high-skilled employees' great mobility'.[88] An in-depth comparison between Silicon Valley and Massachusetts's Route 128 district confirms that this idiosyncrasy handed the West Coast a decisive advantage.[89] While, in the 1970s, the Route 128 district was by far the leader in terms of job numbers, it lost ground from the early 1980s onward due to a closed organisational model, where the firm, imagined to be self-sufficient, existed in a vacuum and without connection to its environment. Things were quite different in Silicon Valley, where the prevalence of the network form and open labour markets encouraged great entrepreneurial flexibility and a high degree of specialisation among firms. This difference is illustrated by a comparison between two start-ups launched in the early 1980s: Apollo Computer in Massachusetts and Sun Microsystems in California. The difference in the profiles of their managers symbolises the gulf that separates the two worlds. While Apollo's CEO, appointed in 1984, was a fifty-three-year-old General Electric executive, Sun

---

88 Bernard Cuneo, Annie Dona Gimenez, and Olivier Weinstein, 'Recherche, développement et production dans l'industrie électronique. Le processus de production et de circulation des connaissances dans la dynamique de la Silicon Valley', GIP 'Mutations industrielles', Paris, 1986.

89 AnnaLee Saxenian, 'Regional Networks and the Resurgence of Silicon Valley', *California Management Review* 33, no. 1, 1990, pp. 89–112.

Microsystems was run by its founders, who were still in their twenties. While the former imposed a strict dress code, discouraging moustaches and beards, the latter organised monthly beer nights; while the former travelled around in a limousine, in the latter case one of the founders saw his Ferrari dumped in the middle of the company's decorative pond for April Fool's Day, amid gleeful employees dressed up as gorillas ... This climate of irreverence goes hand in hand with a radical individualism that absolves each employee of any kind of organisational patriotism: they cannot count on any protection from their employer but are not expected to show any loyalty either; everyone knows that they will set sail for new climes at the first opportunity. If there is just one characteristic of the Silicon Valley experience that needs grasping, it is the atmosphere of free movement of individuals, that encourages the rapid spread of knowledge.

The cultural brew in Silicon Valley in the 1970s and 1980s doubtless played a decisive role in the spread of this mindset – and in this area's leading role in the world of information technology. But, once the valley had achieved a dominant position, this cultural climate was no longer a decisive factor in explaining why it remains one of the world's most vibrant innovation hubs. Geographical economics shows that firms benefit from agglomeration effects when they can draw on a pool of territorially based resources such as infrastructure, a pool of skilled workers and specialist suppliers. This type of cross-fertilisation dynamic is particularly strong in the knowledge economy. Today's Silicon Valley is thus the result of a cumulative process in which, having gleaned a minor initial advantage, the relevant players increasingly benefited from each other's presence, giving this area a major lead over other regions.

This dynamic of social polarisation has been reinforced by the emphasis placed on employee mobility. While for highly qualified staff this can have positive effects, in terms of the dissemination of knowledge, for the rest – the vast majority – flexibility is synonymous with insecurity. Here again, Silicon Valley is emblematic: almost a third of the population has insufficient income to meet its basic needs, and poverty is endemic. The persistence of particularly deep-rooted racial and gender inequalities, often more marked than in the rest of the United States, also undermines the much-vaunted idea of openness to diversity.[90]

Finally, there is a strictly geographical dimension to the relationship between inequalities and innovation. Innovation is about discovering new combinations: it is about connecting things that were not connected before, and codifying things that were not codified before. Proximity and direct interaction are crucial assets which encourage the social pollination that is essential to the discovery process itself. But much of the tacit knowledge needed for this process is embedded in social networks rooted in real life. People who are involved in creative activities thus have an interest in group formation, in order to benefit from informal exchanges and thus boost their productivity and income.[91] But this creates a real dynamic of segregation. Not only is innovation tending to concentrate in the major urban areas, but this polarisation between town and country is accompanied by a deepening of the social divide between the urban areas themselves, and even between different neighbourhoods in the same town or city.[92]

Here, again, the Californian ideology has been wrong-footed by today's realities. The Magna Carta promised that 'putting advanced computing power in the hands of entire populations will alleviate pressure on highways, reduce air pollution, allow people to live further away from crowded or dangerous urban areas, and expand family time'.[93] But exactly the opposite has happened. In fact, it has become crucial to be

90 Molly Turner, 'Homelessness in the Bay Area', *Urbanist* 560, 2017; David Rotman, 'Technology and Inequality', *MIT Technology Review*, 21 October 2014.

91 This point has been demonstrated for the United States over the period 1990–2010. See Enrico Berkes and Ruben Gaetani, 'Income Segregation and Rise of the Knowledge Economy', SSRN, 2018. On the wider relationship between innovation and inequality, also in the United States, see Philippe Aghion et al., 'Innovation and Top Income Inequality', *NBER Working Paper*, 21247, 2015.

92 Pierre-Alexandre Balland et al., 'Complex Economic Activities Concentrate in Large Cities', SSRN, 2018.

93 Dyson et al., 'Cyberspace and the American Dream'. And: 'Does it encourage geographic concentration? Second Wave policies encourage people to congregate physically; Third Wave policies permit people to work at home, and to live wherever they choose.'

'where it's happening': living in the cities and neighbourhoods where the latest ideas are circulating is a key condition for capturing part of the income associated with the global dissemination of intangible goods. The places where the immaterial products valued around the world are made are the same ones where the most attractive professional opportunities are to be found. It may be that future technological developments will erode the informational advantages of proximity, or that the forces of dispersion will eventually win out (via pollution, congestion, high rents, etc.). But, so far, the 'intangible economy' has in fact fuelled spatial polarisation.[94]

Emphasising this spatial dimension underlines the reality that the idea of Silicon Valley is not generalisable, precisely because of the principle on which it is built. It is an experiment in specialisation that has been self-reinforcing over some time, to the point where it has become a unique cluster of global innovation. This also helps to explain why, alongside success stories such as Boston, Tel Aviv, Bangalore, Singapore, and the Chinese provinces of Guangdong and Zhejiang, so many attempts to create other Silicon Valleys around the world have failed. Doubtless, we can always point to mistaken political decisions that seem to explain these broken dreams, but the fundamental reason for these repeated failures is that it is simply impossible for all attempts at imitation to succeed.[95] To put it another way, the islands of Silicon Valley need an ocean of non–Silicon Valley to survive. It is in non–Silicon Valley that goods are assembled, sorted, and moved; it is on this marginal land that animals are reared and killed, and plants grow; it is to these ignored spaces that waste is transported. In short, this entire world where the vast majority of the planet's population lives is reduced to a merely negligible role by a consensus that overlooks the external conditions of possibility for innovation-oriented geographical specialisation. The Silicon Valley consensus is thus based on a fallacy of composition: this

---

94 Jonathan Haskel and Stian Westlake, *Capitalism without Capital: The Rise of the Intangible Economy*, Princeton, NJ: Princeton University Press, 2018, chapter vi.

95 Josh Lerner, *Boulevard of Broken Dreams: Why Public Efforts to Boost Entrepreneurship and Venture Capital Have Failed – and What to Do about It*, Princeton, NJ: Princeton University Press, 2009.

experience is presented as a model to be imitated, whereas it only works precisely because it is almost unique.

The image of openness and free movement also contrasts with the reality of rampant social inequalities. In order to encourage the movement and flexibility of production factors, promote private risk-taking, and attract investors, the authorities are reducing taxation on capital and high incomes, showing a certain leniency towards tax evasion and tightening intellectual property rights. Such a policy inevitably favours the very rich and hurts the public finances. California was also a pioneer in this regard, with a powerful movement to delegitimise social policies. The 1980s were an economic bonanza for this region.[96] Reagan's arrival in the Oval Office brought a windfall of military contracts. At the same time, financial liberalisation fuelled frenzied property speculation. This upstart prosperity encouraged a brutal counter-offensive by the Right, whose first target was public intervention, an area in which the new Left that had emerged from the 1960s was ill-prepared to respond. Hostility to all forms of bureaucracy and a preference for local experimentation left the ideological ground wide open for the champions of massive tax cuts. As early as 1978, they had won a ballot proposition referendum, known as Proposition 13, which introduced an amendment to the Californian constitution drastically limiting property tax levels. This battle was only the prelude to a series of reforms that dramatically reduced the state's tax base and caused a budget crisis in the early 1990s, with the result that all public services were slashed, with the notable exception of prisons.

So, even if the culture of openness and mobility initially gave Silicon Valley a decisive competitive advantage, the most powerful factor in its success was a territorial dynamic through which it built up cumulative advantages in the field of knowledge production. Yet, the result of this combination of developments is a myopia effect which overvalues the latitude for swashbuckling individual ambition while underestimating the importance of regional economies of scale, which are in any case

---

96 Richard Walker, 'California Rages against the Dying of the Light', *New Left Review* 1, no. 209, 1995.

impossible to generalise. This has a doubly paradoxical consequence. On the one hand, the local fluidity that made Silicon Valley such a success in the first place is shrinking under the weight of the inequalities and segregation – that is, the flip side of agglomeration. On the other hand, the pre-eminence of the economic advantage resulting from this same factor prevents the Silicon Valley experience from being set up as a generalisable model. Because territorial distinction is inherently exceptional, it can make no claim to embody the planet's common future.

Innovation without Growth: The Schumpeterian Paradox

With his notion of creative destruction, the economist Joseph Schumpeter formulated one of the most influential economic ideas of the last century. Following in Marx's footsteps, and setting himself against approaches based on equilibrium, he insisted that capitalism's dynamism relies on a tumultuous process of change in economic structures: the 'fundamental impulse that sets and keeps the capitalist engine in motion comes from the new consumer goods, the new methods of production or transportation, the new markets, the new forms of industrial organization that capitalist enterprise creates'.[97] The theory of economic growth that gives the Silicon Valley consensus its scholarly underpinning has taken up this concept and integrated it into its models. Its credo: innovation drives growth by disseminating new technologies and eliminating obsolete methods.[98]

Yet, if we do take such a perspective, the trajectory of capitalism today can only appear as a paradox. On the positive side, various examples of the development of digital technologies do testify to a proliferation of

97 Joseph Schumpeter, *Capitalism, Socialism and Democracy*, London: Routledge, 2003, pp. 82–3.

98 Philippe Aghion and Peter W. Howitt, *The Economics of Growth*, Cambridge, MA: MIT Press, 2009. In reality, these authors have a rather loose hold on ideas rooted in the social sciences of Schumpeter's time. One incidental (if still telling) indicator of this is the fact that they associate the expression 'creative destruction' with the book *Theory of Economic Development* (see p. 474) and not with *Capitalism, Socialism and Democracy*.

innovations, and a multi-form, qualitative change in the ways in which production, consumption, and exchange take place. In short, there are signs of renewed vitality. On the other side of the coin, however, are other tendencies: the slowing of GDP growth and productivity, an increase in the deadweight of the financial sphere, persistent underemployment, and, last but not least, a rapid deterioration in ecological conditions. These phenomena, added up, all point to decline.

As we have seen, since the 2000s the ideas of innovation and competition have played a central role in public policies designed to rejuvenate productive structures deemed increasingly outmoded. In one sense, these policies have succeeded. They have contributed to a qualitative transformation of the techno-economic landscape. The emblematic firms of the digital age are topping the global list for stock market capitalisation, even though most of them have been in existence for less than two decades (Tables 1 and 2) – and they are extending their lead over the former big hitters of the twentieth century. This represents a real upheaval in this elite group, long dominated by a small number of multinationals.[99]

Table 1. The firms with the highest stock market capitalisation worldwide, 2000

Ranking	Company	Sector	Country	Capitalisation in $bn, as of 28 February 2000
1	Exxon Mobile	Hydrocarbons	US	362
2	General Electric	Conglomerate	US	348
3	Microsoft	Tech/software	US	279
4	Citigroup	Finance	US	230
5	BP	Hydrocarbons	UK	225
6	Royal Dutch Shell	Hydrocarbons	Netherlands	203
7	Procter & Gamble	Household/ personal care goods	US	197
8	HSBC Group	Finance	US	193
9	Pfizer	Pharmaceuticals	US	192
10	Wal-Mart	Retailer	US	188

99 Naomi R. Lamoreaux, Daniel M. G. Raff, and Peter Temin, 'Beyond Markets and Hierarchies: Towards a New Synthesis of American Business History', *NBER Working Paper*, 9029, 2002.

Table 2. World's biggest firms by stock market capitalisation, 2023 (companies-marketcap.com)

Ranking	Company	Sector	Capitalisation in $bn, as of 15 November 2023
1	Apple	Tech	2 915
2	Microsoft	Tech	2 751
3	Saudi Aramco	Hydrocarbons	2 162
4	Alphabet (Google)	Tech	1 682
5	Amazon	Tech/retail	1 506
6	NVIDIA	Tech/chips	1 226
7	Meta (Facebook)	Tech	864
8	Berkshire Hathaway	Finance	770
9	Tesla	Tech/automotive	764
10	Johnson & Johnson	Pharmacy/hygiene products	579

But the surprising thing is that this techno-organisational disruption has not renewed the dynamism of the engine of capitalism. Philippe Aghion, one of the most prominent growth economists, has to admit this, albeit only grudgingly. In his inaugural lecture at the Collège de France, he notes, on the basis of standard data on patents, that 'we are indeed seeing an acceleration of innovation, not only in quantity but also in quality'.[100] He goes on to ask: 'Why is this acceleration in innovation not reflected in growth and productivity?' The answer is that this is 'essentially a problem of measurement', linked to the fact that innovations, especially those that result in the creation of new products, take time to be taken into account in the statistics.[101]

---

100 Philippe Aghion, *Repenser la croissance économique*, Paris: Collège de France/Fayard, 'Les leçons inaugurales', 2016, p. 43.

101 Philippe Aghion et al., 'Missing Growth from Creative Destruction', *American Economic Review* 109, no. 8, pp. 2795–822. For a detailed critique of the methodology adopted, see Michel Husson, 'Monsieur Philippe Aghion bouleverse la croissance', *À l'encontre* (blog), 6 July 2017. While Aghion rejects the term 'stagnation', his position has evolved since his inaugural lecture: he acknowledges the secular trend of declining productivity and growth. While not settling on an explanation for the moment, he cites the harmful effect of low interest rates on capital allocation and the weakening of public investment. See the recording of his lectures on the Collège de France website, particularly the one on 17 October 2017.

The technical discussion on the measurement of productivity and growth raises important questions (see Appendix I). However, in terms of the issues of interest here, namely the dynamics of contemporary capitalism, there is no doubt about the trend.[102] Contrary to what Philippe Aghion suggests, the decline cannot be explained in terms of a measurement problem. Reassessing the impact of innovation would not change anything: productivity and growth are slowing.

Yet more interesting, statisticians also point out that many of the effects of digital innovations are not captured by market exchange and the corresponding accounting. This is obviously the case with Wikipedia, which reduces market production by replacing the output of encyclopaedia publishers. But it is also true of the services provided by Google, social networks, and many applications that are only residually commoditised through advertising. Advertising revenues are integrated into the calculation of market production, as intermediate consumption by advertisers, but there is no direct attribution of services rendered to consumers. This may be surprising, given the major benefits to users. But the statisticians are right to say that 'gains in non-market production appear too small to compensate for the loss in overall wellbeing from slower market-sector productivity growth'.[103] The fact that the most powerful and useful effects of digital technology largely escape the grip of the market economy ought not be overlooked. It is one of the symptoms of the fragility of contemporary capitalism.

Surely, there are conceptual and empirical difficulties in capturing the quality of economic activity within a system of prices – crucial though this is. Still, it is clear that the stagnation of the 2010s was not simply a statistical artefact which conceals the (supposed) real dynamism of the market economy. The financial and macroeconomic shock of the 2008 crisis, endemic underemployment, and the ever-increasing debt burden

---

102 David M. Byrne, John G. Fernald, and Marshall B. Reinsdorf, 'Does the United States Have a Productivity Slowdown or a Measurement Problem?', *Brookings Papers on Economic Activity*, March 2016, pp. 109–82; Gustavo Adler et al., 'Gone with the Headwinds: Global Productivity', *IMF Staff Discussion Note*, 17, 2017.

103 Byrne, Fernald, and Reinsdorf, 'Does the United States Have a Productivity Slowdown or a Measurement Problem?', p. 142.

were all symptoms of deeper ills. The Schumpeterian refrain can here be turned around, so that we can speak of a *destructive creation*. For the efforts to roll out the new techno-economic paradigm are accompanied by a breakdown in the social relations characteristic of the previous phase; and they are also making the economic dynamic more fragile in terms of the reproduction of its material and political conditions.

The Resilience of the Entrepreneurial State: The European Paradox

There is something rather forlorn about the European adventure of recent decades, which gives a strong sense of having fallen short. United under the empire of the market and finance, the Old Continent is mired in a morass of rancour and distrust, which relentlessly reduces all discussions on the progress of integration to narrow budgetary calculations. This shared resentment is rooted in broken dreams of European power. On purchasing power parity (PPP) numbers, the European Union's share of global GDP fell from 25.8 per cent in 1980 to 14.5 per cent in 2023. Admittedly, this decline directly reflects the increased weight of certain countries in the Global South, particularly China, whose economic development has accelerated over the same period. But a comparison with the US, whose share has only fallen from 21.32 to 15.4 per cent, shows that Europe is falling behind.[104] This can be seen in particular in the gap between, on the one hand, the EU's institutional sophistication in terms of macroeconomic management, regulation of competition, and monetary policy, which makes it the spearhead of neoliberalism; and, on the other hand, its relative economic failure, reflected not only in chronic underperformance in terms of growth and employment, but also in the absence of European capital in the top tier of key IT companies. It is striking to note that most of the web services used daily by Europeans are provided by US firms. And, yet, even countries that began from a weaker position, such as China and Russia, have managed to

104 IMF, 'GDP Based on PPP – Share of World', *World Economic Outlook*, October 2023, imf.org.

develop extremely rich digital ecosystems of their own, with search engines (Baidu, Yandex), social networks (Vkontakte, Weibo), and e-commerce sites (Tencent, JD.com) that are among the most visited in the world. Conversely, Europe only features three times in the ranking of the fifty most popular websites, and even that is only thanks to three porn sites: xvideos.com, xnxx.com, and xhamster.desi.[105] This may seem an incidental statistic, but it nonetheless offers a cruel judgement on European success. In 2000, European leaders set themselves the goal of making the region the 'most competitive and dynamic knowledge-based economy in the world'. Today, not only is the EU lagging far behind the United States, but it is also lagging far behind China and Russia in this field. So, what happened?

In the late 1990s, the boom of the new economy in the United States was sorely felt in Europe. Despite the completion of the single market and the launch of the single currency, elites noted that the European economy, specialised in the activities of the second industrialisation, was lagging behind the frontier of technology, as the US drove it forward. The EU then adopted the so-called Lisbon Agenda, at the instigation of the social democratic governments then in power in most member states. This ambitious programme combined, on the one hand, reforms aimed at market liberalisation – including in the labour market – and orthodox budgetary policies, and, on the other hand, a keenly advertised desire to support research, education, and training. However, this first focus soon became the dominant one, and innovation policies were themselves subordinated to the neoliberal framework. This was a cold shower for the progressive economists taking part in the discussions. For want of real social forces mobilising behind these economists' positions, the play of politics left the field open to big businesses' natural inclination towards labour flexibility and the non-interference of the state in their investment policies.[106] According

---

105 Ranking of the most popular website in February 2023 carried out by Similarweb and consulted on Wikipedia: 'List of Most-Visited Websites', Wikipedia, 15 November 2023.

106 The economists in question include regulationists Benjamin Coriat and Robert Boyer, and Luc Soete, one of the theorists of national innovation systems. For a critical presentation, see Bruno Amable, *Structural Crisis and Institutional Change*

to Élie Cohen, this decisive moment explains how Europe fell behind on technology:

> In the 2000s, while Europe was forging ahead with its deregulation and liberalisation programmes, which weakened its various national champions (Alcatel, Siemens, Nokia, Philips, STM, FT, DT, TI, etc.), China was building a powerful telecoms, components and consumer electronics industry from scratch, and South Korea was succeeding in becoming one of the world leaders in mobile multimedia thanks to public investment in networks and the consistency of its main industrial players. As for the United States, it constantly reinvents the ICT industry, with world leaders in the internet (Google and Facebook), IT services (IBM), PCs (Apple) and software (Microsoft, Oracle).[107]

Leaving itself wide open to the winds of competition, forbidding itself from making any sectoral intervention, and incapable of sufficient investment in research and education, the EU is seeing its industrial advantages, patiently built up over previous decades, crumble away – and without these strengths being replaced by new ones. Meanwhile, new entrants to the international market are pursuing strategic policies that speed up the accumulation of skills in innovative sectors. For example, in China, public orders, the technology transfers forced on foreign investors, and measures of political control over the web each provide means of ensuring the domestic development of digital productive forces. This starkly contrasts with what is happening at the same time in Europe, where the choice has been made to leave the initiative for innovation up to companies alone, and to prohibit state interventions that would correct or distort the forces of competition. This implies, on the one hand, that public funding for research should remain well upstream of its marketable applications and, on the other hand, that support for

---

in Modern Capitalism: French Capitalism in Transition, Oxford: Oxford University Press, 2017, pp. 118–21.

107 Élie Cohen, 'Stratégie de Lisbonne: l'avenir d'un échec', *Regards croisés sur l'économie* 11, no. 1, 2012, pp. 128–38.

innovation should be indiscriminate – in what are called 'horizontal policies'.

Let us take the French case. The authorities have had to abandon the logic of building up industrial sectors and major projects, which had, until then, been at the heart of the French innovation system. Without doubt, this approach had led to some notable failures – in particular the Calcul plan launched in the 1960s, with the aim of creating a French IT industry – and some problematic successes, such as the nuclear industry. But, without it, the French industrial catch-up, which proceeded into the 1970s, simply would not have happened. As for the new approach, it has its archetypal instrument in the tax credit for research. This generic system gives companies complete control over their chosen type of expenditure. The idea is simply to support and encourage their spontaneous research and development efforts, in the hope that companies will be incentivised to increase their R and D spending if the government takes on part of the cost. This kind of mechanism is extremely costly – around €7 billion in France for the year 2022 – and encourages its treatment as a mere windfall. Companies can, indeed, be highly inventive in their accounting, totting up types of spending that they would have incurred anyway as 'innovation expenditure'. According to the majority of empirical studies, in reality this scheme has no knock-on effect on R and D and does not increase the number of patents filed. What we have here, then, is a policy of public subsidies devoid of any strategic thinking.[108]

To understand the new philosophy guiding policies to support innovation in Europe, and to grasp the error of judgement that has been made, we need to go back to 1994. As the Californian ideology was taking concrete form on the other side of the Atlantic, it was circulated on the Old Continent in the form of a report entitled *Europe and the*

---

108 Evens Salies, 'Études d'impact du crédit d'impôt recherche (CIR): une revue de la littérature', *Rapport à l'attention de Monsieur Thierry Mandon, secrétaire d'État chargé de l'Enseignement supérieur et de la Recherche*, MENESR/OFCE, 2017. Jean-Pierre Moga, *Projet de loi de finances pour 2023: Recherche et enseignement supérieur*, report in the name of the French Senate's economic affairs commission, official statement 17 November 2022, senat.fr.

Global Information Society. Written under the authority of the then European Commissioner for Internal Market and Industry, Martin Bangemann, with the help of eighteen directors of major companies, the text described an industrial revolution pivoting on information technologies – and called on the European Union to commit to market mechanisms, so that it could make its way into this new era:

> This sector is in rapid evolution. *The market will drive, it will decide on winners and losers*. Given the power and pervasiveness of the technology, this market is global. *The prime task of government is to safeguard competitive forces* and ensure a strong and lasting political welcome for the information society, so that demand-pull can finance growth here as elsewhere.[109]

The development of the productive forces associated with ICTs would have to be the result of the market's own selection of winners and losers; and, since it had an immediately global dimension, it could not tolerate the command of the nation-state. Given these assumptions, the report called on governments to act vigorously in favour of competition. This meant that their task was above all about building a suitable regulatory framework, making efforts towards standardisation, mounting domestic and external liberalisation – and strengthening intellectual property rights. The report rejects any recourse to '*dirigisme* or protectionism' and insists that the initiative for funding must come from the private sector; the public sector is deemed incapable of grasping the changes now underway.

With hindsight, this position seems rather naïve. Firstly, because various countries – China, South Korea, and Russia – have relied on public intervention to handle their entry into the digital age. Secondly, and even more importantly, the United States' own leading position is anything but the result of spontaneous market forces, including in the specific context of Silicon Valley.

---

109 Martin Bangemann, 'Report on the Global Information Society', *Bulletin of the European Union*, Supplement 2/94, p. 13.

The history of Silicon Valley and, more generally, of technological development in the United States is inextricably linked to public intervention. This is first and foremost true in the military-industrial complex, but also in the aeronautics and space sector, notably due to the presence in Mountain View of the Ames Research Center, one of NASA's main such facilities. The imagination and the persistence of Stanford University's leaders in obtaining military research contracts played a decisive role in this story. Hewlett Packard, Litton, and Varian each took off during World War II thanks to the orders they raked in from the US military, as their electronic instruments were used to produce radar. In the 1960s, the military still bought the greater part of all output in semiconductors, which had just been developed.[110] Although the electronics industry did grow somewhat independently of government orders, as a consumer market developed in the 1970s, government support was stepped up again in the 1980s with Reagan's Star Wars programme, while semi-protectionist measures were introduced in response to the growing success of Japanese IT. To this day, state intervention, through targeted research programmes or military orders, is an essential element in the dynamism of innovation in the US thanks to a hidden developmental state.[111] In *The Entrepreneurial State*, published in 2013, Mariana Mazzucato shows the decisive role of public programmes in all the major innovations of recent decades, from the internet and genome sequencing to touch screens and geolocation.[112] Her work demystifies the role of the entrepreneur in the progress of technology, for instance showing that Apple's success is largely due to public spending. Above all, it puts the question of strategic thinking back at the heart of the economics of innovation, by demonstrating that the crucial factor is not just the sheer volume of R and D spending, but that of its allocation to the sectors

---

110 AnnaLee Saxenian, *Regional Advantage: Culture and Competition in Silicon Valley and Route 128*, Cambridge, MA: Harvard University Press, 1994, pp. 20–7. Ann R. Markusen et al., *The Rise of the Gunbelt: The Military Remapping of Industrial America*, Oxford: Oxford University Press, 1991.

111 Fred Block, Matthew R. Keller, and Marian Negoita, 'Revisiting the Hidden Developmental State', *Politics and Society*, 14 February 2023.

112 Mazzucato, *The Entrepreneurial State*.

where the opportunities are greatest. This is a clear rejection of the doctrine that has prevailed in Europe. By taking the myth of Silicon Valley at face value, Europe's leaders have wilfully undermined the entrepreneurial functions of the state. They have thus done a great deal to hobble the development of the productive forces and worsen the Old Continent's social and economic difficulties.

At the end of this overview, we see that there is something rather paradoxical about the pervasive use of Silicon Valley as a reference point. The 'start-up spirit' has given way to predation by private monopolies. The ode to autonomy and individual creativity is leading to computerised management tools that intensify employees' subordinate condition. Territorial polarisation, the concentration of gains in the hands of a few 'winners', and barriers to the dissemination of knowledge all feed the dynamics of marginalisation that hinder both innovation and the enjoyment of its potential benefits. As it has grown, Silicon Valley – and, more broadly, the world of innovation of which it is so emblematic – has turned into a reality sharply at odds with the principles that made it such a success to begin with. It has changed so much that the doctrine at its source is now largely outmoded – thus making the political mobilisation of this myth today a complete anachronism. Ultimately, as Jonathan Haskel and Stan Westlake observe with dismay, the policies to support innovation inherited from this era are caught in a vicious circle:

> To help the intangible economy thrive, policymakers will want to encourage trust and strong institutions, encourage opportunity, mitigate divisive social conflict, and prevent powerful firms from indulging in rent-seeking. But at the same time, an effective intangible economy seems to exacerbate all of those problems, creating particularly socially charged forms of inequality, threatening social capital, and creating powerful firms with a strong interest in protecting their contested intangible assets.[113]

---

113 Haskel and Westlake, *Capitalism without Capital*, pp. 237–8.

This is what the cracks in the Silicon Valley consensus show: contrary to predictions, the accelerated socio-economic changes accompanying the rise of digital technology have not offered capitalism a fresh spurt of youth. On the contrary, a massive build-up of evidence points to an involution of this mode of production.

The Refeudalisation of the Public Sphere

> Whereas economy valorizes growth, efficiency, choice, and negative liberty, polity appeals to the public interest, equal citizenship, democratic legitimacy, and popular sovereignty.
>
> Nancy Fraser[114]

The liberal optimism of the 1990s, which promised the growth of democracy in the wake of open markets, has also fizzled out. Three decades on, we instead have to reckon with a democratic winter.[115] This is the result of a combination of two dynamics. The first is the proliferation of non-democratic forms of capitalist rule. While China and Russia represent the paragons of this type of social formation, the electoral victories of authoritarian leaders in Europe and the United States show that highly undemocratic political forces can come to power in the West, too.

The second significant dynamic is the contempt shown by Silicon Valley firms for individual freedoms and democratic rights. Here, it is

---

114 Nancy Fraser, 'Legitimation Crisis? On the Political Contradictions of Financialized Capitalism', *Critical Historical Studies* 2, no. 2, 2015, p. 164.

115 Steven Levitsky and Daniel Ziblatt, *How Democracies Die*, New York: Viking, 2018; Roberto S. Foa and Yascha Mounk, 'The Danger of Deconsolidation', *Journal of Democracy* 27, no. 3, 2016, pp. 5–17; Roberto S. Foa and Yascha Mounk, 'The End of the Consolidation Paradigm, a Response to Our Critics', *Journal of Democracy – Web Exchange*, 28 April 2017; Robert Kuttner, *Can Democracy Survive Global Capitalism?*, New York: Norton, 2018, p. xvii; Yascha Mounk, *The People vs. Democracy: Why Our Freedom Is in Danger and How to Save It*, Cambridge, MA: Harvard University Press, 2018. These works are concisely presented in French by Jean-Fabien Spitz, 'Le capitalisme démocratique. La fin d'une exception historique?', laviedesidées.fr, 10 July 2018.

worth remembering McLuhan's prediction that information technology would crush hierarchical structures, or Google executives' boast of their role in helping to 'reallocate the concentration of power away from states and institutions and transfer it to individuals'. These promises count for little compared to openings for economic growth, particularly those offered by the Chinese market. In summer 2018, Apple announced that it had entrusted a subsidiary of the state-owned operator China Telecom with the iCloud data of its users based in the country, including their emails and SMS messages.[116] Such blatant forms of authoritarianism are superimposed on a more surreptitious erosion of the old Western democracies. Wendy Brown speaks of 'undoing the demos', with reference to the way in which neoliberal policies are hollowing out a democratic life which is caught between the dulling of public debate and the increased remoteness of key economic decisions from any form of popular influence. The convergence of these trends raises questions about the fragility of what has since the mid-twentieth century been known as 'liberal democracy', and calls for a serious reconsideration of the hypothesis of a 'refeudalisation of the public sphere', as formulated in 1962 by the German philosopher Jürgen Habermas.[117]

For Habermas, the mass media's incursion into households' living rooms in this same period was a decisive factor in the consumerist transformation of the family sphere. The public sphere gives way to cultural consumption in 'a sort of superfamilial zone of familiarity', while public conversation becomes more professional as it becomes commodified.[118]

---

116 Wendy Brown, *Undoing the Demos: Neoliberalism's Stealth Revolution*, New York: Zone Books, 2017.

117 In his book *Strukturwandel der Öffentlichkeit*, translated as *The Structural Transformation of the Public Sphere*, Cambridge, MA: MIT Press, 1989. For a summary of the argument and a critical account of its various dimensions, see Craig J. Calhoun, *Habermas and the Public Sphere*, Cambridge, MA: MIT Press, 1992. Stathis Kouvélakis shows how this thesis is rooted in two pessimistic visions, belonging respectively to conservative sociologists and to the Frankfurt School of Adorno and Horkheimer. Stathis Kouvélakis, *La Critique défaite. Émergence et domestication de la théorie critique: Horkheimer, Habermas, Honneth*, Paris: Amsterdam, 2019, pp. 304–7.

118 Habermas, *The Structural Transformation of the Public Sphere*, p. 152.

While the individual is relegated to the position of consumer of public conversation, the latter is transformed into a mass product whose primary aim is to attract an audience so that it can be promoted through the sale of advertising space. 'What can be posed as a problem is defined as a question of etiquette; conflicts, once fought out in public polemics, are demoted to the level of personal incompatibilities.'[119] This transformation profoundly affects the quality of public debate. The business of information and debate seeks to manufacture consensus or, rather, what we might call cognitive centres around which subjectivities converge. These points of recognition are embodied in personalities more than in clearly articulated opinions.

From the young Habermas's perspective, these developments were destroying the conditions of possibility for a critical and rational discussion of public affairs. Long before the twenty-first century, the decline in the quality of public discussion gave rise to a form of 'refeudalisation of the public sphere', to be understood in two senses. Firstly, if the convergence of opinions is the result of a process in which the spectacularisation and personification of political orientations behind the leader-figure echoes the feudal-style incarnation and representation of power, the criterion of rationality disappears:[120] 'The public sphere becomes the court before whose public prestige can be displayed – rather than in which public critical debate is carried on.'[121]

Secondly, the fusion of mass entertainment with advertising leads to a mixture of genres, characteristic of feudalism, from which the state itself is not immune: 'Because private enterprises evoke in their customers the idea that, in their consumption decisions they act in their capacity as citizens, the state has to "address" its citizens like consumers.'[122]

Habermas points out that capitalist development tends to undermine the political structures that have historically gone alongside it – and to erode their democratic potential. Far from a linear course of development,

119 Ibid., p. 164.
120 Ibid., p. 195.
121 Ibid., p. 201.
122 Ibid., p. 195.

the internal dynamics of this system over time produce ebbs and flows that carry with them the ghosts of feudalism.

This analysis foregrounds the political dimension of the liberal imposture that reduces capitalism to the market economy – that is, the fiction that this economic system is based on exchanges between equals. This myth, developed by nineteenth-century liberal theorists, lives on in the rantings of politicians – for instance, Newt Gingrich, who embraced the ideology of Silicon Valley in the 1990s – who promise a smallholder capitalism. But what happens when open competition between start-up founders leads to a new realm of monopolies? Or, more generally, when society is polarised between the owners of the means of production and the proletarianised layers – and, as is happening today, global inequalities widen to the benefit of a tiny ultra-rich minority? These situations point to a radical asymmetry of economic power, which wrecks any possibility of a rational democratic discussion of the general interest. Given this polarisation, the way that the state intervenes in the struggle between economic actors becomes the essential crux of public debate; the sectors left in a weakened position demand corrective action, while the powerful oppose this with all their forces. The structural inequality of capitalism, and more particularly the aggravation of this inequality in the contemporary world, makes it impossible to distinguish between the private sphere and public action, at the same time as it eliminates the category of general interest.

The space for critical-rational debate is stifled by the blending of the two other powers that control resources: money and administrative power. The post-1945 rise of the social state led some to hope that the bourgeois public sphere would be overtaken by the creation of a public meta-sphere – one capable of structuring debate between organisations each having an internal life fed by rich democratic debate. This is clearly not the path that has been followed over the past four decades. As Nancy Fraser puts it:

> The overall effect is to hollow out democracy at every level. Political agendas are everywhere narrowed, both by external fiat (the demands of 'the markets', 'the new constitutionalism') and by internal cooptation

(corporate capture, subcontracting, the spread of neoliberal political rationality). Matters once considered to be squarely within the purview of democratic political action are now declared off-limits and devolved to 'the markets'.[123]

In parallel to this, the dilapidation of public services and social protections, added to the intensified bombardment of advertising, have led to an increased commodification of everyday life. This itself tends to produce atomised subjectivities, confined to the role of passive consumers of social life and obsessed with individual performance.

The changes in the public sphere resulting from the pervasive spread of electronic communications have not counteracted this decline. Hopes that the internet would help to give democracy a new lease on life did, at first, seem to find some sort of confirmation. In France, for example, intense activity online fuelled lively public discussion during the campaign for the referendum on the draft European constitution in 2005. During the Arab revolutions of 2011 and the various 'squares movements', many commentators emphasised the role that electronic communication played in the mobilisations, suggesting that they heralded a renewal of the public sphere. This potential is really there. But there are also strong countervailing dynamics at work. We know, for example, that the sophistication of interaction mechanisms in social networks limits the possibilities for multi-layered conversation and leads to the formation of largely independent feedback loops that show little awareness of each other. This phenomenon is encouraged, for example, by Facebook, which feeds its users' personal information into its system for prioritising content.[124] Moreover, the democratic potential of the internet is now threatened by the appetites of the sector's major

---

123 Fraser, 'Legitimation Crisis?', p. 180.

124 Mark Zuckerberg announced the new algorithm policy in a post published on Facebook on 11 January 2018: 'The first changes you'll see will be in News Feed, where you can expect to see more from your friends, family and groups. As we roll this out, you'll see less public content like posts from businesses, brands, and media. And the public content you see more will be held to the same standard – it should encourage meaningful interactions between people.'

corporations, with the development of digital rights management (DRM) and the undermining of the principle of net neutrality. Finally, the massive appropriation of data by major companies and government security agencies is posing unprecedented threats to individual and collective freedoms. It is against this backdrop that – alluding to Habermas's notion of the refeudalisation of the public sphere – the idea of 'digital feudalism' has gained currency in the field of cultural and media studies.[125]

This idea deserves further exploration. To that end, I am now going to examine the relationship between capitalism and control in the age of Big Data: the phenomena of surveillance, dependence, capture, monopolisation, new forms of rentierism, etc. In small steps, what will emerge, beyond a simple reminiscence of this or that aspect of feudalism, is a configuration that evokes the feudal logic in its entirety. In other words, the possibility of techno-feudalism.

---

125 Sascha D. Meinrath, James W. Losey, and Victor W. Pickard, 'Digital Feudalism: Enclosures and Erasures from Digital Rights Management to the Digital Divide', *Advances in Computers* 81, 2011, pp. 237–87.

2

On Digital Domination

The Age of Conquest

Digital platforms are often described as digital real-estate, hence why what's happening now can be equated to the discovery of a new and highly luscious frontier . . . In classic Wild West terms . . . rents flow to the pioneers who can police and protect those territories . . . If all of the above sounds like a frightfully medieval problem for society, that's probably because it really is an uncanny echo of that era in history. The only real difference now is the digital form of the landscape. The nature of the lords taking tribute payments remain the same.

Izabella Kaminska[1]

It's become a ritual. Each year, Amazon's annual report reproduces the letter Jeff Bezos sent to shareholders when the company was first floated back in 1997. Surely, there is remarkable consistency both in the

---

1 Izabella Kaminska, 'The Sharing Economy Will Go Medieval on You', *Financial Times*, 21 May 2015.

company's project and in the strategy it pursues. In his letter, Bezos explained that Amazon's calling is not just a matter of saving its customers time and money: 'Tomorrow, through personalization, online commerce will accelerate the very process of discovery.'[2] Meaning: through the accumulation of personal and contextual data, Amazon will get one step ahead of the consumer's choice. Its aim is to anticipate demand – or even to generate it by recommending products relevant to the individual customer.

Ever since then, Amazon's core business has not been the book trade, but transforming the cognitive conditions of customers' access to goods, by means of contextualisation. Friedrich Hayek saw competition, and in particular market competition, as a 'discovery procedure' – a means of generating knowledge.[3] Bezos frames Amazon's system in similar terms: the company creates a method for producing knowledge and exploiting data in order to guide customers' access to market goods and services. It is this generic socio-economic function that explains why Amazon has become such a generalist business. The initial ambition to 'create an enduring franchise, even in large and established markets' is based on a radical innovation: the mass collection of digital data, in order to steer economic transactions.[4]

Amazon is not a conglomerate of disparate businesses whose combination could lead to abuses of their dominant position. It is a generalist-specialist firm. This oxymoron stems from the universally indispensable nature of its field of specialisation in complex societies. Amazon produces economic coordination: indicating the right product, at the best price,

---

2 Amazon, *2017 Amazon Annual Report, 2018 Amazon Annual Report*, ir.aboutamazon.com.

3 Friedrich A. von Hayek, 'Competition as a Discovery Procedure', trans. Marcellus S. Snow, *Quarterly Journal of Austrian Economics* 5, no. 3, 2002 (1968), p. 9.

4 This coordinating role, found also in other platforms such as Google or Uber, prompts a series of debates about the nature of algorithmically structured price systems, with some suggesting that the type of knowledge thus generated allows a parallel with centralised planning systems and their cognitive limitations. See Pip Thornton and John Danaher, 'On the Wisdom of Algorithmic Markets: Governance by Algorithmic Price', SSRN, 2018.

and making it available in the right place at the right time. To do this in a more flexible and pinpointed way than the Soviet Gosplan ever could have, Amazon needs data, which demands growth. This thirst for expansion, as a prerequisite for accumulating ever more data, explains why, right from the outset, Bezos's project was designed to build long-term leadership:

> We believe that a fundamental measure of our success will be the shareholder value we create over the *long term*. This value will be a direct result of our ability to extend and solidify our current market leadership position. The stronger our market leadership, the more powerful our economic model. Market leadership can translate directly to higher revenue, higher profitability, greater capital velocity, and correspondingly stronger returns on invested capital.[5]

This emphasis on long-term development has earned Bezos praise even from one of financial capitalism's fiercest critics, Bill Lazonick.[6] A specialist in financialisation, Lazonick is an expert in the distribution of value to shareholders. For the past two decades, he and his team have been studying how company directors distribute profits to the financial markets in the form of dividends and share buybacks rather than reinvesting them in firm development. The researchers see this propensity to distribute profits as one of the main causes of stagnationist trends and rising inequalities. From this standpoint, Amazon is not a financialised company; it is, in fact, one of very few large American companies to hold on to its profits. Over the two decades since its flotation, Amazon has never paid dividends to its shareholders. While Standard & Poor's 500 companies gave away some 98 per cent of their profits between 2012 and 2017, Amazon was investing, innovating, and expanding its business at breakneck speed.

---

5 Amazon, *2017 Amazon Annual Report*.
6 William Lazonick, 'Opinion: The Secret of Amazon's Success', *New York Times*, 23 November 2018.

Cyberspace as a Territorial Space

To understand the logic behind this investment and the emphasis that Amazon places on retaining leadership, we can go back to one of the insights expressed in Magna Carta: the analogy between cyberspace and the conquest of the American West:

> Cyberspace is the latest American frontier . . . The need to affirm the basic principles of freedom [exists] . . . in part because we are entering new territory, where there are as yet no rules – just as there were no rules on the American continent in 1620, or in the Northwest Territory in 1787.[7]

Magna Carta's authors were above all concerned with building ideological continuity between a pre-existing political imaginary – individualism and smallholdings – and the new field of human activity that was being opened up by digital networks. This is why they resorted to the metaphor of conquest. But this image soon took on other connotations, which were first strategic, then geological. As early as 2009, the US armed forces' press service explained: 'Cyber operations simply are another theater of operations for the U.S. military, and the Defense Department must apply the same analytical rigor and resources to it as it would to any other theatre.'[8] Then, a piece published by the *MIT Technological Review* in 2016 reported that digital networks open up access to a new subsoil teeming with resources to be extracted: 'From a data-production perspective, activities are like lands waiting to be discovered. Whoever gets there first and holds them gets their resources – in this case, their data riches.'[9]

---

7 Esther Dyson, George Gilder, George Keyworth, and Alvin Toffler, *Cyberspace and the American Dream: A Magna Carta for the Knowledge Age*, Progress & Freedom Foundation, August 1994, pff.org.

8 Jim Garamone, 'Questions Abound in Cyber Theater of Operations', American Forces Press Service, US Department of Defense, 9 June 2009.

9 MIT Technology Review Insights and Oracle, 'The Rise of Data Capital', *MIT Technology Review*, 21 March 2016.

This new land to be conquered stretches far and wide, and covers everything that can be digitised: images from video surveillance, historical till receipts, usage data from connected devices (mobile phones, audio speakers, fridges, smoke detectors, thermostats, 'smart' meters), transactions and interactions on digital networks (online forms, e-banking services, social media posts), web browsing and location data, feedback from sensors built into objects (industrial equipment; public transport passes), electronic passports, DNA samples, and so on and so forth. The colonisation of these new data-rich lands is the result of a wide variety of technical and legal devices. But, in all cases, it involves a form of territorial appropriation: the idea is to plant markers wherever data can be extracted. This is the extractivist moment in the formation of Big Data, the moment of capturing sources.

As an example of this extractivist logic, we can look to the distribution of the Android operating system. Google has made Android available free of charge to mobile phone makers in order to gain a strategic market position, bypassing Apple's ecosystem of software and becoming the default entry point to the internet from smartphones. In 2023, more than 70 per cent of smartphones ran on Android, and Google applications are among the most widely used. As *Politico* writes – itself using the metaphor of territorial appropriation – this foray into mobile technology via its operating system has allowed Google to 'build prime online real estate', giving the Mountain View firm a growth driver for its advertising revenues.[10]

On Convergence

According to Nick Srnicek, a leading theorist of accelerationism, digital platforms' appetite for data is central to explaining their growth, which follows 'rhizomatic connections driven by a permanent effort to place themselves in key platform positions'. Mergers and acquisitions do not obey a logic of horizontal concentration aimed at increasing market

---

10 Mark Scott, 'What's Really at Stake in Google's Android Antitrust Case', *Politico*, 15 July 2018.

power in a given segment. Nor do they pursue a logic of vertical integration, seeking to combine immediately complementary activities such as, for example, telecommunications networks and the production of audio-visual content. Neither a simple horizontal concentration nor a pure vertical integration, platforms' development follows an expansion strategy guided by the aim of conquering data sources. This observation informs what Srnicek calls his 'convergence thesis', namely

> the tendency for different platform companies to become increasingly similar as they encroach upon the same market and data areas. Currently there is a plethora of different platform models . . . Given the need to expand data extraction and to position oneself in strategic locations, it would appear that companies are tendentially drawn into similar areas. This means that, despite their differences, companies like Facebook, Google, Microsoft, Amazon, Alibaba, Uber, and General Electric (GE) are also direct competitors.[11]

In other words, whatever their original trade may have been, their strategies for conquering cyberspace now all have the same objective: to take control of the spaces used to observe and capture data generated by human activities. So, contrary to what is often claimed, Big Data also faces the problem of scarcity.[12] While Big Data can be reproduced at miniscule costs, *original* data is rare. Hence the logic of cyberspace expansion, over a limited territory, which spans sectoral boundaries. Hence, too, platforms' tendency to become generalist firms, as illustrated by the enormous list of competitors which Amazon identifies in its annual report:

> Our businesses encompass a large variety of product types, service offerings, and delivery channels . . . Our current and potential

---

11 Nick Srnicek, *Platform Capitalism: Theory Redux*, Cambridge: Polity, 2017, p. 108.

12 For instance, Evgeny Morozov writes: 'There is, after all, one important aspect in which data is decisively not like oil: it's not scarce', in 'Capitalism's New Clothes', *Baffler*, 4 February 2019.

competitors include: (1) online, offline, and multichannel retailers, publishers, vendors, distributors, manufacturers, and producers of the products we offer and sell to consumers and businesses; (2) publishers, producers, and distributors of physical, digital, and interactive media of all types and all distribution channels; (3) web search engines, comparison shopping websites, social networks, web portals . . . (4) companies that provide e-commerce services, including website development, advertising, fulfillment, customer service, and payment processing; (5) companies that provide fulfillment and logistics services for themselves or for third parties, whether online or offline; (6) companies that provide information technology services or products, including on-premises or cloud-based infrastructure and other services; and (7) companies that design, manufacture, market, or sell consumer electronics, telecommunication, and electronic devices.[13]

Context Is King

At the end of the 1990s, the web still counted rather little as a site of commerce. In 1997, online purchases accounted for just $1.5 billion – a drop in the ocean of the overall $2,500 billion in sales.[14] In the same year, only $550 million was spent on advertising on the internet. Admittedly, this figure was growing rapidly – it hit $2 billion the following year. But this was still a tiny amount compared to the $285 billion spent on advertising in the United States annually.[15] Back then, commercial activity on the internet was still limited, and it lacked stable business models. Companies' early feedback about online sales was disappointing, and many marketing managers remained sceptical. In 1998, Procter & Gamble, the consumer goods giant (a producer of personal hygiene and beauty products), spent some $3 billion on promoting its wares. In

---

13 Amazon, *2017 Amazon Annual Report*, p. 4.

14 Pradeep K. Korgaonkar and Lori D. Wolin, 'A Multivariate Analysis of Web Usage', *Journal of Advertising Research* 39, no. 2, 1999, p. 53.

15 Brian Kahin and Hal R. Varian, 'Introduction', in Brian Kahin and Hal R. Varian, eds, *Internet Publishing and Beyond: The Economics of Digital Information and Intellectual Property*, Cambridge, MA: MIT Press, 2000.

August of that year, it invited hundreds of marketing and internet profes-
sionals, including its own competitors, to its Cincinnati, Ohio, HQ for a
conference entitled 'Future of Advertising Stakeholders Summit'.[16] This
event was surely unusual. It was motivated by frustration at the difficulties faced by the nascent online advertising industry. Some of the hiccups
were technological: too little bandwidth, non-harmonised norms and
standards, unreliable audience measurement. But the other major issue
was the acceptability of online advertising to consumers, and in particular the question of the right to privacy. The Cincinnati summit helped to
identify the strategic lock that needed to be broken if the web was to be
'commercialised': that is, getting consumers to accept the use of their
personal data for marketing purposes.

In 1999, professors of marketing Donna Hoffman and Thomas Novak
published an article entitled 'Advertising Pricing Models for the World
Wide Web'.[17] The authors distinguished between two types of websites
that would earn advertising revenue: sites with sponsored content, such
as CNN, and then the search engines that guide users around the web, in
this era meaning names such as Yahoo!, Netscape, or Excite. The challenge for these sites' publishers was to create a market for advertising. All
the important parameters remained undefined – the format, the audience, what approaches were most effective . . . But two pricing models
were already emerging.

---

16 Kate Maddox, 'P&G: Interactive Marketer of the Year', *AdAge*, 3 May 1999,
adage.com; Stuart Elliott, 'Procter & Gamble Calls Internet Marketing Executives to
Cincinnati for a Summit Meeting', *New York Times*, 19 August 1998.

17 This article is published in a book with an abstruse title: *Internet Publishing
and Beyond*. It was edited by Brian Kahin, who was founder-director of Harvard's
Information Infrastructure Project (between 1989 and 1997) before holding various
positions linked to the information economy, notably in the US government and at
the OECD. The other editor of this volume was Hal R. Varian: then a dean at the
School of Information Management and Systems at UC Berkeley, he joined Google
in 2002 as a consultant and then chief economist. The book brings together papers
originally presented at a 1997 conference at Harvard attended by Esther Dyson, a
co-author of *Magna Carta for the Knowledge Age*. It is therefore a book at the crossroads of two worlds: the dream of digital capitalism and its realisation. See Donna L.
Hoffman, and Thomas P. Novak, 'Advertising Pricing Models for the World Wide
Web', in Kahin and Varian, *Internet Publishing and Beyond*.

The first, which was more common at the time, was based on page views, using a logic of audience numbers similar to traditional media. This quite simply meant counting the number of internet users who visit a given page. But relying on this measurement technique is unsatisfactory, given the possibilities offered by the web. Banners placed on the home pages of generalist sites should not be valued in the same way as those that directly echo the content of a narrowly defined search. On the internet, from the point of view of promotion, 'context, not the content, is king'.[18]

The second yardstick – clicks – reflects the differentiated effectiveness of advertising in different contexts. Here again, Procter & Gamble was in the lead. As early as 1996, the company told the search engine (Yahoo!, in this case) that it would pay only for internet users' clicks, rather than for the raw number of views of the advertising banners. Simple and straightforward, pay-per-click advertising would be widely adopted. Advertisers were interested in potential customers' response to their messages, and the internet offered 'the first commercial medium in which it is actually possible to measure consumer response, not just to assume it'.[19] The click thus became the measurable yardstick of internet users' reactions.

The two methods based on banners and clicks reflected the distinct positions of the publisher and the advertiser: the former gives up part of its publication space and expects to be remunerated proportionally; the latter is interested in the actual movement of internet users in the desired direction. In the 2000s, this difference led to the emergence of a combined measure: the expected click-through rate – an estimate of the number of clicks that a given advertising impression will receive. This expected click-through rate, supplemented by marketing indicators of message quality, provides the basis on which online advertising space can be allocated to the highest bidder, in auction systems, by the main search engines.[20]

---

18 Kahin and Varian, 'Introduction', p. 2.
19 Ibid., p. 53.
20 Ibid., p. 4.

Admittedly, clicks are hardly a perfect indicator. They do not directly imply engagement with the brand, let alone an actual purchase. However, this did offer the starting point for a new marketing concept based on the creation and measurement of interactivity. The click signals that the internet user is on the move, from the site where she intentionally arrived to the site that the advertiser wants to show her; it is a direct and precisely measurable response to the advertising message. This change in marketing perspective heralded a radical upheaval, which Hoffman and Novak perceived with extraordinary foresight already in 1999. They explain the prospect that lies ahead of online advertising – a contextualised and all-encompassing grasp of the interaction between customer, message, and product.

> It will be necessary to develop a set of integrated response measures, over time and, possibly, over sites that relate exposure and interactivity metrics to consumer response. Exposure and interactivity metrics may take the form, for example, of purchase behavior in an online storefront, attitude change, and the number of visitors who request further information. The development of such metrics, however, requires two things: (1) identified visitors and (2) multi-site data on every Web site involved in the integrated marketing campaign. Until these data are available, the measurement of outcome remains elusive. In addition to the metrics described above, several other behavioral and psychological measures should be considered in the context of Web advertising measurement. These additional measures include primary navigation patterns through the Web site; cross-site navigation patterns; demographic, psychographic, and behavioral characteristics of visitors . . .; cognitive and attitudinal measures, including flow; and visitor loyalty and repeat visits. It is anticipated that innovative future pricing models will incorporate these measures in unique ways.[21]

They thus foresaw cross-site, intertemporal data integrating experiences both in cyberspace and in the real world . . . Yet the data required for these emerging advertising regimes raised complex ethical and political issues, of which the authors were readily aware. On the one hand, there would be

---

21 Ibid., pp. 55–6.

considerable potential for intrusion into private life: 'A networked, distributed computing environment such as the Internet offers unprecedented opportunities for the invasion of privacy. Information about individuals is more accessible and more easily combined and integrated than in the physical world.'

On the other hand, it would be against companies' interests for consumers to be too cautious about these intrusions: 'There is a tension between the marketer's need to have information about individual consumers for the purpose of targeted marketing efforts and the consumer's right to privacy.'[22]

These issues are made all the more delicate because consumer rights and the protection of privacy were 'potential points of entry for government regulators into the Web marketplace.'[23]

We hadn't even entered the new millennium, and tracking and aggregation techniques were still in their infancy, but marketing theorists had already identified the parameters of the central political problem: marketising the web requires an exhaustive surveillance regime, whose political sustainability is uncertain.

Algorithmic Governmentality and Surveillance Capitalism

> This spectral someone other looks at us, we feel ourselves being looked at by it, outside of any synchrony, even before and beyond any look on our part, according to an absolute anteriority . . . and asymmetry, according to an absolutely unmasterable disproportion. Here anach[r]ony makes the law. To feel ourselves seen by a look which it will always be impossible to cross, that is the *visor effect* on the basis of which we inherit from the law.
> Jacques Derrida[24]

Big Data has three main characteristics: it is generated continuously, it aims to be both exhaustive and granular, and it is produced flexibly,

---

22 Ibid., p. 57.
23 Ibid., p. 56.
24 Jacques Derrida, *Specters of Marx*, New York: Routledge, 1994, pp. 6–7, translation corrected.

so that further data sources can always be added in.[25] In other words, Big Data aggregates information from different domains, which had not necessarily been in any way linked beforehand. This heterogeneous data is processed in a characteristically agnostic way: connections and relations are brought to light, without any attempt being made to explain them. These properties of Big Data feed a naïve empiricist epistemology, which imagines that this new regime of knowledge proceeds by purely automatic induction – that the data can deliver the truth without first heading through the diversions of theory. But this is not at all the case.[26] This data expresses a necessarily partial point of view and only makes sense in relation to previously constituted knowledge. It is not innocent. Big Data contains theory, crystallised in the algorithms that organise it, because the search for regularity that governs it depends on the prior construction of hypotheses.

Big Data is also loaded with social biases and relations of domination. Artificial intelligence software not only reflects the racial or gender inequalities embedded in institutions and power relations but can also help to amplify them.[27] The prejudices they contain are, in turn, incorporated into other algorithmic results. It has been shown that Word Embedding, a linguistic analysis programme, classifies names with European American connotations as pleasant, and African American names as unpleasant. Another example: because the databases that train the algorithms of autonomous vehicles to recognise pedestrians are mainly made up of light-skinned people, the machines systematically detect dark-skinned pedestrians less effectively, and they therefore run a greater risk of collisions. The

25 Rob Kitchin, 'Big Data, New Epistemologies and Paradigm Shifts', *Big Data and Society* 1, no. 1, 2014.

26 Ibid., pp. 4–5; Jean-Christophe Plantin and Federica Russo, 'D'abord les données, ensuite la méthode? Big Data et déterminisme en sciences sociales', *Socio. La nouvelle revue des sciences sociales* 6, 2016, pp. 97–115.

27 Safiya Umoja Noble, *Algorithms of Oppression: How Search Engines Reinforce Racism*, New York: New York University Press, 2018; James Zou and Londa Schiebinger, 'AI Can Be Sexist and Racist – It's Time to Make It Fair', nature.com, 18 July 2018.

negative implications of this bias in everyday life are known as 'predictive injustice'.[28]

Big Data is not neutral. But even if the biases and prejudices that it conveys could be corrected, this would still not be the end of our concerns. Antoinette Rouvroy and Thomas Berns have proposed the concept of 'algorithmic governance' to designate 'a certain type of (a) normative or (b) political rationality based on the collection, aggregation and automated analysis of massive quantities of data for the purpose of modelling, anticipating and altering possible behaviour in advance'.[29] This form of governmentality bypasses human subjects and deprives them of reflexivity. Its aim, as Rouvroy and Berns put it, is 'to produce action without the formation or formulation of a desire'.[30] Individuals are absolutised, caught up in the complexity of their multiple determinations, but also disarticulated, reduced to a series of measurements that confine them within probabilistic possibilities. Like Alphaville, the futuristic city imagined by Jean-Luc Godard, the algorithmically governed society begins to resemble 'an entirely technical society . . . like those of ants or termites' in which 'people have become slaves to probability'.[31]

The attempt to reduce human existences to probabilities risks stripping individuals and communities of control over their futures. Deprived of their ability to defy probabilities – in other words, to challenge the existing reality – subjectivities lose all their power. This risk of derealisation is by no means inevitable. Yet, this risk is continually rising, under the pressure of the algorithmic governmentality harnessed by digital firms' profit strategies.

---

28 Benjamin Wilson, Judy Hoffman, and Jamie Morgenstern, 'Predictive Inequity in Object Detection', arXiv.org, 2019.

29 Antoinette Rouvroy and Thomas Berns, 'Gouvernementalité algorithmique et perspectives d'émancipation. Le disparate comme condition d'individuation par la relation?', Réseaux 177, no. 1, 2013, p. 173.

30 Ibid., p. 177.

31 Jean-Luc Godard, Alphaville, 1965.

Big Other Watches Over a World with No Escape

The mobilisation of Big Data by companies is part of a social project that Shoshana Zuboff calls 'surveillance capitalism'.[32] This system is based on a profit strategy which consists of 'predict[ing] and modify[ing] human behaviour as a means to produce revenue and market control'. Surveillance capitalism thus requires a unilateral and exhaustive knowledge of human experience, which it transforms into predictive behavioural data. The suggestion and prescription informed by Big Data make behaviour more predictable for the purposes of targeted marketing. But surveillance capitalism does not stop there. The horizon of the quest for ever more accurate prediction, says Zuboff, is to steer human behaviour.

This Big Other, which absorbs all the data we give it, comes to know us better than we know ourselves. It explores everything from the details of our correspondence to the movements in our bedroom and the inventory of what we have consumed. Through massive online experiments, it learns to guide our actions and ends up embodying a new kind of totalitarianism. Where the totalitarianism of the twentieth century operated through violence, this new power, described by Zuboff as 'instrumentalist', works by altering behaviour.

While opposed on almost every other issue, Hayek and Keynes shared the conviction that economics was ultimately a problem of information and knowledge. This led Keynes to emphasise radical uncertainty and its implications for the psychology of economic actors. He thought that economic policy should account for this psychological dimension of economic behaviour and, through vigorous intervention, counteract the depressive spirals in which negative sentiment turns into self-fulfilling expectations. Conversely, for Hayek, the intrinsically dispersed nature of knowledge is incompatible with public intervention. Only the market

---

32 Shoshana Zuboff, 'Big Other: Surveillance Capitalism and the Prospects of an Information Civilization', *Journal of Information Technology* 30, no. 1, 2015, p. 75; Shoshana Zuboff, *The Age of Surveillance Capitalism: The Fight for the Future at the New Frontier of Power*, New York: PublicAffairs Books, 2019.

can mobilise knowledge that is essentially inaccessible because of its tacit and situated nature. As a result, any disruption to the competitive dynamic can only worsen the quality of the cognitive process at the level of society and, consequently, will lead to poor economic decisions.[33]

Yet, a distinctive feature of the new logic of accumulation turns the preoccupations of Hayek and Keynes on their head. What is central is no longer uncertainty or the unknowable but, on the contrary, the predictable. Zuboff sees in the strategies of surveillance capitalists a 'race for higher degrees of certainty'; they have no choice but to tighten their grip on social activity. Each in their own way, Amazon, Google, and Facebook are heightening this vital link between the extension of surveillance and creating value.

Amazon and the Logic of Recommendation. One of the secrets of Amazon's success lies in its 'recommender' system, and its advantages in personalising the sales context:

> For two decades now, Amazon.com has been building a store for every customer. Each person who comes to Amazon.com sees it differently, because it's individually personalized based on their interests. It's as if you walked into a store and the shelves started rearranging themselves, with what you might want moving to the front, and what you're unlikely to be interested in shuffling further away. From a catalog of hundreds of millions of items, Amazon.com's recommendations pick a small number of items you might enjoy based on your current context and your past behavior.[34]

This personalisation of experience comes from collaborative filtering algorithms that draw on the experience of other users. However, rather than matching customers to other customers with a similar profile, the

33 Philip Mirowski and Edward M. Nik-Khah, *The Knowledge We Have Lost in Information: The History of Information in Modern Economics*, Oxford: Oxford University Press, 2017.

34 Brent Smith and Greg Linden, 'Two Decades of Recommender Systems at Amazon.com', *IEEE Internet Computing* 21, no. 3, 2017, p. 12.

system invented at Amazon is organised on the basis of objects: each item purchased and evaluated by the user is associated with similar items, which are then combined in a list of recommendations based on the degree of proximity between them.[35] This list is refined using various metrics. For example, it integrates a temporal dimension, meaning that the system integrates the sequential logic of certain purchases (such as the successive volumes in a series of novels) or even individuals' socio-biological developments (ageing, the cycle associated with the birth of a child, etc.). One of the main advantages of this technique is that the bulk of the calculations take place offline, making the system both powerful and fast. The system is extremely effective. Click-through rates and conversions into purchases are very high. It is said to generate around 30 per cent of page views on Amazon. On Netflix, which uses the same type of process, 80 per cent of videos watched are accessed through this same intermediary, thus making it an essential factor in this firm's value-creation.[36] So, there is a circular relationship between recommendation and action: the quality of the targeting depends on the quality of the guidance; and, conversely, the guidance will be validated or not by the user's action, which in turn informs the cycle of future recommendations.

Google and Context-Aware Ranking. Google's parent company, Alphabet, is first and foremost an advertising giant. In 2022, this activity generated about 80 per cent of its revenue and the company controlled 28 per cent of the total online advertising market in the United States.[37] The system for selling advertising space that has made Google's fortune is based on two elements, whose power combines. The first is the performance of the search engine itself. The ranking system invented by Sergey Brin and Lawrence Page is built on the web's architecture of hypertext

35 Greg Linden, Brent Smith, and Jeremy York, 'Amazon.com Recommendations: Item-to-Item Collaborative Filtering', *IEEE Internet Computing* 1, no. 1, 2003, pp. 76–80.

36 Smith and Linden, 'Two Decades of Recommender Systems at Amazon.com', p. 14.

37 Patience Haggin, 'Google and Meta's Advertising Dominance Fades as TikTok, Streamers Emerge', *Wall Street Journal*, 3 January 2023.

links.[38] Unlike early search engines, which mainly worked on the basis of keyword analysis, Google's prototype takes into account both the number of links pointing to a page and the relative importance of the pages containing these links, as well as other factors such as the link text, the locality of the request itself, and visual characteristics such as font size. The success it encountered as a new search engine comes from the power of its ranking principle, which is capable of offering the most relevant results – that is, not merely eliminating junk links, but also discriminating between those that are only of moderate interest relative to the specific search. Google's economic success has been built upon this functional bedrock.

The second decisive factor is the ads' relevance to the particular browsing context. This makes sure that, in the worst-case scenario, the ad will cause limited annoyance during the web user's browsing experience, and, at best, that they will perceive it positively. The honing of the ad targeting depends on an analysis of keywords, browsing history, and a host of other data collected in the Google ecosystem. This wealth of contextual information allows for pinpointed ad targeting, which increases the likelihood that it will prompt the user to click on the link. Maximising the behavioural effect sought by the advertiser increases the value of the advertising space. Alphabet diversified its activities in the 2010s as it extended its reach into cybersecurity (Chronicle), artificial intelligence (DeepMind), the smart home (Nest thermostats, cameras, sensors, alarms, and video doorbells) and self-driving cars (Waymo). The Google subsidiary's robot taxis first hit the road in Arizona only in 2018, but it already has an estimated value of $30 billion.[39] Waymo's profit strategy is not to build better cars, but to take control of the car as a living space, a mobility space, and therefore a 'data derrick' as explained in a note from UBS bank examined by the *Financial Times*:

---

38 Sergey Brin and Lawrence Page, 'The Anatomy of a Large-Scale Hypertextual Web Search Engine', *Computer Networks and ISDN Systems* 30, nos. 1–7, 1998, pp. 107–17.

39 Patrick McGee, 'Microsoft Invests in $30bn Driverless Car Company Cruise', *Financial Times*, 19 January 2021.

The threat of Waymo is not that it will build better cars. It has no need to. Instead it is ordering vehicles from Chrysler and Jaguar – effectively turning them into suppliers – and then fitting them out with self-driving software and hardware built in-house. But its potential goes beyond superior self-driving capabilities. Once robotaxis are mainstream, Alphabet can collect data from Google Maps and Search, entertain with YouTube and the Play Store, offer advice through Google Home smart speakers and use its software knowhow to manage fleets. Aside from the vehicle itself, Waymo is a vertically-integrated 'closed system', says UBS. 'This will influence advertising, the media and the entertainment business,' Mr Thill says. 'It's not just the autonomous technology, it's all the components that Google brings to the car. This is why it is putting so much investment into the living room, because it wants the car to feel like your living room.'[40]

Google's expansion is guided by the quest to collect, combine, and process data, with the constant aim of offering the most relevant products for the particular individual and the given context. According to Lawrence Page, the firm's founder and CEO, 'the problem with Google is that you have to ask it questions; it should know what you want and tell you even before you ask.'[41] So, targeting is aimed at anticipating behaviour, but more than that, at steering it.

Facebook and Extensive Integration. This principle of data contextualisation has been the focus of constant refinement. It strives to integrate all the digital traces left by each person's activities, including data relating to their social network, their movements, their purchasing history and – even their most private – administrative, financial, and occupational information. It is public knowledge that Facebook has directly received data from certain mobile apps, without users being informed. This was particularly the case with a meditation programme called

---

40 Patrick McGee, 'Robotaxis: Can Automakers Catch Up with Google in Driverless Cars?', *Financial Times*, 31 January 2019.
41 Hal R. Varian, 'Beyond Big Data', *Business Economics* 49, no. 1, 2014, p. 28.

Breethe, another called Instant Heart Rate, touted as 'the first, fastest and most accurate mobile heart rate monitor', and the Flo health app. The latter offers to record over thirty symptoms and activities 'in order to get the most precise AI-based overview' of the menstrual cycle and ovulation, and get to know your body better by detecting recurrent physical and emotional patterns. In each of these instances, the information – whether on meditations, heart rate, or ovulation date – is communicated to Facebook.

The data collected comes from small programmes integrated into applications or websites called Software Development Kits (SDKs). These allow for their enhancement with advanced functionalities: they transmit data to an analysis platform, including such information as the number and duration of sessions, the location and the type of terminal used, and information which users enter into the app, enabling companies to gain a better understanding of user behaviour and target their ads more effectively. Facebook Analytics offers 'people-first analytics for an omni-channel world'. It promises entrepreneurs a 'deeper understanding of where and how people interact with your business across your website, app, Facebook Page, and more' thanks to statistics collected from a 'community' of some '2 billion people'.[42] In line with the thesis of so-called 'unscaling', which points to the possibility of combining small-scale operations with the power of Big Data, this giant firm offers sophisticated IT services that no medium-sized company could match.[43]

Through SDKs, Facebook gains access to additional sources of personal data, which it links to the user data it already possesses, thereby increasing its knowledge of individual lives. This enables it to conduct sophisticated market research, feed the algorithmic process to finely select the content to be displayed on users' profiles and, of course, sell increasingly targeted advertising. According to the *Wall Street Journal*,

---

42 Facebook, 'Facebook Analytics: Drive Growth to Web, Mobile and More', February 2019, analytics.facebook.com.

43 Hemant Taneja, *Unscaled: How AI and a New Generation of Upstarts Are Creating the Economy of the Future*, New York: PublicAffairs Books, 2018.

which investigated these SDKs, this mobile application data is crucial to Facebook's profits:

> Advertising buyers say that because of Facebook's insights into users' behavior, it can offer marketers better return on their investment than most other companies when they seek users who are, say, exercise enthusiasts, or in the market for a new sports car. Such ads fetch a higher cost per click. That is partly why Facebook's revenue is soaring.[44]

In this race to extract relevant information, the web giants jealously guard the data they collect or appropriate from their partners. But to supplement this, they also draw on brokers specialising in the compilation of databases:

> Oracle owns and works with more than 80 data brokers who funnel in an ocean of data . . . including consumer shopping behaviour at brick-and-mortar stores, financial transactions, social media behaviours and demographic information. The company claims to sell data on more than 300m people globally, with 30,000 data attributes per individual, covering 'over 80 per cent of the entire US internet population at your fingertips'.[45]

With 30,000 attributes per individual, and multiple, overlapping tracking devices, Oracle knows a great deal about each person. This informational advantage, derived from the systematic exploration of data, provides what Zuboff calls a 'behavioural surplus'. This holistic knowledge allows the business in control of it an oversight position, meaning that the firm is able to restrict the use of the data to its own specific objectives. In this way, user-relevant information will only

---

44 Sam Scheschner and Mark Secada, 'You Give Apps Sensitive Personal Information: Then They Tell Facebook,' *Wall Street Journal*, 22 February 2019.

45 Madhumita Murgia and Aliya Ram, 'Data Brokers: Regulators Try to Rein in the "Privacy Deathstars"', *Financial Times*, 8 January 2019.

be disclosed if it converges with the higher imperative of producing value.

The novelty and the strength of Zuboff's argument is that it shows where this dynamic is leading us: the goal of surveillance capitalism is not to make behaviour more predictable, but to control it. This can be achieved through subtle incentives, such as the game Pokémon Go, whose business model is based on the idea of charging businesses to guide crowds of people towards their favoured destinations. Zuboff shows that surveillance capitalism can also be more intrusive, for example by offering companies the opportunity to remotely shut off the engine if the owner falls behind with their loan or insurance payments. Telematic technologies – remote computerised management processes – have a clear objective:

> Telematics are not intended merely to know but also to do ...
> Behavioral underwriting promises to reduce risk through machine processes designed to modify behavior in the direction of maximum profitability. Behavioral surplus is used to trigger punishments, such as real-time rate hikes, financial penalties, curfews, and engine lock-downs, or rewards, such as rate discounts, coupons, and gold stars to redeem for future benefits.[46]

According to Zuboff, surveillance capitalism firms are building the infrastructure of a Big Other that limitlessly draws resources from our social experience (which it itself rearranges) and then returns them to us in the form of behavioural injunctions. The effect is to radically reduce our autonomy. This Big Other is a spectre, in the sense that Jacques Derrida meant it. There is a radical asymmetry of power between the individual and this spectre. It has 'the supreme insignia of power: the power to see without being seen' while as individuals we are caught in a 'visor effect: we do not see who is watching us'.[47] Yet, unlike most spectres, the Big Other does not settle for inhabiting our lives but plays with

---

46 Zuboff, *The Age of Surveillance Capitalism*, p. 216.
47 Derrida, *Specters of Marx*, pp. 6–7, translation edited.

them. It activates its power in a labour of modelling our existences, through recommendations, suggestions, and obligations that profoundly influence our behaviour. Zuboff shows that surveillance capitalism thrives at the expense of the integrity of the autonomous individual. Which is to say, it strikes at the heart of the human condition.

Who Controls the Experimenter?

This Big Other has 'the tangible intangibility of a proper body without flesh'. It is elusive and everywhere at once: it is 'paradoxical incorporation, the becoming-body, a certain phenomenal and carnal form of the spirit'.[48] But what kind of spirit is this? How is it produced? What is the source of its power? One first answer to these questions can be found in the type of knowledge from which Big Data derives and, more specifically, in the role of controlled random experiments.

The Internet as a Laboratory. Randomised controlled trials are made up of three elements.[49] The first is the experiment itself – the trial, the treatment whose effects we want to test. The second is control: it refers to the idea of having a point of comparison. The third, randomisation, aims to improve the quality of the control by mobilising the statistical properties of chance.

This experimental method has a long history, at the crossroads of several disciplines. While its roots go back to the experimental medicine of the nineteenth century, it was first formalised in the 1920s. In his work assessing the effectiveness of a fertiliser on plots used for oat crops, the geneticist and agronomist Ronald Fischer had the idea of randomly selecting which plots would be treated with it and which would not be. He explained his approach in detail in an article published in 1926, which earned him a place in the history of science as the first theorist of

---

48 Ibid., pp. 6, 5.

49 On the genealogy of these practices and their use in economics, see Arthur Jatteau's thesis, 'Faire preuve par le chiffre? Le cas des expérimentations aléatoires en économie', Université Paris-Saclay, 2017.

this experimental method. After World War II, the practice became widespread and standardised, particularly in the context of medical clinical trials. It is also widely used in the United States and Canada to evaluate public policies, particularly in the field of employment. Finally, at the beginning of the twenty-first century, these methods were rediscovered in the field of development economics with the work of Esther Duflo and the JPAL team at MIT.[50]

What is rather less well known is that experiments of this type are now being conducted at an unprecedented scale online. We are regularly used as guinea pigs for experiments which we know nothing about, as Ron Kohavi and Roger Longbotham, two Microsoft researchers specialising in these experiments, reveal:

> Online-controlled experiments started to be used in the late 1990s with the growth of the Internet. Today, many large sites, including Amazon, Bing, Facebook, Google, LinkedIn, and Yahoo!, run thousands to tens of thousands of experiments each year testing user interface (UI) changes, enhancements to algorithms (search, ads, personalization, recommendation, etc.), changes to apps, content management system, etc. Online-controlled experiments are now considered an indispensable tool, and their use is growing for start-ups and smaller websites.[51]

There is a simple reason why such experiments are conducted en masse: the proliferation of connected objects allows for a large-scale evaluation of the effects of different devices on individual behaviours. The aim of these experiments, unlike other data mining techniques, is

---

50 For a critical overview, see Agnès Labrousse, 'Nouvelle économie du développement et essais cliniques randomisés: une mise en perspective d'un outil de preuve et de gouvernement', *Revue de la régulation* 7, 2010; Cédric Durand and Charlotte Nordmann, 'Misère de l'économie du développement', *La Revue des livres* 1, 2011.

51 Ron Kohavi and Roger Longbotham, 'Online Controlled Experiments and A/B Testing', in Claude Sammut and Geoffrey I. Webb, eds, *Encyclopedia of Machine Learning and Data Mining*, Boston: Springer, 2017, p. 922.

not simply to display spontaneous statistical regularities, but to establish controlled correlations with a very high degree of probability.

The experimenters, who are often economists, can explore hypotheses such as: If a specific change is made, will it improve key indicators?[52] A typical experiment might involve marginally changing the form of an advertisement on a search engine, then randomly distributing the stand-ard view and the modified view to users in order to observe whether there are any changes in their behaviour. Often, only minor variations are introduced – for example, in the case of a test carried out on Microsoft's search engine Bing, it meant the inclusion of an internal link in an advertising banner, or a change in font size, or even the number of ads on a page. Yet even this can have an effect counted in the millions of dollars.

One of the difficulties lies in defining the correct indicator to measure the desired effect – a synthetic metric that specialists call the Overall Evaluation Criterion. For example, an effect on the click-through rate may be a false positive if it leads to a drop in site traffic. So, it is necessary to find a satisfactory way of capturing both these aspects. It is also impor-tant to make sure that the results are reliable, in particular by ruling out false signals that result from the activity of software robots. Still, so long as these difficulties are taken into account, the experiments produce conclusive results.

For Hal Varian, Google's chief economist, random experiments 'are the gold standard for causality ... If you really want to understand causality, you have to run experiments. And if you run experiments continuously, you can continuously improve your system.'[53] Technically, Varian is wrong, here. Tests do not allow us to understand causality: they indicate the statistical robustness of a correlation, but they do not explain anything. For example, it can be firmly established that changing the colour of an ad increases the click-through rate. But why does this link exist – and what cultural, social, or biological mechanisms are at work

---

52 Susan Athey and Michael Luca, 'Economists (and Economics) in Tech Companies', NBER Working Paper 25064, 2018, p. 7.

53 Varian, 'Beyond Big Data', p. 29.

here? We don't know. The only thing that has been demonstrated is the link. From an instrumental point of view, however, that is enough. These correlations provide a sufficient basis for building profitable systems.

Initially confined to large companies, 'test and learn' is becoming the norm in cycles of digital innovation, with platforms offering third-party companies the tools to conduct their own online tests. But should we be concerned about these new methods? An experiment conducted on Facebook during the week of 11 to 18 January 2012 sparked the debate. It sought to find out whether emotional contagion, a phenomenon which has been studied in social psychology, can be found in social networks.[54] The results corroborated the hypotheses. Individuals who had less positive content in their news feed used a higher percentage of negative words and a lower percentage of positive ones in their status updates. The opposite trend was observed for those whose negative content had been reduced. Admittedly, the measured impact was quite small (a variation of the order of 0.1 per cent), but it does indicate that hundreds of thousands of emotions expressed every day can be altered by such filtering processes. The study also showed that lessening the number of messages with positive or negative emotional content reduces the number of words a person subsequently posts on the social network. In other words, there is a lever that Facebook can use to influence people's engagement. Favouring emotionally charged content tends to increase the rate of content, meaning that it is in the business's interest to prioritise more hysterical content in order to boost user engagement. This study therefore establishes a link between the capacity for emotional manipulation and engagement on the social network and Facebook's own profitability . . .

This experiment stirred up a wave of disapproving reactions. Might not individuals have been affected by this, even though they never explicitly consented to take part in the experiment?[55] But unlike

---

54 Adam D. I. Kramer, Jamie E. Guillory, and Jeffrey T. Hancock, 'Experimental Evidence of Massive-Scale Emotional Contagion through Social Networks,' *Proceedings of the National Academy of Sciences* 111, no. 24, 2014, pp. 1–3.

55 Robinson Meyer, 'Everything We Know about Facebook's Secret Mood Manipulation Experiment', *Atlantic*, 28 June 2014.

scientific institutions, Facebook is not bound by codified ethical standards regarding the experiments it may choose to carry out. As with other internet firms, it sets out its data policy in its Terms of Use, and most of us click past the page without ever reading it. That is, terms such as: 'We conduct surveys and research, test features in development, and analyze the information we have to evaluate and improve products and services [and] develop new products or features . . .'[56]

Such a vague warning gives the company a free hand. But this is just the tip of an iceberg, the bulk of which remains protected by business secrecy. These mass experimental manipulations on the internet are the daily bread of research teams working on digital apps. They are even their main means of innovation. Most of the time, companies simply do not publish the protocols and results of the experiments, since they are decisive factors in building their competitive advantage.

When Machines Put Us to the Test. The stakes of online experiments are getting ever higher, with the development of machine learning in artificial intelligence. In October 2015, AlphaGo, a programme developed by DeepMind, an Alphabet company, beat a professional Go player, Fan Hui, the reigning European champion, for the first time. In March 2016, the programme repeated its feat against one of the best players in the world, South Korea's Lee Sedol. Until then, the game of Go was considered to be one of the most difficult for artificial intelligence programmes to master. The computer's victory is not just down to greater computational capacity. It does not calculate the consequences of every move, but learns, through its accumulated experience, what kind of move leads to the best results.[57] As well as examining vast numbers of games already played by others, the machine learns to select the best moves by playing against itself. That is, it experiments on itself.

This 'reinforcement learning' method is a technology well advanced in the domain of artificial intelligence, with developed applications in

---

56 Facebook, 'Data Policy', facebook.com.

57 David Silver et al., 'Mastering the Game of Go with Deep Neural Networks and Tree Search', *Nature* 529, no. 7587, 2016, pp. 484–9.

a wide range of fields such as robotics, computer vision, and gaming, as well as finance, education, transport, energy networks, and health care.[58] Experiments are carried out by machines on humans with a view to maximising some non-immediate outcome. Just like when it is playing Go, the computer is testing moves and exploring unknown strategies. The difference is that here the machine is not playing against itself. It is testing the effectiveness of arrangements that it imposes on humans, in the aim of producing the behaviour that the study's sponsors are trying to promote. For example, an experiment was carried out to encourage type 2 diabetes patients to do physical exercise.[59] The machine was set learning how to personalise the messages sent to the participants, in particular by adjusting their content, whether positive – in some cases even involving efforts at 'social' interaction – or negative, as well as their frequency. Over time, the programme fine-tuned its interactions with each individual according to how they reacted to the signals sent. In this way, the machine learned to adapt the messages to the individual patients and succeeded in significantly increasing their level of activity.

After World War II and the Nuremberg trials, informed consent was established as an ethical prerequisite for experiments on human subjects. In the case of online experiments, however, this principle is widely flouted – usually, this consent is extorted from users via the general terms of use to which they agree when they sign up to a given platform. In the digital age, the massification of experience and the extension of control go hand in hand. If, in the nineteenth century, 'there was in fact a deep affinity between experimental knowledge and the power of disciplinary institutions', it could be said that, in the twenty-first century, the development of online experiments is associated with the power of total surveillance.[60]

---

58 Yuxi Li, 'Deep Reinforcement Learning', arXiv.org, 15 October 2018.

59 Irit Hochberg et al., 'Encouraging Physical Activity in Patients with Diabetes through Automatic Personalized Feedback via Reinforcement Learning Improves Glycemic Control: Table 1', *Diabetes Care* 39, no. 4, 2016, pp. 59–60.

60 Grégoire Chamayou, *Les Corps vils. Expérimenter sur les êtres humains aux xviiie et xixe siècles*, Paris: La Découverte, 2008, p. 291.

This worrying overview of the Big Other's grip over our lives points to very real threats. And yet it only sheds light on part of the problem. The risk, warns Evgeny Morozov, is that 'by seeking to explicate, and denounce, the novel dynamics of surveillance capitalism, Zuboff normalizes too much in capitalism itself'.[61] In other words, if we fixate too much on the disciplinary dimension of the systems that are being rolled out, we risk overlooking their economic underpinnings. What the 'surveillance capitalism' thesis is missing is an interrogation of these systems' political economy. What changes in the mode of production have taken us to this point? Why do the dynamics of competition validate profit strategies based on surveillance?

To this first criticism, Morozov adds a second more immediately political one. The normative a priori of Zuboff's book, Morozov points out, is built on a sanctification of the liberal individual: in seeking to rein in the excesses of surveillance capitalism, its essential goal is to protect the isolated consumer's sovereignty in making choices for themselves. But isn't there another, more collective dimension to this that we ought to be thinking about?

A New Digital Glebe

> As a typical millennial constantly glued to my phone, my virtual life has fully merged with my real life. There is no difference any more.
>
> Judith Duportail[62]

An Immanent Transcendence Effect

Zuboff's theory is underpinned by the liberal atomistic premise of a free and autonomous human being. This is the presupposition that Frédéric Lordon tears apart in *Imperium*, as he subjects to critique the

---

61 Morozov, 'Capitalism's New Clothes'.

62 Judith Duportail, 'I Asked Tinder for My Data. It Sent Me 800 Pages of My Deepest, Darkest Secrets', *Guardian*, 26 September 2017.

idea that the social sphere is merely a gathering of fundamentally sovereign individuals, bound together only by their own voluntary choice. Taking up the holistic stance of a sociology in the tradition of Émile Durkheim, Lordon instead speaks of 'an *exceedance* of the whole in relation to the parts':

> The social is necessarily transcendence, albeit of a special kind: an immanent transcendence. No human collectivity of significant size can form without projecting, over and above its members, symbolic productions of every type which they have all contributed to creating, even if they are dominated by those productions and unable to recognise their own hand in them.[63]

Researchers Brent Smith and Greg Linden – working for Amazon and Microsoft, respectively – suggest that Big Data abides by a similar logic:

> Recommendations and personalization live in the sea of data we all create as we move through the world, including what we find, what we discover, and what we love . . . The algorithms aren't magic; they simply share with you what other people have already discovered.[64]

Big Data consists of symbolic productions that emanate from individuals but which, through their multiplication and aggregation, take on a form that becomes unrecognisable to these same individuals. It is a 'sea of data' which algorithms draw on, an 'exceedance' which emanates from individuals' actions and yet, through the process of aggregation, comes to transcend them and returns to them metamorphosed.

There is more than just an analogy between the social and Big Data. Of course, Big Data does not make up the entirety of this dimension

---

63 Frédéric Lordon, *Imperium: Structures and Affects of Political Bodies*, London: Verso, 2022, p. 36.
64 Smith and Linden, 'Two Decades of Recommender Systems at Amazon.com', pp. 18, 12.

– but it does belong to it. It is the result of a dialectical movement: first, the symbolic crystallisation of the collective power captured in statistical regularities; then, the feedback effect of this power upon individuals and their behaviour. It is a common characteristic of most platforms that the data they collect from users makes possible the service that they provide. 'Whether that data is search terms, voice samples, or product reviews, the users are in a feedback loop in which they contribute to the products they use. That's the beginning of data science.'[65] Data capture feeds algorithms, which in turn guide behaviour, each reinforcing the other in a feedback loop.

Big Data owes its power to its sheer size. In other words, the greater the 'exceedance' of algorithms, the greater the transcendence-effect resulting from the collection and processing of immanent data. But the downside of this power of large numbers is the risk of a loss of control.[66] At the scale of small numbers, it is possible to share in a full awareness of the driving forces and effects of collective life. Yet on the scale of large numbers this becomes a matter for specialists, a job for data scientists. It is hard for the multitude to take its power into its own hands, once it has become estranged from it and thus unrecognisable. 'Composition . . . is more than a simple matter of adding up. Rather, it is a process that gives rise to something additional', writes Lordon.[67] The tragedy is that, in this vertical movement of social composition, the power that manifests itself risks being dispossessed:

> The *potentia multitudinis* is the very stuff of capture, the 'thing' to be captured . . . The origin of the authority of institutions – their normative and tangible power to make us behave a certain way and do certain things as dictated by their norms – is none other than the

---

65 Mike Loukides, 'What Is Data Science? The Future Belongs to the Companies and People That Turn Data into Products', *O'Reilly Radar Report*, 2010.

66 'Immanent transcendence is precisely that something extra which grows out of the affective synergies of large numbers of people, whereas small groups that satisfy the synoptic condition are able to aspire to the complete control of their collective productions': Lordon, *Imperium*, p. 46.

67 Ibid., p. 168.

power of the multitude, which they capture by crystallising it, so to speak: institutions are crystallisations of the *potentia multitudinis*.[68]

Replace 'institutions' with 'Big Data' and you'll understand what the Big Other is all about. Or rather, you will see Big Data not as a set of technical facts, but rather as an institutional reality. In the words of one of the fathers of institutionalism, John R. Commons, an institution should be defined as 'collective action in control, liberation, and expansion of individual action'.[69]

In the 'upswing' movement of the quest for data, the fundamental aim is not to capture the data itself, but rather its substance in terms of social power. In the 'downswing' movement, this power has a direct impact on the individual, extending their capacity for action by endowing them with the cognitive resources drawn from the collective strength. But when the power of the social dimension is thus returned to the individual level, this takes place under the influence of the powers that shape it. The individual is thus simultaneously augmented by the power of the social, as fed back by the algorithm – but also loses autonomy, because of the modes in which this takes place. This two-sided movement is itself a form of domination, since the institutional capture is organised by firms pursuing their own agenda, which has nothing to do with that of the communities affected.

Big Data is the product of a special kind of immanent transcendence, placed under the empire of capital and digital companies. The bottom-up process of symbolic crystallisation of collective power (*potentia*) retroacts in the form of power (*potestas*) exercised over individuals by organisations pursuing their own ends. This is the core of a device (*dispositif*) which Zuboff only partially grasps in her concept of 'surveillance capitalism'.

---

68 Ibid., p. 166.
69 John R. Commons, *Institutional Economics: Its Place in Political Economy*, vol. 1, London: Transaction, 1990, pp. 73–4; Marie-Claire Villeval, 'Une théorie économique des institutions', in Robert Boyer and Yves Saillard, eds, *Théorie de la régulation. L'état des savoirs*, Paris: La Découverte, 1995, pp. 479–89.

Platforms as Fiefs

The augmented human being of our digital age does not escape the empire of algorithms, any more than the socialised human being escapes the empire of institutions. The crystallisation of social 'exceedance' in the Cloud permeates individual existences, binding them to it in the same way that serfs were once bound to the glebe of the lordly domain. This social force, which emanates from human communities and shapes individuals, is partly objectivated in Big Data. We should see it as a new kind of means of production, a field of experience to which the subjectivities of the twenty-first century are pinned.

Our complementarities are now embodied in a narrow range of hegemonic IT devices and systems, which have a considerable force of attraction. For a basic illustration of how this mechanism works, we need only look to the place still occupied by Microsoft Word. Obviously, Word is useful to me because it gives me a way of writing and formatting my work – but, most of all, it is useful because my editors, my colleagues, my co-authors, my students, my university administration, and over 1.2 billion potential correspondents also rely on the same software, and this guarantees the proper formatting of the documents I want to send or receive.[70] The effort already devoted to understanding the Office interface, the routines that we have picked up by using it, and the user data that we have agreed to pass on to this software's publisher, all make us part of a socio-technical ecosystem controlled by Microsoft, which there is a high bar to exiting. What is more, there is no simple co-ordination mechanism that would allow everyone using Word to migrate to some other software package at the same time. In the end, Word's influence persists because its gradual spread since its first version in 1983 has created a 'path dependency', a 'lock-in effect'.[71]

---

70 The number of Microsoft Office users in March 2016, according to John Callaham, 'There Are Now 1.2 Billion Office Users and 60 Million Office 365 Commercial Customers', Windows Central, 31 March 2016, windowscentral.com.

71 Economists talk about a 'lock-in' resulting from increasing returns and network effects. For the classic article highlighting the role of initial advantages in the historical dynamics of technological development, see W. Brian Arthur,

If it is so difficult to give up the Microsoft Office suite – despite the existence of well-performing and indeed free alternatives – this is the reverse side of the network complementarities that bind us together. For the Seattle-based company, this offers a windfall that has little relation to the intrinsic quality of its products. Users are encouraged to subscribe to the Office suite to ensure business continuity. This involves activating a specific code, which is Microsoft's intellectual property and yields it some tens of billions of dollars annually.[72] The economic power derived from such an embeddedness in organisational routines could be turbocharged by its coupling with AI capabilities, following Microsoft's investment in OpenAI: by making the technology behind ChatGPT available as a standard feature in a widely used software product, it could potentially transform the working lives of millions and deepen Microsoft's grip on unnumerable business processes.[73]

However, for the moment our attachment to the Office suite pales in comparison to the force of attraction generated within other giant digital ecosystems. For most Westerners, Google has become an indispensable part of everyday life. Google Maps can give me the best route because it is already drawing on real-time geolocation data supplied by other devices using its software. By analysing my e-mails or my diary, Google can deduce what my destination is and tells me where I am going before I even ask. It will also be able to tell me – again, without my needing to ask – the result of a sports event which I had looked up the previous day.

As platforms observe and test us, they provide us with powerful – and useful – results. What they are feeding back to us, here, is the power of our own complementarities. We can already see how strong a grip this allows them to exert. In summer 2014, when Facebook suffered outages lasting a few hours in various localities in the United States, the

'Competing Technologies, Increasing Returns, and Lock-in by Historical Events', *Economic Journal* 99, no. 394, 1989, pp. 116–31.

72 Office generated $44.9 billion in 2022. Daniel Shvartsman, 'Microsoft: The Most Enduring Tech Superstar', investing.com, 25 October 2023.

73 Richard Waters, 'Microsoft Pioneers Use of Generative AI in Software – at a Price', *Financial Times*, 1 November 2023.

emergency services were inundated with calls.[74] Platforms have become indispensable; they ought to be considered as infrastructure, in the same manner as electricity, rail, or telecoms networks.[75] Their management raises the same type of issues as the management of critical infrastructures, whose importance to society can be measured by the disturbances that their malfunctioning can cause.

The architecture of these digital infrastructures is organised around three key elements: central components with low variability, complementary components with high variability, and interfaces that manage the modularity between the central and the complementary. This way of structuring these infrastructures affords the possibility of maintaining their fundamental robustness while also allowing flexibility in the way that they evolve. But this also comes at a cost: a radical asymmetry between the players who are in charge of the central components, those who intervene on the complementary elements, and – at the end of the chain – the users who can navigate between the modules but remain attached to the platform to whom they have handed almost every trace of themselves. Over time, they have entrusted the platform with a whole set of elements that mark them out: their network of acquaintances, their browsing habits, their search histories, their centres of interest, their passwords, their addresses, etc. In this sense, they have become the platform's captive.

The development of these app ecosystems based on closed platforms represents a fundamental break with the organisational principle behind the initial design of the World Wide Web. The web is based on a decentralised architecture in which a generic transaction protocol (http) and a uniform resource identifier (URI/URL) create a 'flat' content space which human and computer agents can access in a uniform and unmediated way. The platform, however, recreates mediation: it sets up feedback loops in which interactions become ever denser. The technical object

---

74 '911 Calls about Facebook Outage Angers [sic] LA County Sheriff's Officials', *Los Angeles Times*, 1 August 2014.

75 Jean-Christophe Plantin et al., 'Infrastructure Studies Meet Platform Studies in the Age of Google and Facebook', *New Media and Society* 20, no. 1, 2018, pp. 293–310.

underlying this hierarchical architecture is the application programming
interface (API) owned by the platform. Via APIs, the major platforms
provide the applications nestled within them with the basic data that
they need to thrive; but the platform also accesses the additional information that these applications generate. And, as the ecosystem grows,
the platform accumulates more and more data. This is illustrated by the
example of Google Maps:

> In 2005, Google released Google Maps and almost immediately
> provided an API. The API permitted third parties to add or overlay
> other data onto the Google base map, thus creating mapping 'mash-
> ups'. In other words, Google transformed maps into programmable
> objects, with Google Maps as the platform. Similar examples are
> proliferated via the addition of APIs to most Google products. As with
> Facebook, the principal benefits to Google are the user activity data
> returned by the API and the ubiquity of its branded interface, while
> the myriad applications connected to the Google platform benefit
> from the ability to build on Google-provided data.[76]

The transition from the open, horizontal architecture of the web to
the hierarchical, layered structure of platforms coincides with the accumulation of a socio-digital surplus in the Cloud. The individualised and
instantaneous availability of these collective resources is turning our
personal and social lives upside down. Our permanently connected
'cyborg-being' is becoming richer and denser. Algorithms aim to relieve
us of the most mechanical aspects of our cognitive activities, with the
effect that each of the roles we fulfil can rely on the immediate and
continuous support of a common strength.[77] As these interventions
become more widespread, our lives become more closely linked to the
Cloud.

---

76 Ibid. This also hampers the work of app developers, who must either confine
themselves to a single platform, or maintain multiple versions of the same product.

77 Dominique Cardon, À quoi rêvent les algorithmes. Nos vies à l'heure des Big
Data, Paris: Seuil, 2015.

If consumers are sinking more roots in these platforms' layered digital structures, the forms of this attachment are also modelled by firms' profit strategies. The quality of the service on offer increases in tandem with their profits, as users generate more data. It is thus in platforms' interests to lock users into their ecosystems by limiting interoperability with their competitors.[78] Their growing strength thus goes hand in hand with a logic by which the internet itself becomes more fragmented.

Platforms are becoming fiefdoms. As well as the territorial logic of platforms' efforts to monopolise original data sources, the feedback loop inherent in digital services creates a situation in which subjects become dependent. This is not only because the algorithms that feed on the observation of our practices are becoming indispensable means of production for our everyday existence. It is also because individuals' registration on platforms becomes a permanent fact, due to a lock-in effect owing to the personalisation of the interface and the high exit costs.[79]

Ultimately, the digital territory organised by platforms is fragmented into rival infrastructures that are relatively independent of each other. Whoever controls these infrastructures concentrates both political and economic power over the individuals somehow connected with them. The flip side of the logic of surveillance inherent in algorithmic governmentality is the attachment of subjects to the digital glebe.

A Deceptive Autonomy

In the age of algorithmic management, the nature of the link between ride platforms and workers has given rise to major controversies about employment relations. Uber is paradigmatic in this respect, and a case which poses a recurrent question for the 3.9 million drivers registered on this platform: Are they, as Uber claims, self-employed workers who

---

78 Plantin et al., 'Infrastructure Studies Meet Platform Studies', pp. 299–300.

79 Adam Candeub, 'Behavioral Economics, Internet Search, and Antitrust', *I/S: A Journal of Law and Policy for the Information Society* 9, 2014, p. 409.

freely contract with it?[80] Or should they be considered employees of the platform, who therefore ought to benefit from the protections afforded by this status?

The answer remains uncertain from a legal point of view, especially seeing as the problem has not been addressed in the same way in different local and national contexts. For example, in 2019, the Californian state legislature ruled in favour of the second interpretation, stating that platform workers are employees and that platforms must therefore take their responsibilities as employers in terms of social security, unemployment insurance, payroll taxes, workers' compensation coverage, and compliance with minimum wage regulations. In Switzerland, the federal court found in February 2023 that there was an employment relationship between drivers and Uber, and ruled that the company should pay social security contributions.[81]

For their part, French authorities have tended to abide by the arguments put forward by platforms such as Uber, which deny that they are traditional service firms and present themselves as tech companies connecting consumers and individual entrepreneurs. Since 2016, a series of legislative measures have been adopted in France to 'secure the platform model'.[82]

At root, this is a matter of whether work gets paid. Uber places great emphasis on drivers' independence because reclassifying them as

---

80 As of 31 December 2018.

81 Swiss Federal Tribunal, 'Sociétés néerlandaises tenues de payer les cotisation AVS pour les chauffeurs Uber', press release, 23 March 2023, bger.ch. Conversely, platform drivers and delivery personnel will continue to be considered as self-employed in California, following the adoption by referendum of Proposition 22, which legalises their status as self-employed workers. Miriam A. Cherry, 'Dispatch – United States: "Proposition 22: A Vote on Gig Worker Status in California"', *Saint Louis U. Legal Studies Research Paper*, No. 2021–03, SSRN.

82 The concept of platforms' 'social responsibility' has been wielded in the attempt to limit any prospect of these relations being reclassified as employment contracts. See Yves Struillou, 'Annexe N°4: De nouvelles dispositions législatives pour "réguler socialement" les plateformes de mobilité et sécuriser leur modèle économique', in *Salaire minimum interprofessionnel de croissance: Rapport du groupe d'experts*, 2019, tresor.economie.gouv.fr, pp. 144–8; Coralie Larrazet, 'Régime des plateformes numériques, du non-salariat au projet de charte sociale', *Droit social* 2, 2019, pp. 167–76.

employees would represent a major additional cost, of the order of 20 to 30 per cent in the US case.[83] Uber's model, which is still financially fragile, is only viable through the use of low-paid labour – that is, hourly incomes around the same low levels as the food service and retail sectors, without the cost of employers' obligations.[84]

Justifications for this contractual arrangement are based on one main argument: autonomy. Drivers use their own vehicles, choose their own working days and hours, and are free to switch to another platform at any time. This flexibility is undeniably an important aspect of the relationship, as is also clear from surveys among the workers involved. As one Uber driver in New York put it: 'You are your own boss. If you want, you work; if you don't want, you stay home. It depends on you.'[85] To drive the point home, researchers, including an economist working for Uber, carried out an empirical modelling exercise to quantify the value of this flexibility, which they estimated at 40 per cent of drivers' income.[86] In the eyes of Uber and the devotees of the gig economy model, this flexibility and the opportunity it represents for drivers imply an absence of subordination and – in correlation with this – a non-waged relationship to work.

83 Kate Conger and Noam Scheiber, 'California Bill Makes App-Based Companies Treat Workers as Employees', *New York Times*, 11 September 2019.

84 As part of the documentation accompanying its initial public offering (IPO), Uber admits to its future shareholders that drivers are dissatisfied with their low compensation and anticipates that this situation will worsen: 'While we aim to provide an earnings opportunity comparable to that available in retail, wholesale, or restaurant services or other similar work, we continue to experience dissatisfaction with our platform from a significant number of Drivers. In particular, as we aim to reduce Driver incentives to improve our financial performance, we expect Driver dissatisfaction will generally increase', cf. 'Uber technologies, inc. form s-1 – Registration statement under the Securities Act of 1933', United States Securities and Exchange Commission, 11 April 2019, p. 30.

85 Mareike Möhlmann and Lior Zalmanson, 'Hands on the Wheel: Navigating Algorithmic Management and Uber Drivers' Autonomy', International Conference on Information Systems (ICIS), Association for Information Systems, 2017, p. 7.

86 M. Keith Chen, Judith A. Chevalier, Peter E. Rossi, and Emily Oehlsen, 'The Value of Flexible Work: Evidence from Uber Drivers', *Journal of Political Economy* 127, no. 6, 2019, pp. 2735–94.

But if the question of subordination is not posed in quite the same terms as in traditional employment, it remains clear that the relationship between workers and platforms is based on a radical asymmetry, both from the perspective of information systems and from a legal standpoint.

Information systems specialists use the term 'algorithmic management' to describe remote, software-assisted practices of 'oversight, governance and control'. This form of management is 'characterized by continuously tracking and evaluating worker behavior and performance, as well as automatic implementation of algorithmic decisions'.[87] In this way, these agents interact not with human supervisors but mainly with a rigid and little-transparent system, in which much of the rules controlling the algorithms are inaccessible to them. In the case of Uber drivers, this leads to a paradoxical situation, where the aspiration to autonomy comes up against the platform's intense hold over their working activity: real-time monitoring of journeys, passenger assessments, opaque pricing structures, a ban on taking customers' details, incentive bonuses aimed at building driver loyalty or increasing supply in certain areas, penalties that can go as far as deactivation, etc.[88] The radical asymmetry built into the architecture of the software drastically weakens workers' bargaining power, making it impossible to believe the fiction that Uber only plays the role of an intermediary.[89]

Yet Uber's directors are devoting all their energies to keeping this fiction alive. In its efforts to avoid tighter regulation, it has sometimes reconfigured the parameters governing the app's operation, in order to give drivers greater autonomy. For instance, in 2020, California drivers secured the possibility of knowing in advance the time, distance,

---

87 Möhlmann and Zalmanson, 'Hands on the Wheel', p. 3.

88 Lawrence Mishel and Celine McNicholas, *Uber Drivers Are Not Entrepreneurs: NLRB General Counsel Ignores the Realities of Driving for Uber*, Washington, DC: Economic Policy Institute, 2019, epi.org.

89 On this see the interpretation given by the European Court of Justice: Barbara Gomes, 'Les plateformes en droit social: l'apport de l'arrêt "Elite Taxi contre Uber"', *Revue de droit du travail* 2, 2018, pp. 150–6; Vassilis Hatzopoulos, 'After Uber Spain: The EU's Approach on the Sharing Economy in Need of Review', *European Law Review* 44, no. 1, 2019, pp. 88–98.

destination, and estimated price of the journey that they will be offered. They can also reject requests without any risk of being penalised. Finally, a reverse auction mechanism, whereby drivers set their own prices, has also been introduced in various cities, on a trial basis.[90]

The convoluted reworkings of Uber's algorithmic management process in California, and the difficulties that French authorities have faced in providing it with a secure legal footing, show that the platform workers are 'on the edge of the relationship of subordination inherent in employment contracts'.[91] But, beyond the question of subordination, the question of economic dependence remains. Platforms for passenger transport, delivery, or odd jobs in the home enable the offering of services that could not exist without the intervention of software systems. Indeed, it is the data power of algorithmic feedback loops – their reputation, real-time adjustment, simplicity, behaviour history, etc. – that gives these services a particular quality that scattered individual producers could never achieve. In other words, even if we consider that workers have a substantial margin of autonomy to produce the services in question, they could not reach the same level of quality outside of their attachment to the platform. This attachment is precisely the reason why the platform is in a position to draw a profit from their work.

This is an essential point, recognised by French social law. The criterion of 'economic profit from the activity of others' applies even in the absence of a relationship of subordination. This itself justifies the order-giver's contribution to funding social protections, for example for the social security of artists.[92] So, even if it implies only a very partial subordination, the production of a service mediated by algorithmic devices does not rule out a relationship of total economic dependence between labour and the capital which exploits it. This possible disjuncture is precisely what distinguishes the relationship to work in ride platforms. Whereas the question of *subordination* lies at the heart of the classic

90 Preetika Rana, 'Uber Tests Feature Allowing Some California Drivers to Set Fares', *Wall Street Journal*, 21 January 2020.

91 Étude d'impact. Projet de loi pour la liberté de choisir son avenir professionnel', Assemblée nationale, 27 April 2018, art. 28, p. 234.

92 Larrazet, 'Régime des plateformes numériques'.

wage relationship, the relationship of economic *dependence* is pre-eminent in the context of the platform economy.

Automating Social Control

> Are we prepared for the administrative truth, for cold reports on the gods' well-guarded Tablet?
>
> Mathias Énard[93]

Making Trustworthiness Objective

In a now-classic 1970 article, George Akerlof takes the example of used cars to demonstrate that uncertainty about the quality of a good can jeopardise certain markets' very existence. Since the used-car buyer faces an impossible task in knowing what shape the vehicle is really in, and the vendor may be concealing certain defects, this leads buyers only to accept prices corresponding to worse-quality vehicles (lemons, in US slang). But since this price is unacceptable to those who wish to sell a good-quality vehicle, they leave the second-hand market, which is eventually reduced to 'lemons' alone.[94]

Dishonesty on the part of vendors is a serious problem for economic theory. Even though there may be potential buyers for certain categories of goods, information asymmetries can nonetheless prevent transactions from taking place. From an economic point of view, the main cost tied to the existence of rogue traders is not so much the loss suffered by the buyers who are materially defrauded, as the fact that, due to a lack of trust, a large number of other potential transactions are never completed at all.

In the 1990s, when e-commerce was still in its infancy, these problems of information asymmetry looked like near-insurmountable

---

93 Mathias Énard, *Zone*, Arles: Actes Sud, 2013, p. 505.

94 George A. Akerlof, 'The Market for "Lemons": Quality Uncertainty and the Market Mechanism', *Quarterly Journal of Economics* 84, no. 3, 1970, pp. 488–500.

obstacles to its development. Unlike when you buy something in a shop, it is impossible to examine, touch, or weigh an item before you buy it online. It is also impossible to check the seller's identity. Of course, the legal system provides for measures to be taken against fraudsters and swindlers. But this is also an expensive road to go down. In everyday life, trust is built above all through repeated exchanges, through close ties, and over time. While the rise of the internet promised to vastly widen the field of transactions by reducing communication costs, there was no guarantee that the trust essential to exchanges would follow. So, if these new economic links were ever to be activated, this required the invention of a means of establishing trust, appropriate to the new medium. Without such a mechanism, the proliferation of scams would have dried up the online market, just as Akerlof's lemons chased good cars out of the used car market.

It was eBay that first came up with the solution: a reputation system based on users rating each other.[95] Users are invited to leave positive, negative, or neutral feedback. These responses are then aggregated and translated into an overall score and percentage of positive ratings. Buyers and sellers can also write public comments. Finally, a star system provides a detailed assessment of different aspects of the process. These tools offering feedback on the quality of the exchange have a long-run effect on both parties, beyond the particular transaction concerned. The aim is to encourage them not to act opportunistically – not to exploit the information asymmetry to their own advantage. In other words, eBay offers public recognition for good-faith behaviour, in order to encourage the vendor to sell what he promises and to do so under the advertised conditions. The establishment of such a benchmark allows potential future buyers to find out about the seller's past behaviour before doing business with him. Based on feedback from past transactions, reputation becomes a powerful incentive, facilitating trust despite user anonymity.

On Airbnb, guests are rated as well as hosts – after all, you will only allow someone to use your accommodation if you can trust them. Studies

95 Steven Tadelis, 'Reputation and Feedback Systems in Online Platform Markets', *Annual Review of Economics* 8, no. 1, 2016, p. 332.

show how much value is based on reciprocal good behaviour: attention to detail, thoughtful decorations, the sharing of stories, etc. The length of the comments left by guests is a demonstration of this desire for transactions with a social depth – as confirmed by the fact that non-professional hosts average better ratings than professional ones do.[96]

Similarly, according to Uber, 'ratings encourage mutual respect between passengers and drivers. This strengthens our community and allows everyone to get the most out of the service'. The rating is supposed to summarise the quality of individuals' experience of interactions.

In their efforts to maximise transactions, platforms have gradually made their reputation measurement processes more complex. They have supplemented the explicit feedback given by users by examining implicit indications given by the traces of their interactions – for example, on the Airbnb direct messaging system, by a syntactic analysis of the content of the correspondence between renters and tenants. This case is unlike the methods used to measure reputation directly, since the logic behind the ranking is unknown to users. As economist Steven Tadelis explains, platforms 'can benefit from a more paternalistic, or regulator-like approach, that does not assume that market participants can decipher information effectively'.[97] Rather than letting participants interpret the information available, the platforms summarise it for them in the form of recommendations.

This slippage from reputation to recommendation represents a shift in the site of judgement: it is now the algorithms that decide on the best matches for us, like the dating app Tinder. It shamelessly draws on our personal data to evaluate us and decide – based on criteria which are its own company secret – which potential partners it will present to us.

Of course, platforms claim that all they are doing is trying to achieve better user satisfaction. But there is no small risk of abuse. A platform can manipulate its reputation system for purposes that are less readily

96 Davide Proserpio, Wendy Xu, and Georgios Zervas, 'You Get What You Give: Theory and Evidence of Reciprocity in the Sharing Economy', *Quantitative Marketing and Economics* 16, no. 4, 2018, pp. 371–407.
97 Tadelis, 'Reputation and Feedback Systems in Online Platform Markets', p. 336.

admitted, for instance when Amazon's rankings highlight its own products to the detriment of those of other sellers.

In the context of social networks, reputation management poses directly political problems. Facebook has begun to assign its users a score predicting their reliability on a scale of zero to one. This score, whose stated aim is to combat fake news, affects the way in which individuals' publications are made visible by the algorithm. This amounts to entrusting the supervision of public expression to a private company, which is itself likely to incorporate its own biases into the filtering of opinions. The problem is that the criteria on which the evaluation is based are not transparent. And 'the irony', says one researcher, 'is that they can't tell us how they're judging us – because if they do, the algorithms that they build will be gamed'.[98]

Solvency, Integrity, Morality

We may well imagine that these new ratings mechanisms could spread far beyond individual platforms to social relationships in general. An episode of the *Black Mirror* series entitled 'Nosedive', broadcast in 2016, puts this dystopian possibility on the small screen. The story plays out in a society where all individuals are continually rating each other. The constant flow of these reciprocal ratings makes up a score which determines access to goods and services, thus moulding an ever-shifting social hierarchy. Each interaction is thus the subject of an implicit bargaining, with the aim of improving one's score rather than risk being downgraded. In the series, Lacie's rating slips below four following an argument with her brother; this low score prevents her from taking a plane and prompts her descent into the social hell reserved for bad subjects. The strength of this system, its legitimising principle, is that social stratification does not derive from any overarching authority or normative framework. It is a bottom-up mode of evaluation, in which the accumulation of the opinions of the multitude produces an

---

98 Elizabeth Dwoskin, 'Facebook Is Rating the Trustworthiness of Its Users on a Scale from Zero to 1', *Washington Post*, 21 August 2018.

immanent social judgement, a reputation system in which all individuals participate and which directly applies to them.

But there is no need to rely on science fiction. To grasp the implications of such practices, we need only look to China.[99] The authorities in Beijing are planning to roll out a system of 'social credit' designed to cover every human being and organisation nationwide. Whether individuals, companies, or public authorities, each of them will gradually be integrated into this hybrid public-private system. The programme was officially launched in 2013 under the motto 'Commend sincerity and punish insincerity'.[100] As detailed in a resolution by the State Council, the highest government authority, the aim is to encourage behaviour that is deemed to be financially, economically, and socio-politically responsible, and to punish those who do not reach this standard:

> It uses encouragement to keep trust and constraints against breaking trust as incentive mechanisms, and its objective is raising the honest mentality and credit levels of the entire society . . . It is an important method to perfect the Socialist market economy system, accelerating and innovating social governance.[101]

The social credit system has a primarily economic objective. Until recently, Chinese households had only limited access to bank credit. The creation of a rating register is intended to develop the financial system, as was the case in the United States with the rise of the credit score after World War II.[102] The idea is to accumulate and centralise information on borrowers

---

99 Responding to a series of press articles making this striking analogy, the *New Statesman* explained that this easily made comparison was misleading and, indeed, euphemistic: see Ed Jefferson, 'No, China Isn't Black Mirror: Social Credit Scores Are More Complex and Sinister than That', *New Statesman*, 27 April 2018.

100 Third plenum of the 18th Congress of the Chinese Communist Party, November 2013, cited in Rogier Creemers, 'Planning Outline for the Construction of a Social Credit System (2014–2020)', *China Copyright and Media* (blog), 14 June 2017.

101 Ibid.

102 In the United States, the most widely used system is managed by the Fair Isaac Corporation. It is based on a weighting of five elements: regularity of repayments, level of indebtedness, length of credit history, type of credit used, and applications for credit.

in order to facilitate households' access to bank credit. But the term used, *shehui xinyong*, which is usually translated as social credit, means something broader: trustworthy, reliable, and honest. As former prime minister Li Keqiang explained, a market economy is based on trustworthiness, and the social credit system corresponds to this way of operating:

> A fine credit system provides market entities with the information they need for business operations. A blacklist should be established. Access to and sharing of information, which can serve to incentivize or discipline, helps reduce transaction costs and improve the business environment.[103]

In fact, embezzlement, violation of environmental regulations, and failure to observe food-safety standards are endemic problems in Chinese society. Fraud and corruption are part of a widespread climate of mistrust that must be seen in the context of the privatisation and the liberalisation of large parts of the economy. These reforms have contributed to a sharp rise in inequality since the 1980s.[104] The more unequal societies are, the less individuals can expect others to behave cooperatively, and the less trust there is.[105]

So, the leadership of the Chinese Communist Party is attempting to tackle the decline in trust. Its chosen method is to discipline and punish. The key idea is 'lose trust in one area, face restrictions everywhere'.[106]

The combination of these different metrics results in a score, recorded in a national register, which bankers use to decide whether or not to grant a loan and to set its conditions.

103 Zhang Yue, 'Social Credit System Work Progressing', chinadaily.com, 7 June 2018.

104 Thomas Piketty, Li Yang, and Gabriel Zucman, 'Capital Accumulation, Private Property and Rising Inequality in China, 1978–2015', NBER Working Paper 23368, 2017.

105 Henrik Jordahl, 'Inequality and Trust', under the title 'Economic Inequality', in Gert Tinggaard Svendsen and Gunnar Lind Haase Svendsen, eds, *Handbook of Social Capital*, London: Edward Elgar, 2009.

106 Mareike Ohlberg, Ahmed Shazeda, and Bertrand Lang, 'The Complex Implementation of China's Social Credit System', *China Monitor*, Mercator Institute for China Studies, 12 December 2017, p. 14, fn 21.

Whoever is caught falling short in some particular area will suffer the consequences of this in all their activities.

The Chinese planning system is highly decentralised. It sets objectives for the country as a whole but leaves great latitude to local governments to decide the appropriate means for achieving them.[107] This has led to a kind of 'inventors' competition' between local governments, in devising innovative means of social control. Often, their chosen schemes go beyond the purely economic and financial spheres, to also encompass a very broad concept of trust. In the country's largest city, for example, the Honest Shanghai app cross-references data from more than a hundred government sources, including facial recognition data, and assigns scores to individuals and businesses, particularly restaurants. For bad performers, administrative procedures are more onerous, inspections more frequent, and access to certain jobs restricted. Businesses and professional associations are also invited to take their own initiative in redoubling the effects of these public decisions, by adopting 'reward measures for trustworthy entities such as key recommendations or raising the rank of members; and adopt[ing] punitive measures such as industry warnings, circulation of criticism, reducing membership rank, cancelling membership credentials, for untrustworthy entities.'[108]

In Rongcheng, in Shandong province, the rating system integrates everyday actions: leaving rubbish on the public highway or committing minor traffic infractions will lower one's score, while model behaviour such as visiting an elderly person will improve it. In Zhejiang and Henan provinces, two district administrations have created a partnership with telecoms firms: when a person phones someone who has not paid a fine, an automated message informs them that their correspondent is blacklisted and invites them to enjoin the offender to comply with the court order.[109]

---

107 Nathan Sperber, 'La planification chinoise à l'ombre du capitalisme d'état', *Actuel Marx* 65, no. 1, 2019, pp. 35–53.

108 Standing Committee of the Shanghai People's Congress.

109 Ohlberg, Shazeda, and Lang, 'The Complex Implementation of China's Social Credit System'.

The integration of data between different administrative levels and different organisations is still very imperfect. As well as the technical difficulties they face, there is also considerable resistance from various sectors of the bureaucracy. But the effectiveness of the Chinese plan relies on its selection of the most categorical experiments and its perseverance in pursuing the objectives set. The annual report of the National Public Credit Information Centre, a body affiliated to the planning agency, gives an idea of the system's growing importance.[110] In 2018, 3.59 million Chinese companies were added to the blacklist of untrustworthy entities, which prohibits them from bidding for public contracts. In the same year, 17.46 million 'discredited' people were prevented from buying airline tickets, and 5.47 million from buying high-speed train tickets. These bad subjects were also denied access to premium insurance, wealth management products, and property.

Seeing as these lists are public, humiliation is an integral part of the penalty system. Indeed, a cartoon on the government credit platform shows a man holding a bouquet of flowers, whom a young woman turns away from because he is mentioned on the list of public shame. Accusations of fraud, loan defaults, illegal fundraising, misleading advertising, and minor incivilities (such as sitting in reserved seats on trains) are the main grievances identified in the National Public Credit Information Centre report. It also states that some 3.51 million untrustworthy individuals and entities who had repaid their debts or paid their taxes and fines in the previous year were taken off the blacklists.

Managing Social Issues with 'Foresight and Wisdom'

The rollout of the social credit system is part of the implementation of what the PRC's former president Jiang Zemin referred to in 1995 as 'the informatization, automation, and intelligentization of economic and social management'.[111]

---

110 He Huifeng, 'China's Social Credit System Shows Its Teeth, Banning Millions from Taking Flights, Trains', *South China Morning Post*, 18 February 2019.

111 Simina Mistreanu, 'Life Inside China's Social Credit Laboratory', *Foreign Policy*, 3 April 2018.

In a report published by the US Defense Department, consultant Samantha Hoffman provides an instructive genealogy of the social credit system from the point of view of Communist Party ideology.[112] The project of cybernetic social management has been discussed for decades in China. An article in the *People's Daily* of 13 September 1984 explains that, in this area, 'only if we fully grasp [the concepts of] information, data, systems analysis, and decision modeling, can we truly possess "foresight and sagacity", and generate the courage and a bold vision consistent with the flow of history'.[113]

For Hoffman, social management in general, and the social credit system in particular, are an extension of the Maoist 'mass line'. Its principle of starting *from* the masses to go back *to* the masses is what connects the political process in a mass party with the algorithmic processing of behaviour allowed by mass data. In 1945, Mao set out this point of doctrine as follows:

> In all the practical work of our Party, all correct leadership is necessarily 'from the masses, to the masses'. This means: take the ideas of the masses (scattered and unsystematic ideas) and concentrate them (through study turn them into concentrated and systematic ideas), then go to the masses and propagate and explain these ideas until the masses embrace them as their own, hold fast to them and translate them into action, and test the correctness of these ideas in such action. Then once again concentrate ideas from the masses and once again go to the masses so that the ideas are persevered in and carried through.[114]

This comparison has its limits. In Mao, the mass line is presented as a method for mobilising and politicising the population. The aim of algorithmic social control is quite the opposite: to automate, and thereby depoliticise, the workings of economic and social life. It is clear, however, that the

---

112 Samantha Hoffman, 'Managing the State: Social Credit, Surveillance and the CCP's Plan for China', in *AI, China, Russia, and the Global Order: Technological, Political, Global, and Creative*, SMA Report, 2018, p. 42.

113 Cited in ibid., p. 147.

114 Mao Tse-Tung, 'The Mass Line', in *Quotations from Chairman Mao Tse-Tung*, Peking: Foreign Languages Press, 1966, available at marxists.org.

perspective adopted – a holistic approach, which raises the question of how society as a whole should be managed – diverges greatly from the individualistic thinking characteristic of liberalism, which sees society only through the prism of its constituent individualities. So, it is possible that, in adopting such a viewpoint on the totality of society, the CCP is gaining an epistemic advantage over liberalism in thinking about the developments connected to the pervasive spread of algorithms in the age of Big Data.

The fact is that the Chinese authorities are attempting to build a surveillance apparatus for the purposes of a part-automated social control. This is what emerges from the in-depth study that Fan Liang and his co-authors have dedicated to the technical and institutional mechanisms of the social credit system.[115]

This catch-all system aims to record more than 500 variables for each entity based in China (individuals, companies, various organisations). The goal is to centralise robust identification data and compare it with a register of discreditable or else commendable activities. It is quite clear that even if the primary aim is to monitor economic agents, this surveillance also has a political and social dimension.

The overall logic of this programme is based on three phases, as shown in figure 2. The first involves collecting data from various private and public institutions. Financial data includes banking and tax information, as well as transaction data relating to online or credit card payments. The non-financial data includes a wide range of personal information, such as education and training, criminal and medical records, employment, and social media use. Seeing as the data flows come from a vast number of sources, their integration raises certain technical and administrative difficulties. Hence the social credit system is not a homogeneous body, but rather a multiform system. Its backbone is the National Credit Information Sharing Platform (NCISP) developed by the central planning agency – the National Development and Reform Commission. According to China's official news agency, Xinhua, as of

---

115 Fan Liang et al., 'Constructing a Data-Driven Society: China's Social Credit System as a State Surveillance Infrastructure', *Policy and Internet* 10, no. 4, 2018, pp. 415–53.

2017 it was already gathering more than 10.7 billion data points from forty-two central government agencies, thirty-two local governments, and fifty market players. Major technology firms such as Baidu and Alibaba share data with the NCISP. Of the 400 databases handled by this platform, two-thirds relate to companies, one-fifth to individuals, and the rest to various public and social bodies.

Figure 2. Organisation of the Chinese social credit system

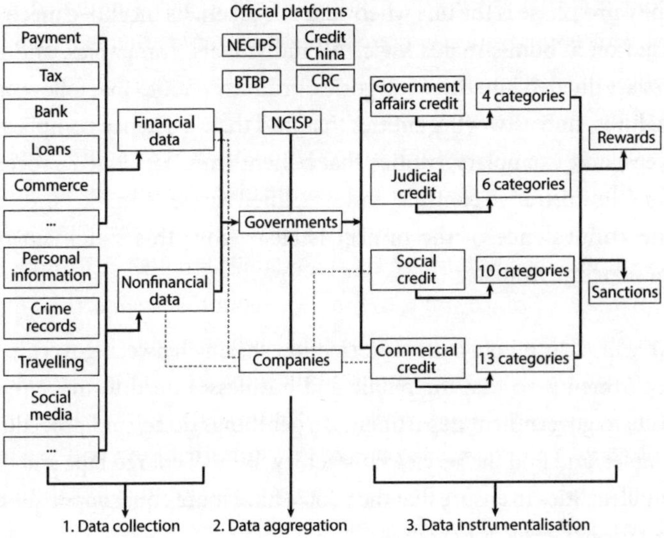

The dotted lines indicate the unofficial but anticipated roles of private firms in the construction of the official social credit system; their private credit systems focus on social and commercial credit.

NCISP: national credit information sharing platform; CRC: credit reference centre; NECIPS: national enterprise credit information publicity system; BTBP: blacklist of trust-breaking platforms.

Source: Fan Liang et al, 'Constructing a Data-Driven Society: China's Social Credit System as a State Surveillance Infrastructure', *Policy and Internet* 10, no. 4, 2018, p. 427.

Matters are rather murkier in the second phase, which involves the aggregating and processing of data. We know that, as well as the NCISP, there are five platforms responsible for compiling the information gathered. But the specific mechanisms of the aggregation and processing of the data are kept a secret. While this system is vast in its sheer scale, it remains relatively unsophisticated, and exists mainly for the sake of interconnecting the data scattered across various administrative bodies. So, this little resembles the single social rating we see in *Black Mirror*. And there is nothing to tell us that administrative action at the central level is guided by behavioural prediction models of the kind used by online marketing – and denounced by Shoshana Zuboff. Still, the Chinese authorities make no secret of their aim of achieving a semi-automated management of social life.

The third phase is the one when action is taken. Its incentive mechanism is based on a 'bonus-malus logic'. All individuals, companies, and public bodies are divided into three categories: ordinary entities that follow normal procedures, untrustworthy entities that find their existence complicated in all areas, and exemplary entities that benefit from facilitated procedures, lighter administrative controls, and simplified access to markets.

The ambivalence of the project is clear from this statement by the Chinese prime minister:

> We will . . . promote better information sharing between government departments, so that the public and businesses need to make fewer visits to government departments to get things done, find procedures simpler, and find the service satisfactory. We will cut red tape and root out illegalities to ensure that the people have more equal opportunities and greater space for creativity.[116]

The Chinese system offers a 'state-capitalist' version of the Silicon Valley consensus. Here, the automation of administration thanks to information technology is meant to free individuals from the burden of bureaucratic procedures even as it intensifies social control. The fantasy of the cybernetic state is here fully at work.

---

116 State Council of the People's Republic of China, 'China's Promotion of "Internet Plus Governance"', english.gov.cn, 1 February 2017.

The Corporate-State Nexus

The most radical aspect of the system being rolled out in China cuts across these three phases of collecting, aggregating, and making use of data. It involves the construction of a symbiotic relationship between the Chinese state apparatus and digital firms – what Liang and his co-authors call the corporate-state nexus.

Companies have set up their own ratings systems, connected in various ways to the public system. There are around ten large-scale private structures of this type operating in China. The largest of them is called Sesame. Developed by Ant Financial, Alibaba's financial subsidiary, it reached more than 520 million individuals in 2018. In some respects, these private programmes are comparable to big Western firms' loyalty programmes. Their primary function is to provide access to credit, but high-rated members enjoy a wide variety of benefits: they range from being able to hire a bicycle or car without paying a deposit, to fast-tracked visa applications and preferential treatment at hospitals. Sesame combines five main elements: borrowing history; user behaviour (types of purchase: someone who buys nappies or makes charitable donations will be favoured over a gamer); asset stability; personal characteristics (education, employment); and, finally, the quality of their social networks (with whom money is exchanged).[117] These elements are the subject of automatic ratings, which have tangible consequences for users in terms of differentiated access to many services.

These private programmes have a double advantage for planners. On the one hand, they act as a sounding board for the national social credit system: because private operators take the Credit China lists into consideration, they amplify this system's own power. Since three-quarters of the databases created as part of the social credit system are accessible to the public, their information is gradually being integrated into private firms' routine operations. For example, 80 per cent of the

---

117 Creemers, 'Planning Outline for the Construction of a Social Credit System'; Genia Kostka, 'China's Social Credit Systems and Public Opinion: Explaining High Levels of Approval', *New Media and Society* 21, no. 7, 2018, pp. 1565–93.

data used by Alibaba to inform individuals' personal credit scores comes from sources external to the firm, mainly government databases.[118] On the other hand, the government relies on private firms to hone its own system. The experience that they accumulate constitutes a reservoir of resources on which the planning agency can draw to fuel the engine of public social credit. The authorities attach such importance to the financial and social importance of private credit systems that they are now seeking to exercise a direct and permanent oversight over their operations, via a combined meta-system. This was the objective behind the 2018 creation of Baihang Credit, a consortium involving the eight main private credit systems, but which is de facto controlled by China's Central Bank.[119]

Fluid Automation

Under the planning agency's leadership, the various players are working together to build a surveillance infrastructure that is inextricably both public and private, economic, and political. The aim is to police economic exchanges in a manner that presents itself as neutral and impartial, indeed in a manner not unlike ordoliberal concerns. The presuppositions behind the norms that structure this black box tend to be glossed over, carried away by the fluidity and obvious necessity of automation.[120] Yet, in reality, the social credit system is brimming with politics in all its dimensions – starting with the relative weighting of positive and negative, reward and sanction, hidden and transparent. These are all choices

---

118 To make this lever more effective, the planning agency launched a project called 'Xinyi +' in 2018. The firms taking part, including Alibaba and its Sesame programme, are committed to promoting model behaviour by offering benefits to people on Credit China's red list. See Shazeda, 'Credit Cities and the Limits of the Social Credit System', p. 48.

119 Xin Dai, 'Toward a Reputation State: The Social Credit System Project of China', SSRN, 2018, p. 18; Lucy Hornby, Louise Lucas, and Sherry Fei Ju, 'China Cracks Down on Tech Credit Scoring', *Financial Times*, 4 February 2018.

120 Ramon Salim Diab, 'Becoming-Infrastructure: Datafication, Deactivation, and the Social Credit System', *Journal of Critical Library and Information Studies* 1, no. 1, 2017, pp. 16–17.

that respond to the requirements of the decision-makers within the architecture of this system.

As far as we can tell, a significant proportion of the Chinese population support the reduction in uncertainty that these control systems allow for. At least, this is what we learn from a survey in which 80 per cent of those questioned approved of this type of system. Genia Kostka, the researcher at the Free University of Berlin who supervised the study, sees this as a reaction to the widespread climate of mistrust prevailing in China after three decades of unbridled capitalist development. In such a context, she notes:

> the survey findings suggest that citizens perceive [social credit systems] not as an instrument of 'surveillance' but instead as an instrument to improve 'quality of life' and to close 'institutional and regulatory gaps' leading to more honest and law-abiding behavior in society.[121]

From a Polanyian perspective, the acceptance of the social credit system can be understood as a movement to reintegrate the economy into the properly social dimension. Its apparent aim is to counterbalance the development of opportunistic behaviour that has accompanied the extension of market relations. It purports to do this by means of an incentive structure that reintegrates into individual calculations both positive and negative effects which stand outside actors' field of vision and which market signals are unable to communicate. From this point of view, the party-state system has no trouble posing as a calculator of society's well-being. It starts with the masses and goes back to the masses in an algorithmic loop, whose political authority is both openly vaunted in its advertising and invisibilised by its automation.

China's social credit system is not just a techno-Maoist curiosity, a repellent counterexample that could conveniently be reduced to the regime's authoritarianism. In the age of algorithms, the proliferation of

---

121 Kostka, 'China's Social Credit Systems and Public Opinion', p. 20.

more or less decentralised, automatic, and transparent evaluation systems is becoming a pervasive problem. Who designs these systems? To what end? To what effect? The questions around China's social credit system also concern the many administrative and commercial ratings systems today being developed in Western societies.[122]

122 Daithi Mac Sithigh and Mathias Siems, 'The Chinese Social Credit System: A Model for Other Countries?', *EUI Department of Law Research Paper*, SSRN, 2019. On these problems more generally, see Cathy O'Neil, *Weapons of Math Destruction*, New York: Crown, 2016; Evgeny Morozov, 'The Case for Publicly Enforced Online Rights', *Financial Times*, 27 September 2018.

3
The Rentiers of the Intangible

Making Globalisation an Intellectual Monopoly

> The monstrous brute was not a dead weight. On the contrary, it
> wrapped round and oppressed the man with its powerful and elastic
> muscles.
>
> Charles Baudelaire[1]

The Rise of Intangibles

There are some means of production that you can touch: machines,
buildings, vehicles, raw materials, and so on. Then there are the other
kind that economists call 'intangible assets'. This term refers to means of
production such as computer codes, designs, databases, or procedures
that can be replicated infinitely without losing any of their intrinsic

---

1 'Everyone Has His Chimera', in Charles Baudelaire, *Little Poems in Prose*,
Chicago: Teitan Press, 1995, p. 10.

qualities.[2] There is no 'rivalry' over these assets: if you Google the time-table for the boat from Dakar to Gorée island, or watch an episode of *Stranger Things* on Netflix, it will not affect my ability to do the same, at least so long as the network does not become saturated. But, if we both want to buy an old moped at a flea market, we cannot both get our way if there's only one of them on sale.

The distinction between tangibles and intangibles is not new. For example, already in the mid-nineteenth century, when Friedrich List was considering the conditions on which German industry could catch up with Britain, he pointed to the role of 'the sciences and the arts' as opposed to 'bodily labour' in the development process – and went so far as to suggest the notion of an 'intellectual capital of living humanity'.[3] This distinction is also ubiquitous in our everyday lives, though it is so mundane that generally we pay it little attention. It goes without saying that to make a vinaigrette, you need the recipe (which is intangible) as well as ingredients and utensils (which are tangible); or that the impromptu piano piece you are planning to play will fall flat if you have forgotten the notes (intangible) or if your instrument is out of tune (tangible). In short, intangibles and tangibles are nothing without each other. The fact that they need to be combined, if they are going to have any useful effect, remains as true as ever.

But one thing surely has changed: technological advances have dramatically reduced the cost of reproducing, manipulating, and disseminating information. The cost of computer processing operations has fallen 100 billion times over since the middle of the last century.[4] Communication is now almost free and instantaneous, and storage costs are minimal. As Hegel noted, 'this seemingly innocuous alteration of the

---

2 Many recent works in economics and management have looked at the question of intangibles. For an overview of the subject, including the related definitional problems and accounting issues, see Jonathan Haskel and Stian Westlake, *Capitalism without Capital: The Rise of the Intangible Economy*, Princeton, NJ: Princeton University Press, 2018, 157.

3 Friedrich List, *Système national d'économie politique*, ed. Henri Richelot, Paris: Capelle, 1857, p. 248.

4 William D. Nordhaus, 'Are We Approaching an Economic Singularity? Information Technology and the Future of Economic Growth', NBER Working Paper 21547, 2015, p. 4.

quantitative is so to speak a ruse through which the qualitative is captured'.[5] The rising power of computer processing corresponds to just this kind of leap from quantity to quality.

The accelerating flow of information has affected the way in which intangibles are integrated into social arrangements. Back when intangibles could only be passed from one person to another by word of mouth, the printed word, or even, later on, by radio and telephone, their non-rivalry was somewhat limited. Their expansive capacities continued to be held back by the size of interpersonal and commercial networks, by the scarcity of opportunities for contact, by the time and costs involved in their transmission, and by the rigidity of the communications system. Now that the system of information is powerful enough, their being everywhere at once amounts to an absence of rivalry. But what consequences does this have for the mode of production?

A Second Unbundling

In his work describing the link between the information technology revolution and globalisation, Richard Baldwin speaks of a 'second unbundling'. The idea is simple enough. A first 'unbundling' arrived at the end of the nineteenth century, then developed more forcefully starting in the 1960s. As transport costs fell, it was no longer necessary to manufacture goods close to where they were consumed. But since the late 1980s, we have had a new, second wave of unbundling. As communication costs have fallen, the possibilities for remote coordination have increased exponentially. As a result, most stages of manufacturing no longer need to be carried out in close proximity.

There are plenty of examples of this. Cars, telephones, turbines for power stations, but also clothes, food products, software, and even some management or medical analysis services are produced in a combination of stages across multiple countries or even continents. The work process is dispersed. Production activities that are closely interdependent can be

---

5 G. W. F. Hegel, *Encyclopaedia of the Philosophical Sciences in Basic Outline*, vol. 1, Cambridge: Cambridge University Press, 2010, p. 170.

synchronised across thousands of miles' distance. So, as economist Baldwin shows, 'to ensure the operation operated as one, the off-shoring firms moved their managerial, marketing, and technical know-how along with the off shored stages'.[6]

The possibility of this new way of arranging production owes much to information technology. It is ICT that allows for the matching up of managerial skills and technical specifications across large distances. Yet, the drive behind this movement is not technological in nature, but economic. The quest for profit is driving what David Harvey calls a spatial fix: a new spatial-geographic arrangement that allows for improved capital valorisation.[7] This involves offshoring work geographically by relocating certain tasks – the simplest, or at least the most easily standardised and controlled ones – to countries where labour costs are lower. Apple, for example, no longer owns any factories and has all its devices produced by subcontractors. Many of these subcontractors are in China, where device assembly is concentrated. But there are also other cases. When the Rana Plaza building collapsed in Dhaka, Bangladesh, on 24 April 2013, among the bodies of the 1,134 women textile workers killed were labels from such brands as Benetton, Bonmarché, Prada, Gucci, Versace, Moncler, Mango, Primark, Walmart, Carrefour, Auchan, Camaïeu . . .[8]

The 'smile curve' offers a stylised representation of the effects of this fragmentation of production on the distribution of value (figure 3).[9] In the middle of the curve are the most standardised and least knowledge-intensive activities, which have been offshored en masse since the 1990s. These are the segments in which competition is fiercest and, as a result, the ability to capture value is lowest. At either end of the curve are the activities furthest upstream and downstream of production – design tasks, on the one hand, and the interface with customers, on the other. These are the most knowledge-intensive segments, where value capture is at its highest.

---

6 Richard E. Baldwin, *The Great Convergence: Information Technology and the New Globalization*, Cambridge, MA: Belknap Press, 2016, p. 134.

7 David Harvey, *The Limits to Capital*, London: Verso, 2006, chapter 7.

8 'Rana Plaza Collapse', Wikipedia, French-language version consulted 22 March 2019.

9 An image owing to Acer's founder Stan Shih: 'Me-too is not my style: challenge difficulties, break through bottlenecks, create values', Acer Foundation, Taipei, 1996.

Figure 3. The smile curve of the distribution of value across global value chains

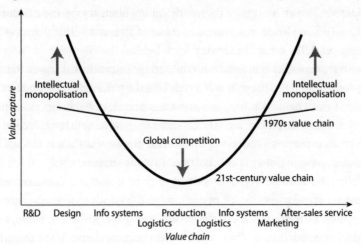

Babbage's Principle, Magnified

Charles Babbage was a polymath who designed the first mechanical prototype of the computer, called the difference engine, back in 1821. His starting point was a simple observation: any given production process requires the mobilisation of multiple different skills. But some of these are rarer, or more expensive to acquire, than others. For the employer, there is an advantage to be had in dividing up these tasks and paying for them separately, allowing for a differentiation of workers in which each focuses on some particular task according to their skills:

> The master manufacturer, by dividing the work to be executed into different processes, each requiring different degrees of skill and force, can purchase exactly that precise quantity of both which is necessary for each process; whereas, if the whole work were executed by one workman, that person must have sufficient skill to perform the most difficult, and sufficient strength to execute the most laborious, of the operations into which the art is divided.[10]

---

10 Charles Babbage, *On the Economy of Machinery and Manufactures*, Cambridge: Cambridge University Press, 2009, pp. 137–8.

In short, the division of labour reduces the cost of labour for the employer. This encourages a relative deskilling of most jobs and a concentration of knowledge in a limited number of functions. This principle of saving on skills is still the driving force behind the cognitive division of labour that goes hand in hand with the current international segmentation of production.[11] But the dynamic producing the polarisation of incomes in global value chains is more than just an extension of Babbage's principle. Rather, it is its magnification. The concentration of value at the extremes of the chain expresses a process of intellectual monopolisation, at the end of which economic power is concentrated in a few strategic sites.

The international fragmentation of work processes is accompanied by a greater standardisation of operations and by a more intensive use of information technology. As the production process becomes increasingly dispersed, information systems must become denser if the integrity of the production process is to be maintained. So, this polarisation is not simply a separation between more and less knowledge-intensive tasks. Rather, the integration is itself becoming an autonomous factor of production. On a global scale, the forces of labour organisation are concentrated in the form of intangible forces of production. Intellectual monopolisation centralises the will to produce.

The Mechanisms of Rent

Everything that ripens is teeming with bandits.

Henri Michaux[12]

The Italian economist Ugo Pagano uses the concept of intellectual monopoly capitalism[13] to describe the economic system that emerged from the

11 Philippe Moati and El Mouhoub Mouhoud, 'Les nouvelles logiques de décomposition internationale des processus productifs', *Revue d'économie politique* 115, no. 5, 2005, pp. 573–89.

12 Henri Michaux, 'Tranches de savoir', in *Face aux verrous*, Paris: Gallimard, 1992 [1951], p. 64.

13 Ugo Pagano, 'The Crisis of Intellectual Monopoly Capitalism', *Cambridge Journal of Economics* 38, no. 6, 2014, pp. 1409–29.

drastic hardening of property rights in the last decades of the twentieth century.[14] In the case of intellectual property rights, he explains, 'monopoly is not simply based on the market power due to the concentration of skills in machines and management; it becomes also a *legal monopoly* over some items of knowledge'.[15] And since 'knowledge is not an object defined in a limited physical space . . . the full-blown private ownership of knowledge means a global monopoly that limits the liberty of many individuals in multiple locations'.[16]

One illustration of this harmful dynamic comes in the rise of patent trolls. Firms specialise in holding patents, not in order to exploit them but to charge for the use of the knowledge which they keep under lock and key, with the effect of holding back innovation.[17] For Pagano, while, in the 1990s, there may have been a Schumpeterian effect of stimulating investment through the search for innovation rents, this is no longer the case. The new barriers are now drastically limiting investment opportunities. This is slowing accumulation and growth in the rich countries and hampering development in the countries of the Global South – and this dynamic also explains the huge rise in the amount of capital sitting idle, which is fuelling financial instability.[18]

It is no coincidence that tougher intellectual property rules have come at the same time as globalisation. On the one hand, companies wishing to take full advantage of international opportunities are pushing for stricter rules in this area.[19] On the other hand, the dissemination of

14 Benjamin Coriat and Fabienne Orsi, 'Establishing a New Intellectual Property Rights Regime in the United States: Origins, Content and Problems', *Research Policy* 31, nos. 8–9, 2002, pp. 1491–507; Christopher May, *The Global Political Economy of Intellectual Property Rights: The New Enclosures*, London: Routledge, RIPE Series in Global Political Economy, 2010.

15 Pagano, 'The Crisis of Intellectual Monopoly Capitalism', p. 1413.

16 Ibid.

17 Lauren Cohen, Umit G. Gurun, and Scott Duke Kominers, 'Patent Trolls: Evidence from Targeted Firms', *Management Science* 65, no. 12, 2019, pp. 5449–956.

18 Ugo Pagano and Maria Alessandra Rossi, 'The Crash of the Knowledge Economy', *Cambridge Journal of Economics* 33, no. 4, 2009, pp. 665–83.

19 Susan K. Sell, 'TRIPS Was Never Enough: Vertical Forum Shifting, FTAS, ACTA, and TPP', *Journal of Intellectual Property Law* 18, no. 2, 2010, pp. 104–60; Susan K. Sell and Aseem Prakash, 'Using Ideas Strategically: The Contest between

rigorous standards reduces the risk that their innovations will be appropriated by others, and this in turn strengthens their resolve to fragment production internationally.[20]

Rents from Natural Monopolies

The strengthening of exclusive control over standards, technologies, and brands is thus a powerful driving force behind intellectual monopolisation in globalisation. But it is not the only one. In another study, I showed together with my co-author, William Milberg, that three additional mechanisms are also at work therein.[21]

The first is what economists call a natural monopoly situation – a market structure that itself stems from three elements: network complementarities, economies of scale, and sunk investments.[22] A typical example is a railway network: the more extensive it is, the more useful it is (network complementarities); however, the organisation of the network involves fixed costs (economies of scale); finally, once the railway lines have been built, it is impossible to go back and recover the money invested (sunk costs). In such situations, management by a single company is more economical than a market open to competition.

Business and NGO Networks in Intellectual Property Rights', *International Studies Quarterly* 48, no. 1, 2004, pp. 143–75.

20 Various empirical studies have shown that an increase in trade is associated with a tightening of intellectual property rights. See Titus O. Awokuse and Hong Yin, 'Does Stronger Intellectual Property Rights Protection Induce More Bilateral Trade? Evidence from China's Imports', *World Development* 38, no. 8, 2010, pp. 1094–104; Rod Falvey, Neil Foster, and David Greenaway, 'Trade, Imitative Ability and Intellectual Property Rights', *Review of World Economics* 145, no. 3, 2009, pp. 373–404; Yungho Weng, Chih-Hai Yang, and Yi-Ju Huang, 'Intellectual Property Rights and US Information Goods Exports: The Role of Imitation Threat', *Journal of Cultural Economics* 33, no. 2, 2009, p. 109.

21 Cédric Durand and William Milberg, 'Intellectual Monopoly in Global Value Chains', *Review of International Political Economy* 27, no. 2, 2020, pp. 404–29.

22 Manuela Mosca, 'On the Origins of the Concept of Natural Monopoly: Economies of Scale and Competition', *European Journal of the History of Economic Thought* 15, no. 2, 2008, pp. 317–53.

We can see these same characteristics in global value chains: the inter-play of complementarities between firms; economies of scale on func-tions that organise the integration of dispersed activities; and the sunk investments needed to make operations compatible. The dynamic behind Apple's success is archetypal of the logic of the natural monopoly. After abandoning its factories at Fountain in Colorado Springs and Elk Grove in Sacramento in 1996 and 2004, the firm enjoyed a return to fortune, owing to its rigorous value chain management. All manufactur-ing is carried out by facilities based outside the US, mainly in China, but this does not mean that the company has relaxed its control over produc-tion. Quite the opposite is true: Apple has built a closed ecosystem where it exercises control over almost every link in the supply chain, from design to retail.[23]

What is at issue, in this remote supervision, is the firm's ability to maintain its distinction over the devices produced by its competitors. From the viewpoint of Apple's suppliers, being part of such a complex and well-managed value chain means that they can benefit from these network complementarities. But it also puts them in a position where they depend on the Californian company, which controls them and is thus in a position to appropriate the lion's share of the value produced.

Differential Rents on Intangibles

Beyond these two widely analysed types of rent, there is a rather less well-known third one. It is associated with intangibles – or, more precisely, with the difference between the returns to scale associated with the classic mobilisation of tangible assets, and the highly intensive production phases of intangible assets.

To explain: intangible assets, such as software or organisational know-how, are generally scalable. Once the initial investment has been made,

23 Donald L. Barlett and James B. Steele, 'Apple's American Job Disaster – Philly', philly.com, 20 November 2011; Andrew B. Bernard and Teresa C. Fort, 'Factoryless Goods Producing Firms', *American Economic Review* 105, no. 5, 2015, pp. 518–23; Adam Satariano and Peter Burrows, 'Apple's Supply-Chain Secret? Hoard Lasers', *Bloomberg Businessweek*, 3 November 2011, pp. 50–4.

they can be reproduced at negligible marginal costs, so that the returns to scale tend towards infinity. However, this is not the case for tangible assets such as buildings or machinery. In these cases, even if economies of scale do exist, they are much lesser: each additional material operation involves a non-trivial additional cost, if only because of the expenditure on energy and raw materials that it entails.

These differentiated returns are one of the keys to understanding the specific features of today's competitive logic, for example, the growing rivalry between Walmart and Amazon, as reported in the *New York Times*:

> Retailers need to figure out how to manage sophisticated supply chains connecting Southeast Asia with stores in big American cities so that they rarely run out of product. They need mobile apps and websites that offer a seamless user experience so that nothing stands between a would-be purchaser and an order ... Companies that are good at supply chain management and technology can spread those more-or-less fixed costs around more total sales.[24]

There is, of course, a decisive advantage in being able to amortise the (approximately) fixed cost of intangible assets over the broadest possible sales base. But another aspect also comes into play: the more a business operates in segments intensive in intangible assets, the more potentially profitable it is. Global value chains combine segments that are intensive in tangible assets and/or labour, and other segments that are intensive in intangible ones. The former include, for example, garment manufacturing, the assembly of telephones, semiconductor casting, and rail transport. The latter include the design of integrated circuits, websites, clothing design, marketing strategies, software coding, database management, etc. But consider what happens when total production in the value chain concerned increases: for the costs of segments intensive in intangible assets and those of segments

---

24 Neil Irwin, 'The Amazon-Walmart Showdown That Explains the Modern Economy', *New York Times*, 7 June 2017.

intensive in tangible assets and labour will increase at different rates. As a result of the uneven distribution of fixed costs and differentiated marginal costs, total costs increase rapidly for material-intensive segments, while average costs fall much faster for information-intensive segments. This is illustrated in figure 4.

The difference in economies of scale between tangible and intangible assets means that companies that control the intangible links in the chain receive a disproportionate share of gains as total production increases.

Figure 4. Dynamic of total and average costs for segments intensive in tangible and intangible assets

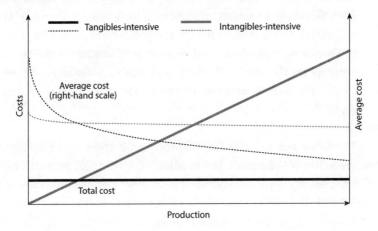

Dynamic Innovation Rent

One last force of intellectual monopolisation is associated with what we can call 'dynamic innovation rent'. It works like this: the more integrated the value chains and the greater the development of their activity, the larger the quantities of data produced. This information accumulates in very specific sites – that is, where the integration functions are focused. The firms that organise the value chains control the information systems, and so it is they who centralise the data. But this data is an essential raw material for modern research and development processes: it makes it possible to pinpoint weaknesses, identify sources of improvement, and test innovative solutions virtually. In the words of former Siemens CEO Joseph Kaeser, data is 'the holy grail of innovation'.[25]

We have seen already that accumulating data is the core of the internet giants' business model. User-generated data enables these companies to improve their user experience, design targeted advertising, or sell personalised services. But the importance of data in innovation processes is not limited to these companies alone. Kaeser explains:

> We manufacture products that generate power, that automate manufacturing processes, that scan people (like CT and MRI machines), and that move people and goods from place A to place B. That's a lot of products, and all those products have sensors . . . Once we get the data, we have the data analytics platform and the cloud. We have a proprietary cloud, for example, an on-site cloud.[26]

The data generated by industrial processes, particularly in the context of predictive maintenance, is the object of intellectual property rights that are fiercely negotiated between equipment manufacturers and their customers. This owes to the simple – but crucial – reason that this data is an essential input into the R and D process.

In the case of the relationship between Walmart and its subcontractors, Walmart has an overwhelming advantage. The company, based in Bentonville, Arkansas, collects activity data from its 245 million customers at a rate of one million transactions per hour. This is in addition to the logistical and operational data coming from more than 17,500 suppliers. Suppliers can improve their operations by accessing point of sale data on their own products. But the benefit reaped by Walmart is

---

25 Joseph Kaeser and Daniel Gross, 'Siemens CEO Joe Kaeser on the Next Industrial Revolution', *Strategy and Business*, 9 February 2016.
    26 Ibid.

much greater, as the company has insight into the operations of all its suppliers: production planning, product design and packaging, and, of course, customer information.[27]

Walmart's informational advantage lies in its central position, in relation to both its suppliers and its customers. Using software called the HANA Business Intelligence Platform, supplied by the German company SAP, the retailer gathers real-time data from its various stakeholders. According to CEO Karenann Terrell, 'HANA is floating on our [Enterprise Resource Planning] system' – meaning that 'innovation doesn't rest in the back office'.[28] At the firm's HQ, a Data Café centralises data provided in real time by 200 internal and external feeds (including weather reports, social media, and local events). The idea is to exploit this unique mass of information by enabling teams in the various departments to put their hypotheses to the test by calling on the aid of experts at the analysis centre.[29]

In value chains, there is a vertical struggle over the control over data. Data circulation is a prerequisite for the integration and optimisation of business processes within fragmented workflows. But this grants disproportionate data access to those who initiate and organise this integration itself. Because of the asymmetry inherent in information systems and the unequal bargaining power between firms, dominant companies are able to learn from their partners' production and commercial processes and use this information to sharpen their own capacity for innovation. So, we see that the dynamic of intellectual monopolisation is fuelled by the centralisation of the data generated with the help of the digital tools that enable the integration of value chains.

~

27 Nada R. Sanders, 'How to Use Big Data to Drive Your Supply Chain', *California Management Review* 58, no. 3, 2016, pp. 26–48; Jianfeng Wang, 'Economies of IT Systems at Wal-Mart: An Historical Perspective', *Journal of Management Information and Decision Sciences* 9, no. 1, 2006, p. 45.

28 Marianne Wilson, 'Wal-Mart Focuses on Speed, Innovation with SAP's HANA Technology', chainstoreage.com, 6 May 2015.

29 Bernard Marr, 'Really Big Data at Walmart: Real-Time Insights from Their 40 + Petabyte Data Cloud', *Forbes*, 23 January 2017.

The process of monopolising knowledge involves the massive enclosure of knowledge within intellectual property rights, which are becoming increasingly strict on a global scale. But it does not stop at that. The international fragmentation of production processes and the increased unbundling of design and execution activities that it requires through integration functions are creating new sources of intellectual rents, as can be seen in table 3.

Table 3. Taxonomy of rents linked to intangibles

Type	Description	Example
Intellectual property rents		
Patents, copyright, trademarks	Rationing through exclusive rights on productions and processes, cultural and scientific assets, and marketing investments	Patents on pharmaceutical products, the characteristics and coding of software, brand protection: Nike, Louis Vuitton
Natural monopoly rent		
Toll on global-value-chain (GVC) integration	Return on intangible assets underlying the integration Complementarities of networks within the GVC Sunk costs resulting from the specific nature of the assets	Supply chain management: Apple, Valeo, Bosch for car parts
Differential rents on intangibles		
Unequal returns to scale	The unequal returns to scale for intangible assets compared to tangible assets enable intangibles-intensive segments of the chain to capture a larger share of gains	Factory-less manufacturing: Apple and Nike vs. assembly plants, Nespresso vs. coffee producers
Dynamic innovation rents		
Schumpeter Mark II *via* data collection	Centralisation of data generated along value chains via asymmetric information systems. Data fuels the path to Schumpeter Mark II innovation	Siemens's sensors on machines, Goodyear's tyre censors, Walmart's information system, Amazon's purchase histories

The digital boom is fuelling a gigantic rentier economy; and this not because information is a new source of value, but because the control of information and knowledge – intellectual monopolisation – has become the most powerful means of capturing value.

Trouble among the Monopolies

In our situation free market means not competition, but rather monopoly, and on a world scale; or perhaps feudal capitalism.

Fredric Jameson[30]

On 21 June 2018, Anne-Marie Slaughter, head of the influential New America Foundation, published an article in the *Financial Times* entitled 'Vertical Media Mergers Are Just So 19th Century'.[31] Slaughter is a former White House adviser to Barack Obama, and her column criticised the aggressive mergers taking place in the media sector between infrastructure magnates and content producers. She was writing against the backdrop of the birth of a new giant, after the merger between telecoms group AT&T and Time Warner, which owns CNN, the HBO channel, and film studios, among others.

Since the 1990s, the telecommunications sector has undergone massive concentration processes, with AT&T, Comcast, and Verizon forming a de facto cartel. Since the late 2000s, they have gone to war against net neutrality: indeed, they seek to use their telecoms networks to form vertically integrated conglomerates, in order to control all the layers of a media empire, from underground cables and airborne terminals to content creation.

Slaughter argues that, in the twenty-first century, this strategy is doomed to failure. It is a manoeuvre worthy of the nineteenth century, when steel magnate Andrew Carnegie sought to control the railways, as

---

30 Fredric Jameson, 'In Soviet Arcadia', *New Left Review* 75, 2012, p. 124.

31 Anne-Marie Slaughter, 'Vertical Media Mergers Are Just So 19th Century', *Financial Times*, 21 June 2018.

well as coal mines and steelworks, in order to keep his competitors at bay. Such a project no longer makes sense in the information age: 'Vertical integration amounts to building silos in an era that will be dominated by platforms – owning in an era of renting – and looking for mass markets when customers want individualised products.' To support her argument, she cites *Unscaled*, the aforementioned book just published by Silicon Valley venture capitalist Hemant Taneja, in which he promises the rebirth of an entrepreneurial capitalism of small, innovative firms thanks to artificial intelligence (AI):

> In an economy driven by AI and digital technology, small, focused, and nimble companies can leverage technology platforms to effectively compete against big, mass-market entities. The small can do this because they can rent scale that companies used to need to build. The small can rent computing in the cloud, rent access to consumers on social media, rent production from contract manufacturers all over the world ... The old mass markets are giving way to micromarkets. This is the essence of unscaling: technology is devaluing mass production and mass marketing and empowering customized microproduction and finely targeted marketing.[32]

This is the same argument that Hal Varian had made in the *American Economic Review* in 2010, with regard to the 'platform as service' model:

> Nowadays, it is possible for a small company to purchase data storage, hosting services, an applications development environment, and Internet connectivity 'off the shelf' from vendors such as Amazon, Google, IBM, Microsoft, Sun and others. The 'platform as service' model turns what used to be a fixed cost for small

---

32 Hemant Taneja, *Unscaled: How AI and a New Generation of Upstarts Are Creating the Economy of the Future*, New York: PublicAffairs Books, 2018, p. 13.

Web applications into a variable cost, dramatically reducing entry costs.[33]

Anne-Marie Slaughter embraces this argument without qualification:

> Companies will become smaller, because it will no longer be as efficient to organise human activity centrally. The future is more likely to belong to companies that have a small number of managers overseeing machines and freelancers, the gig economy writ large.

In this context, the old monopolists embodied by the AT&T–Warner alliance have only one card left to play in order to turn back the clock. In a 14 December 2017 decision, the US Federal Communications Commission put an end to net neutrality – the guarantee of equal treatment of data flows by operators. For infrastructure owners like AT&T, this is a godsend. Thanks to their control over the physical mobile and cable internet network, they will be able to charge content providers more, or encourage the distribution of their own creations. But Slaughter sees this as nothing more than a reprieve: 'Behemoths, beware!' she warns, because this haphazard strategy will not hold up against the onslaught by a myriad of nimble new entrants.

Slaughter's column kills two birds with one stone. On the one hand, she attacks the telecoms firms that are at war over net neutrality with West Coast big tech firms (who are also among the main backers of her foundation). On the other, she lights a backfire to the revival of the anti-monopolistic critique of digital firms. At a time when this issue is taking centre stage in the public debate, she attacks the old-style monopolies (the telecoms networks) in order to let the new ones off the hook. In so doing, she is attempting to revive the ideological core of the Silicon Valley consensus: the myth that information technologies are inseparable from entrepreneurial capitalism.

---

33 Hal R. Varian, 'Computer Mediated Transactions', *American Economic Review* 100, no. 2, 2010, p. 7.

But less than a week later, there was a reply, also on the *Financial Times* site. Alexandra Scaggs, then a columnist for Alphaville (the *FT*'s 'markets and finance' blog), slammed the New America Foundation chairwoman's article. She began by correcting a few facts. The historical analogy with the end of the nineteenth century was built on rather shaky premises: Slaughter seemed to have confused Carnegie's defensive vertical integration with the strategy of Rockefeller's Standard Oil, which did indeed squeeze out its competitors by forcing them to pay higher costs for the railways. But, if this mistake was symptomatic of a certain ideological zeal, this was not the main point. What Scaggs shows is that by denouncing the threat posed by an old kind of monopoly, she is promoting an even more dangerous model:

> When she recommends renting tech capabilities instead of developing them internally, she neglects to mention from whom these nimble companies would be renting. Someone owns those capabilities, of course, and that someone is Big Tech. Keeping your work files in the cloud? You're paying Amazon or Google for the ability to work anywhere, any time. The structure she recommends ('the gig economy writ large') hearkens back to an economic structure that preceded robber-baron capitalism. In that system, servants and workers of varying rank paid for the privilege of owning nothing and working in a specific territory controlled entirely by a person/entity with extreme power over all who dwelled there, and little to no accountability. We are speaking of course of feudalism. There have been compelling arguments that tech is bringing us into a new feudal era where individuals must provide *robota* – which means free work, and happens to be the root of the word robot – just to maintain effective access to the Big-Tech platforms where an ever-growing portion of people's lives are spent.[34]

This is a hard-hitting charge against Slaughter's argument. It mixes two registers. The first draws on a new generation of anti-monopolistic

---

34 Alexandra Scaggs, 'The Node to Serfdom', *Financial Times*, Alphaville (blog), 27 June 2018.

arguments whose theses have been brought to the fore by the work of the young lawyer Lina Khan – later nominated as the chairperson of the Federal Trade Commission under the Biden administration – and the so-called 'hipster antitrust school' (see Appendix II). The second is the critique of Big Tech based on the issue of data extraction and exploitation, discussed above. But, above all, Scaggs's argument sketches out an avenue worth pursuing further, that of a paradoxically feudal future for the new economy – what I call the techno-feudal hypothesis.

4

The Techno-feudal Hypothesis

What Is Feudalism?

> Economists have a singular method of procedure. There are only two
> kinds of institutions for them, artificial and natural. The institutions of
> feudalism are artificial institutions, those of the bourgeoisie are natu-
> ral institutions.
>
> Karl Marx[1]

Karl Marx observed that economic science is generally unable to grasp
changes in the fundamental ways in which societies are organised. The
classical economists of his day, like mainstream economists in our own
time, regard the market relationships that structure contemporary economies as natural. It is as if their principles had applied since time imme-
morial. What is rational, in these observers' view, is what conforms to
the rules of operation of an industrial market capitalist economy.

---

1 Karl Marx, *The Poverty of Philosophy*, in *Marx and Engels Collected Works*, vol.
6, London: Lawrence & Wishart, 1976, p. 174.

Anything that does not conform must be irrational, archaic – and ultimately, unintelligible.[2] So, if we want a chance to refresh our perspective, and perhaps to get a better grasp of the changes in front of us, we need to take a closer look at what appear as persistent 'anomalies' compared to a capitalist idea of what is 'natural'.

Today, for anyone paying attention, the spectres of feudalism are legion.[3] Philosophers, lawyers, and anthropologists have no hesitation in referring to this bygone age in order to reflect on the problems of our time. The connection can be made with such phenomena as the decrepitude of democratic processes in Western countries, the fragmentation of the juridical order in the context of globalisation, or indeed the ubiquity of the theme of appropriation in discussion of managerial practices.[4]

---

2 Maurice Godelier, *Rationality and Irrationality in Economics*, London: Verso, 2012, chapter 4.

3 I owe this idea to an unpublished text by Thierry Labica, '"Neofeudalism" or the Insights of Neoliberalism Dystopianized', 2011.

4 In addition to Habermas's concept of the refeudalisation of the public sphere discussed in chapter 3, we can mention three other notable uses. The anthropologist Katherine Verdery has hypothesised a 'transition from socialism to feudalism' in the context of economic involution in central and eastern Europe in the early 1990s. She highlights the fragmentation of economic space and the re-creation of local networks of allegiance in response to the shocks of economic liberalisation.

In France, legal experts have noted symptoms of feudalism in the growth of independent self-regulatory bodies, the increasing variety of laws applying to criminal procedure, and the extended possibilities for self-regulation in the fields of social law and sporting activities. This diversification of the sources of law and the social and institutional players involved in its creation leads to a lack of unity and a weakening of the regulatory idea of the general interest. The plurality of the law was a characteristic feature of the *ancien régime*, in opposition to which post-1789 legal principles were built. This plurality corresponded to the diversity of seigneurial rights, which themselves reflected the pre-eminence of personal bonds and dependencies in the feudal system.

Finally, David Graeber looks at the rise of 'bullshit jobs', even in societies so obsessed with the quest for performance and its objective measurement. He argues that this phenomenon is the result of a new form of indistinction between politics and economics. In a break with properly capitalist principles, this is giving rise to a 'managerial feudalism' in which the process of appropriating, distributing, and allocating resources predominates.

See Katherine Verdery, *What Was Socialism, and What Comes Next?*, Princeton, NJ: Princeton University Press, 1996, chapter 8; José Lefebvre, ed., *L'Hypothèse du*

My question is more specific. It is about how relevant the category of feudalism is in accounting for certain types of contemporary economic trends. To answer this question, we need to start by looking at the original meaning of the term. Feudalism is first and foremost a historical concept that relates to the organisation of western European societies in the Middle Ages. As we shall see, it is also the name of a particular socio-economic form.

The aim here is not to give an exhaustive account, but to sketch a stylised picture of this mode of production and provide a schema of its logical structure. By this, I mean the articulation of the fundamental social relationships which, starting from a limited number of characteristic features, structure the typical aspects of its socio-economic dynamics.

Power over Men and the Land

In the ninth and tenth centuries, the medieval West was 'a highly stratified society, in which power was vested in a small group of people who controlled from above the activities of the vast mass of country folk'.[5]

According to Georges Duby, the main effect of feudal organisation was that it allowed a situation in which

in this poverty-stricken society, where men worked themselves to the bone for their wretched crops, the mere presence of the great estate and the power it conferred on the lord and his steward combined to drain away for the use of the lords and their parasites the miserable surpluses won from minute patches of ground by the grim privation of peasant households. The extravagance of an aristocracy totally

néo-féodalisme. Le droit à une nouvelle croisée des chemins, Paris: Presses universitaires de France, 2006; Alain Supiot, *La Gouvernance par les nombres*, course at the Collège de France, 2012–2014; Alain Supiot, *Poids et mesures du monde*, Paris: Fayard 2015; David Graeber, *Bullshit Jobs*, New York: Simon & Schuster, chapter 5.

5 Georges Duby, *Rural Economy and Country Life in the Medieval West*, London: Edward Arnold, 1962, p. 34.

dominated by a love of luxury and a desire for conspicuous display speedily disposed of these surpluses.[6]

This acute social polarisation thus resulted from a process in which a minority cornered and centralised wealth for the purposes of consumption. 'It was the privilege of the noble', Duby tells us, 'at all times to avoid any appearance of shortage. He had to be prodigal in the midst of famine.'[7] So power, ostentation, and profligacy went hand in hand. The reason for this was that the masters' material affluence was a prerequisite of their ability to reproduce their power over men. They needed, 'without anxiety for the morrow, [to] have something always in hand to provide for the "family" and if need be to increase the number of their dependents'.[8] The powerful reigned over domains from which they derived economic security, which was inextricably linked to political security.

The aristocracy exercised a power that Alain Guerreau calls *dominium*, which is the primordial feudal tie. It is 'a social relationship between the dominant and the dominated, in which the dominant simultaneously exercised power over men and over land'.[9] The relationship between the lords and the producers obliged to them was thus spatial and territorial. It concerned all the inhabitants of a manor, who, while diverse in terms of their status and type of habitat, were subject to the local master's domination through their attachment to the land. The church was also fully part of this *dominium* relationship. Depending on the period and the region, ecclesiastical institutions owned between a quarter and a third of the land. As a result, the episcopal and monastic authorities were full-fledged feudal lords, whose power was magnified by their spiritual offices, which underpinned the entire edifice of society.

However, feudal domination was far from total. The lack of centralisation of power and the overlapping of seigneuries resulted in the

6 Ibid., p. 58.
7 Ibid., p. 36.
8 Ibid.
9 Alain Guerreau, 'Le concept de féodalisme: genèse, évolution et signification actuelle', *HAL*, 1997, p. 2.

fragmentation of sovereignty and the persistence of margins of peasant autonomy. In particular, as Friedrich Engels noted, communal owner-ship of land gave 'the oppressed class, the peasants, even under the harshest medieval serfdom a local centre of solidarity and a means of resistance such as neither the slaves of classical times nor the modern proletariat found ready to their hand'.[10] The medieval commons were economic and political resources.

While *dominium* is feudalism's pivotal institution, it is of course not the only one. One of the related forms is serfdom. This persistent feature of feudal societies affected between 10 and 20 per cent of the rural popu-lation. Unlike slaves, serfs were not their masters' property. However, their freedom was strictly limited, particularly at key moments in their social existence such as marriage and inheritance. As the saying goes, 'the serf is attached to the soil' – that is, the land of the estate, on which he was obliged to remain. What is more, the extent of their *corvée*, or unpaid compulsory labour, was more up to the lord's discretion than was true of other dependent populations.

Vassalage, another essential institution of feudalism, affected only a tiny proportion of the population, since it was restricted to the aristoc-racy alone. Nonetheless, it was important because it regulated a large proportion of relationships by organising, alongside other forms of asso-ciation, ties of solidarity and the distribution of power. A significant part of the control exercised over the land was thus exercised through ties of vassalage. This was an asymmetrical relationship. The vassal was granted a fiefdom, a concession of seigneurial power over a territory and its inhabitants, which enabled him to maintain his rank and fulfil his obli-gations. He also benefited from the lord's protection. In return, the vassal was bound by obligations to him: he had to join his military endeavours, but also support him financially or through his advice. This first aspect was crucial, as it was on him that the formation of feudal armies depended. However, seigneurial authority remained highly precarious. As Max Weber points out, it was

---

10 Friedrich Engels, *The Origin of the Family, Private Property and the State*, London: Penguin, 2010.

very dependent on the voluntary obedience and hence the purely personal loyalty of the members of the administrative staff, who, by virtue of the feudal structure, are themselves in possession of the means of administration. Hence, the latent struggle for authority becomes chronic between the lord and his vassal.[11]

War played an essential role in the regulation and reproduction of the seigneurial system. It put the solidarity within the aristocracy to the test and settled rivalries between competing lords. Jérôme Baschet shows that it also played an essential role in reproducing the submission of the peasants, demonstrating how much these latter – the main victims of pillage – relied on their masters' protection.[12] War defined the boundaries of the lands controlled by the lords and established their domination over the people who lived on them. The lords' function as a public authority was expressed in the exercise of justice and the maintenance of order within the domain; this was matched, in their relations with the outside world, by a protective function that took on a vital character precisely because of military instability.

Dominium, serfdom, and vassalage are the basic categories that historians use to think about feudal society. In such a society, politics and economics are essentially indistinguishable, and violence is the dominant regulating principle – hence why feudal relations are organised around the question of domination/protection.

Serfdom: A Case of Predation, or an Effective Contract?

Neo-institutionalist theorists of economic history and Marxist authors adopt a different general perspective than historians do. Their interest is not in gaining insight into all the multiple dimensions and variations of the feudal era; rather their aim is to isolate a limited kernel of

---

11 Max Weber, *Economy and Society*, Berkeley: University of California Press, 1978, p. 57.

12 Jérôme Baschet, *La Civilisation féodale. De l'an mil à la colonisation de l'Amérique*, Paris: Flammarion, 2018, e-book, position 2195.

relations that can be used for analytical purposes – that is, to characterise a social configuration distinct from the capitalist one. This leads them to focus on serfdom, considered the decisive institution for grasping the essence of feudalism. This is a questionable premise, from a historian's standpoint, but it is highly fruitful from a theoretical point of view.

In a 1971 article, Douglass North and Robert Thomas proposed applying the new economic theories of property rights and institutional change to the analysis of feudalism, its crisis, and the subsequent economic rise of the Western world. To this end, they draw on the economic theory of contracts. Their hypothesis is that continued economic growth required that 'fundamental institutional developments created or simulated or approximated private property in land and a free labor market'.[13] An economic analysis of 'the rise and fall of the manorial system' is thus essential to understanding the acceleration of economic growth in the Western world from the end of the eighteenth century onwards.

These neo-institutionalist economists look at feudalism through the prism of serfdom. In their assessment, it was neither a 'form of involuntary servitude' nor 'an exploitative arrangement'. They see it as something else, 'essentially a contractual arrangement where labor services were exchanged for the public good of protection and justice'.[14] This is how they summarise their thesis:

> The general lack of order compelled dependence on specialized individuals possessing superior military skills and equipment ...
> This affords the classic case of a public good, since protection of one peasant family involved protection of his neighbors as well. Each peasant therefore would have been inclined to let his neighbor pay the costs; in such a case, some form of coercion was required to raise the resources necessary for defense. The military power of the

---

13 Douglass C. North and Robert P. Thomas, 'The Rise and Fall of the Manorial System: A Theoretical Model', *Journal of Economic History* 31, no. 4, 1971, p. 778.
14 Ibid.

lord provided him with the force to insure the collection of these resources. It also made him the logical person to settle disputes . . . Thus, the dispensing of justice was early added to the lord's role of protector.[15]

This contractual theory of serfdom within the seigneurial domain is based on three presuppositions describing the initial situation:

1) a context of widespread insecurity resulting from a situation of political anarchy;
2) the existence of two classes of agents, some with military capabilities and others without them who needed protection;
3) the public good nature of seigneurial protection – its non-rivalry and non-excludability.

In addition to these three premises, there are two assumptions that are essential to the contractual logic:

4) the existence of 'a rudimentary labour market', which implies that the serfs were fundamentally free.[16] Indeed, North and Thomas in fact consider that competition between lords for control of labour, the absence of centralised authority, and the existence of vast tracts of free land combined to give the serfs an exit option;
5) the fact that the peasant was 'generally protected from arbitrary changes in the terms of the contract' by the lord.[17]

It is based on these five points that North and Thomas believe they can assert that serfdom represents 'an efficient solution' to a situation characterised by 'anarchy, local autarchy, and differential military capacities'.[18]

---

15 Ibid., p. 788.
16 Ibid., p. 790.
17 Ibid., p. 778.
18 Ibid., p. 802.

While the first two statements can be regarded as acceptable simplifications, the other three are highly problematic. The first response is that protection was not a public good, but a service that could be rationed.[19] Unlike the mutual deterrent between modern states, or the fortifications of the medieval commune, the fortified castle did not protect the peasants' possessions against pillage. The village and farms were located outside the fortified area. What is more, the individuals themselves enjoyed no indiscriminate guarantees: space in the castles was limited and, above all, the lord could decide whether or not to accord protection to particular individuals. Because of these characteristics of rivalry and excludability, the protection of peasants was not at all a public good, but rather placed each of them at the mercy of the lord's discretion. Nor was justice a public good. Individuals had no guarantees and could be treated as outlaws, also at the whim of the lord.

Secondly, the idea that there was a rudimentary labour market is incorrect. Peasants were not in a position to choose between the forms of protection offered by lords, or still less set them in competition. In particular, they faced high exit costs, starting with the cost of moving and setting up elsewhere, in an era when communication routes were difficult and risky. Moreover, because of the limited circulation of money, the peasants would have had to take with them the tools and food reserves they needed to survive until the next harvest. Fleeing would also have entailed high costs in terms of lost income, because even if there was unused arable land, it would have had to be cleared and prepared before offering yields equivalent to land which was already occupied.

Finally, if the escape was organised as a group, and if it succeeded in eluding the lord's vigilance and reprisals, it would inevitably attract the attention of a new self-proclaimed protector, which would bring the peasants back to their original condition. As one of North and Thomas's early critics summarises: 'The serfs' options were thus to

---

19 Stefano Fenoaltea, 'The Rise and Fall of a Theoretical Model: The Manorial System', *Journal of Economic History* 35, no. 2, 1975, p. 388.

bear serfdom where they were, or to bear significant moving and setting-up costs for either isolation (with its attendant costs) or probable serfdom elsewhere.'[20]

As for the last point put forward by the two authors — the idea that peasants were protected from arbitrary changes in the terms of the contract — Robert Brenner reminds us that this directly contradicts feudalism's defining characteristic:

> It is precisely the interrelated characteristics of arbitrary exactions by the lords from the peasants and control by landlords over peasant mobility that gave the medieval serf-economy its special traits: surplus extraction through the direct application of force rather than equal exchange via contract.[21]

North and Thomas contradicted themselves on this essential point, when they refer to the lords needing a form of 'coercion' to obtain from the peasants the resources necessary for the common defence. But a useful analysis has to choose one or the other: Was it 'contractual', or 'coercive'? The authors' ambivalence on this point reveals the dead end that their approach leads into.

The reality is that, given the high exit costs and the rationing of the offer of protection, the peasants were at their lord's mercy. Protection and the exercise of justice were not services that they freely acquired as part of a contractual arrangement. On the contrary, as Mehrdad Vahabi puts it, 'extortion was the price of protection for peasants'.[22] Another way of looking at serfdom is based on the notion of predation, defined as an appropriative allocation mechanism supported by violence.[23] From the outset, the predator is in a dominant position relative to his prey. This

---

20 Ibid., p. 389.

21 Robert Brenner, 'Agrarian Class Structure and Economic Development in Pre-industrial Europe', *Past and Present* 70, no. 1, 1976, p. 35.

22 Mehrdad Vahabi, *The Political Economy of Predation: Manhunting and the Economics of Escape*, Cambridge: Cambridge University Press, 2016, p. 295.

23 Ibid.

primordial asymmetry is constitutive of this type of relationship.[24] Using this definition, feudalism can be characterised in terms of the predominance of predatory relationships between lords and their subjects: the former protect the latter but simultaneously exert on them an extraeconomic constraint – one of actual or potential violence – which is the condition for extorting payment. Yet, while the idea of predation is surely a better way of characterising feudalism than the notion of contract, it is not enough to grasp the structure as a whole.

The Socio-political Causes of the Crisis of Feudalism

In a groundbreaking contribution, Mathieu Arnoux argues that the decisive factor in the growth dynamics of the eleventh to thirteenth centuries was neither demographic nor technological, but rather related to 'a massive and lasting increase in the supply of peasant labour'. What thus needs understanding is 'what led the inhabitants of the countryside to intensify their efforts'.[25] According to Arnoux, this revolution in industriousness was part of a transformation in the place of work in medieval society. The consolidation, during this period, of a socio-political structure built on three distinct orders combined a moral recognition of the dignity of work and an institutionalisation of redistribution mechanisms – in particular the ecclesiastical tithe, which played a role in assisting the poor. These factors acted in concert to increase the value of work, in turn leading to its intensification.[26] However, this highly stimulating interpretation fails to shed light on the reasons for the economic stagnation

---

24 Ibid.

25 Mathieu Arnoux, *Le Temps des laboureurs. Travail, ordre social et croissance en Europe (xie-xive siècle)*, Paris: Albin Michel, 'L'évolution de l'humanité', 2012, p. 13. An interesting discussion of this argument, from the perspective of an institutionalist economist, appears in Martino Nieddu, 'Pourquoi lire Le Temps des laboureurs lorsqu'on est économiste, de surcroît régulationniste et travaillant sur les patrimoines économiques collectifs?', *Revue de la régulation* 14, 2013.

26 This same logic is at work in the surprising resilience of European societies during the crisis of the fourteenth and fifteenth centuries, in the wake of the Black Death. See Mathieu Arnoux, 'Croissance et crises dans le monde médiéval, xive-xve siècle', *Les Cahiers du monde russe* 46, nos. 1–2, 2005, pp. 115–32.

that marked the early years of the fourteenth century, before the economic situation then took a catastrophic turn.

To account for the growth of these centuries, Isaac Johsua proposes an analysis that partly differs from Arnoux's. In his *La Face cachée du Moyen Âge*, he shows that both the quantitative and qualitative transformation of the productive forces during this period was essentially due to the appearance of a *seigneurial capital*. From the early Middle Ages onwards, the small proportion of their income that lords devoted to the acquisition of equipment (ploughs, windmill building, etc.) went hand in hand with their growing insertion within market logics, an orientation that would develop into a properly capitalist logic of investment for profit, thus leading to the hiring of a waged workforce. Thus 'the development of the productive forces is inversely proportional to the share of the seigneurial income occupied by his two properties, i.e. the land and the person'.[27] In other words, the (limited) progress of the productive forces in the Middle Ages only took place insofar as economic domination began to turn from control over labour to control over the means of production. For Johsua, it is this timid shift towards a capitalist logic that lies at the root of the marked phase of expansion between the tenth and thirteenth centuries. Conversely, the brake on the development of productive forces that led to the feudal crisis in the fourteenth century was due to the persistence of rents on land and people, based on the coercive power of the lords.

Robert Brenner has himself focused on this question of the impasse of economic development, explaining the role that extortion played in this state of affairs. Writing at the same level of abstraction and generality as North and Thomas, he also considers serfdom to be the fundamental relationship in feudal society, but unlike them, he does not think that this relationship is at all contractual. Rather, it is 'a relationship of power' in which peasants are forced into an 'unequal exchange' through the lords' strict exercise of extra-economic power. Starting out from this definition of serfdom, Brenner lays the foundations for an explanation

---

27 Isaac Johsua, *La Face cachée du Moyen Âge. Les premiers pas du capital*, Montreuil: La Brèche, 1988, p. 219.

based on the arrangement of class relations, rather than on demographic dynamics alone.

For a long time, the stagnation of the medieval economy that began at the end of the thirteenth century was explained in Malthusian terms. On this reading, because feudal society was unable to improve its productivity, it became caught in a bind between its demographic dynamics and the lack of available land. Population growth initially allowed for expansion, but this soon led to overuse of the land, resulting in weaker agricultural yields and the annexation of less fertile land. This resulted in lower incomes for farmers and higher food prices. In the absence of any improvement in agricultural production, overpopulation ultimately produced famine. This reading gives the impression of a self-regulating system, with alternating phases of expansion and impoverishment in response to variations in population. In his history of the peasants of Languedoc, Emmanuel Le Roy Ladurie vouches for the soundness of this cyclical model, across almost six centuries of the High Middle Ages. For him, Malthus 'came too late'[28] – meaning, while the Malthusian model was unable to explain the economic growth of the industrial era, it did offer a good account of the dynamics of older societies.

While the Malthusian analysis is persuasive at an empirical level, it fails to answer the essential question: Why was the medieval economy incapable of improving its productivity? Le Roy cites the absence of capital, entrepreneurship, and innovation, but does not tell us what the origin of these shortcomings might have been. This is exactly the point that Brenner zeroes in on, explaining economic dynamics in terms of the relations between peasants and lords. Here is his thesis:

> The Malthusian cycle of long-term stagnation . . . can only be fully understood as the product of established structures of class relations (particularly 'surplus extraction relations'), just as economic development can only be fully understood as the outcome of the

---

28 Emmanuel Le Roy Ladurie, *Les Paysans de Languedoc*, vol. 1, Berlin: De Gruyter Mouton, 2017 [1977], p. 652.

emergence of new class relations more favourable to new organiza-
tions of production, technical innovations, and increasing levels of
productive investment.[29]

In other words, it is the class structure that determines how changes
in demography or trade affect long-term variations in income distribution and economic development – and not the other way around. For
Brenner, two factors explain the Malthusian trap of repeating demographic cycles of enrichment and impoverishment.[30]

The first lies in the lordly extortion of the surplus. Left with just
enough to survive, the peasants were unable to invest in improving or
even just preserving the quality of the soil. Crushed under the burdens
imposed by the lords, whether in kind or in money, they lacked sufficient resources to accumulate surpluses. One crucial consideration in
this regard is livestock: acquiring animals aids productivity, because
they help to plough and enrich the soil. But when the food supply is
running short, crops are spread onto the land hitherto allocated to
grazing, and this exacerbates the fall in crop yields and fuels the demographic crisis.

The second factor was that the surplus captured by the lords was
largely unproductive, squandered as it was on ostentatious consumption
and military expenses. Such spending was necessary to maintain their
rank, reproduce the circle of their dependents, and maintain or even
extend the territorial control on which their social position ultimately
relied. But medieval lords, when they could, invested in buying up land:

A gentleman's or a baron's standing in his region or in the country as a
whole; the following he was able to recruit and the power he could
mobilize in times of political and military stress; his ability to provide
for daughters or to form family alliances, and even to ensure salvation
by religious or charitable endowments – in effect every benefit and
privilege a feudal lord esteemed most – were best measured and

29 Brenner, 'Agrarian Class Structure', p. 37.
30 Ibid., pp. 47–51.

secured by the size of his landed estate. It is for this reason that land-lords failed to channel into productive use the bulk of the savings they were able to make.[31]

Lordly *dominium* was driven by the extensive logic of investing in land or in the military equipment needed to take control of it. Under feudalism, as Perry Anderson points out, the brutal appropriation of wealth appeared to offer greater advantages than production:

> It can be argued that war was possibly the most rational and rapid single mode of expansion of surplus extraction available for any given ruling class under feudalism. Agricultural productivity was, as we have seen, by no means stagnant during the Middle Ages: nor was the volume of trade. But both grew very slowly for the lords, compared with the sudden and massive 'yields' afforded by territorial conquest . . . It was thus logical that the social definition of the feudal ruling class was military.[32]

Joining wars of conquest offered feudal lords far more attractive prospects for gains than the returns that they could ever have counted on from agricultural investments. The pre-eminence of military competition made feudal rivalry a zero-sum game: the main concern was not to make production more efficient, but to control the land and the men who toiled on it.

According to Brenner, another reason for slow productivity gains lay in the obstacles to labour mobility and land ownership. The control that the lords exercised over the peasants created a situation of capture, in which it was easier to try and increase their income through intensified pressure on this workforce, than to embark upon difficult and uncertain efforts reorganising production. Nor could peasants freely cede the land

---

31 Michael M. Postan and John Hatcher, 'Population and Class Relations in Feudal Society', in Trevor Henry Aston and Charles H. E. Philpin, *The Brenner Debate: Agrarian Class Structure and Economic Development in Pre-industrial Europe*, vol. 1, Cambridge: Cambridge University Press, 1987, pp. 77–8.

32 Perry Anderson, *Lineages of the Absolutist State*, London: NLB, 1974, p. 31.

they cultivated to other, more efficient peasants, and this prevented the creation of larger estates.

The two decisive causes of sluggish productivity under feudalism were thus (i) the concentration of the surplus in the hands of the lords, who kept a distance from the production process and used it unproductively, and (ii) the lack of mobility in the factors of production. These were mutually reinforcing processes: the increased pressure on the direct producers – the easiest way to increase the nobles' incomes – stifled any desire for emancipation that the peasants might have had; but, by depriving the producers of the resources necessary for investment, this pressure hindered the improvement of the productive process.

Brenner's approach is materialist without being mechanistic: it leaves the historical process open-ended and undetermined as to the outcome of the peasants' struggle against lordly domination.[33] This fight over the level of *corvée* obligations, freedom of movement, and control over land lasted all the way through the Middle Ages. In the fourteenth century, the decline in agricultural productivity left weakened populations at the mercy of a series of plagues that decimated between a third and half of

---

33 Recent economic theorisations of forced labour do not invalidate Brenner's thesis. Two contradictory effects connect the relative scarcity of labour and forced labour. On the one hand, the scarcity of labour increases its value: it raises the price of production and thus increases the value of effort, which in turn incentivises coercion. On the other hand, the scarcity of labour increases the marginal product of labour in non-coercive sectors, which expands the opportunities that exist outside of forced labour; the relative cost of exiting forced labour thus tends to fall, implying that the level of coercion and thus the cost of coercion must be increased, tending to disincentivise this practice. In short, the price mechanism leaves undetermined the impact of labour scarcity on the incentives to coercion. This conclusion converges with the idea that, in the final analysis, it is political conflict that determines transformations in social arrangements and the corresponding economic dynamics. Daron Acemoglu and Alexander Wolitzky, 'The Economics of Labor Coercion', *Econometrica* 79, no. 2, 2011, pp. 555–600. The fact that there can be two possible reactions to the scarcity of labour is something that escapes Thomas Piketty when he writes, in opposition to Brenner, that 'scarcity of labor after the Great Plague is often cited as the reason why serfdom ended in Western Europe (and sometimes, notwithstanding the inconsistency, to explain its persistence in the east as well)'. See Thomas Piketty, *Capital and Ideology*, Cambridge, MA: Belknap Press, 2020, p. 68.

the population. This demographic shock led to a resurgence of class conflicts, which had the most varied outcomes in England, France, and eastern Europe over the centuries that followed. In France, the peasants' victorious struggles led to the domination of the small independent peasantry. In eastern Europe, on the other hand, the crushing of the peasants led to a revival of serfdom. In England, however, the defeat of the peasants resulted in their expulsion from the land and the creation of vast estates leased by the lords to farmers. This new partnership between landowners and farmer-entrepreneurs was based on widespread, market-based dependence; farmers took on salaried workers and were encouraged to invest, introducing the characteristically capitalist dynamic of investment and innovation which, according to Brenner, created the conditions necessary for industrial development.

Feudalism, Slavery, and Capitalism

From this point of view, the logic that most defines the structure of feudalism is not about the legal relations between vassal and suzerain. Nor does it centre on the low priority given to market exchange, or on the emergence of seigneurial capital. We could hardly say that these aspects are devoid of importance. In fact, in many respects, they are crucial elements in feudalism's variations across space and time. But they are not decisive in distinguishing feudalism as a mode of production.

A Combinatorial Approach to Modes of Production. A mode of production is a way of producing on the scale of a given society. In class societies, it is always a particular combination of the following elements: first, a labour process – workers who, independently or as subordinates, use the instruments of production and transform the objects of labour; second, a relation of appropriation – the methods by which non-producers capture a share of the economic surplus.[34] The way in which these relationships are arranged varies according to the

34 Étienne Balibar, 'The Basic Concepts of Historical Materialism', in *Reading Capital*, London: NLB, 1970.

mode of production, and this itself leads to distinct economic, social, and political dynamics.

The historian Guy Bois, author of a monograph on the economy of Normandy in the late Middle Ages, sums up feudalism as a mode of production: 'It is the hegemony of small-scale individual production (and therefore the level of productive forces that this hegemony implies), plus the seigneurial levy ensured by a constraint of political (or extra-economic) origin.'[35] This sentence contains four essential elements already found in Marx:

1) the hegemony of small-scale production corresponds to the fact that the direct producer individually has 'the material means necessary to carry out his work and produce his means of subsistence';

2) the level of productive forces that this hegemony implies relates to an absence of social cooperation in production. The producer 'pursues his agriculture independently'.[36] The horizon of this social mode of production remains the relative security provided by the individual sphere of production;

3) the seigneurial levy creates a tension between the landowner and the independent producer;

4) this tension is resolved by the intervention of force – coercion: without it, the independent producer has no reason to consent to the seigneurial levy:

There must be extra-economic reasons of some kind to force them to do work for the landowner in title . . . Relations of personal dependence are therefore necessary, in other words personal unfreedom, to whatever degree, and being chained to the land as its accessory – bondage in the true sense.[37]

---

35 Guy Bois, 'Crise du féodalisme: économie rurale et démographie en Normandie orientale du début du xive siècle au milieu du xvie siècle', *Cahiers de la Fondation nationale des sciences politiques* 202, 1976, p. 355.

36 Karl Marx, *Capital*, vol. 3, London: Penguin, 1981, p. 926.

37 Ibid., pp. 926–7.

We can use these considerations to draw up a summary typology of production methods. This will allow us to highlight which characteristics distinguish the feudal mode of production from both modern slavery and capitalist wage-labour.

Property, Labour, and Appropriation of Surpluses. Before we get to that, it is worth emphasising what feudalism, slavery, and capitalism have in common. In all three cases, legal ownership of at least some of the assets essential to production is monopolised by a dominant class. In the case of feudalism, it is the land that is monopolised by feudal lords, whereas the direct producers own only the instruments necessary to produce their means of subsistence. In capitalism and slavery, all the means of production belong to the ruling class. This legal monopoly of one class over the assets essential to the reproduction of the conditions of subsistence is the basis for the appropriation of a surplus – a surplus labour beyond what goes to the direct producers.

The second dimension they have in common concerns labour. In both feudalism and slaving, labour is not free, and a form of coercion binds producers to their masters. In capitalism, on the other hand, proletarians are considered 'free' to sell their labour power to whomever they please. They have to do this to survive, so they *do* depend on capitalists in general – but they can choose their particular capitalist. There is no direct relationship of interpersonal dependence.

The third dimension concerns the labour process itself. In the cases of capitalism and plantation slavery, workers are subordinate to the owners of the means of production. It is these owners who organise the work, define its rhythm, and give it a collective character. The use of the term 'plant' for 'factory' indicates this link between the collective organisation of work on slave plantations and capitalist industry. In the tightly coordinated labour on the sugar plantations of the late eighteenth century, as in the industrial plants of the nineteenth and twentieth, we find the effort to precisely calibrate quantities of labour and the submission of the workforce to mechanised rhythms.[38] This was not the case with feudalism. There, producers were independent, working as they saw fit, as long as this complied with their master's demands in terms of service or payment. This (relative) autonomy corresponded to an only partial monopolisation of the means of production: while the lords only granted them the use of the land, the peasants owned other means of production, for instance tools, the built environment, and livestock.

The fourth dimension concerns the appropriation of surplus, that is, the relationship between labour and surplus labour. In capitalism and slavery, the labour and surplus labour appropriated by the ruling class coincide 'in space and time'. This is not the case in feudalism.[39] The surplus labour for the benefit of the lord is carried out in the form of *corvée* or payments, but, in all cases, in a distinct temporality and space, which makes the exploitation itself transparent:

> It needs no further analysis here that surplus-value coincides with the unpaid labour of others, since this still exists in its visible, palpable form, the labour of the direct producer for himself being still separate both in time and space from his work for the landlord, with the latter appearing directly in the brutal form of forced labour for a third party.[40]

The Dynamics of the Productive Forces. The fifth and final dimension concerns the dynamics of the productive forces, which result from the combination of the four previous coordinates.

Unlike in capitalism, in slaving and feudalism, there is no systematic tendency to increase productivity by introducing labour-saving technologies. There are several reasons for this.

Firstly, as we have seen, under feudalism, the direct producers have virtually no means of investment. When labour is mainly subjugated by

---

38 Robin Blackburn, *The Overthrow of Colonial Slavery, 1776–1848*, London: Verso, 1988, p. 8.

39 Balibar, 'The Basic Concepts of Historical Materialism'.

40 Marx, *Capital*, vol. 3, p. 928.

force, there is no incentive for them to collaborate in improving the production process.[41]

The second obstacle results from the lack of incentive for the owners to pursue labour-saving. Neither feudal lords nor slavers pay their workforce: so, there is nothing for them to save.[42] While 'capitalists can and do respond to falling prices by "expelling labour" from production – by reducing output through lay-offs or introducing labour-saving machinery', slave-owners are unable to get rid of their workforce without risking a loss of capital. So, their incentive is not to save labour but, on the contrary, to use it as much as possible: they react to a fall in prices by trying to step up production and increase the slaves' labour to the point of exhaustion, much as feudal lords tried to increase levies when yields fell. As a general rule, neither of them invested in labour-saving machinery and tools.

A third obstacle to increasing productivity in slave societies was the tendency towards self-sufficiency – the only limited recourse to the market. It was in the owners' interest to employ their slaves on a permanent basis, and not just during the most intense periods of cotton or sugar cane cultivation. Slaves were therefore also employed in other jobs, such as growing maize, rearing pigs, or making or repairing objects, with the effect that the plantations were largely self-sufficient, particularly in their food supply. Coupled with a lack of investment in production goods, this lack of demand for consumer goods tended to fetter the further development of the division of labour and the expansion of a domestic market for local industry. Not only did productivity stagnate within the plantations themselves, but the local economy was deprived of outlets.

41 In such an order, 'force can be of only limited utility in affecting the quality and consistency of labour in connection with increasing, and increasingly complex, tools'. Robert Brenner, 'The Origins of Capitalist Development: A Critique of Neo-Smithian Marxism', *New Left Review* 1, 104, 1977, p. 36.

42 Charles Post analyses this question in the context of the slave plantations of America: 'Because the slave entered the production-process as a constant or fixed element of production, planters experienced inflexible costs of reproducing their labour-force.' Charles Post, *The American Road to Capitalism: Studies in Class-Structure, Economic Development and Political Conflict, 1620–1877*, Leiden: Brill, 2011, pp. 146–7.

This principle of self-sufficiency was also essential to the operation of the feudal manor until around the eleventh century. 'The lords', writes Duby, 'set before themselves the ideal of supplying all their needs from their own property, and that they believed that "it should not be necessary to seek for, or to buy anything from outside"'.[43] The same was true later for feudal farmers and, more broadly, for small independent peasants. When the lords' levies became less onerous and farmers became more independent, the direct producers disposed of resources beyond those strictly necessary for their own subsistence. They then used this surplus to satisfy new needs by widening the scope of their activity – this, in obedience to an autarkic logic, rather than in terms of investment in improving the productive process with a view to exchange.

But why does the principle of satisfying internal needs prevail over the principle of efficiency in production? Quite simply because self-production is less risky than exchange. When producers have direct access to the means of ensuring their own subsistence, they are not forced to conform to the discipline of the market and its uncertainties. Hence 'small property tends to dictate individualized and unspecialized production'.[44] With no generalised dependence on the market, it bears a logic of diversification that is radically different from the capitalist logic of investment for profits, in which increased productive efficiency is achieved through specialisation.

So, we can see that the capitalist logic results from an exceptional configuration. It takes the form of generalised market production, in the sense that the means of production, like labour, are free to be exchanged and their use must imperatively correspond to the prevailing level of productivity. When social property relations are structured in this manner, Brenner explains, a generalised dependence on the market makes investment and innovation compulsory:

Only where labour has been separated from possession of the means of production, and where labourers have been emancipated from any

---

43 Duby, *Rural Economy and Country Life in the Medieval West*, p. 44.
44 Brenner, 'The Origins of Capitalist Development', p. 36.

direct relation of domination (such as slavery or serfdom), are both capital and labour power 'free' to make possible their combination at the highest possible level of technology . . . Only under conditions of free wage labour will the individual producing units . . . be forced to sell in order to buy, to buy in order to survive and reproduce, and ultimately to expand and innovate in order to maintain this position in relationship to other competing productive units. Only under such a system, where both capital and labour power are thus commodities – and which which Marx therefore called 'generalized commodity production' – is there the necessity of producing at the 'socially necessary' labour time in order to survive, and to surpass this level of productivity to ensure continued survival.[45]

To conclude, let us pull together the main elements that make up the logical structure of feudalism:

1) the inextricably both political and economic nature of the relationships of domination, which crystallised in a central institution, the *dominium*, where power over men fused with power over the land;

2) a general principle of concentration and consumption of wealth, whose 'apex was an all-powerful and spendthrift aristocracy', 'concentrat[ing] in the lords' hands the new income generated by agricultural expansion' and 'channell[ing] the money towards the purchase of items of luxury'.[46]

3) the economic exploitation of the bulk of the population by the aristocracy relied on coercion rather than a contractual-type exchange of services in return for protection, such as would have presupposed a form of symmetry between the parties. More precisely, the lordly levy was based on a logic of predation, an appropriative allocation mechanism whose maintenance and extension of a situation of inequality relies on violence.

---

45 Ibid., p. 32.
46 Duby, *Rural Economy and Country Life in the Medieval West*, p. 127.

Table 4. Comparison of modes of production: slavery, feudalism, and capitalism

	Slavery	Feudalism	Capitalism
Means of production	Monopolised by slavers	Land owned by lords, instruments by dependants	Monopolised by capitalists
Labour	Unfree	Unfree	Free
Work process	Subordinate, cooperative	Independent, individual	Subordinate, cooperative
Surplus extraction	Takes place in production	Separate from production	Takes place in production
Productivity	Weak	Weak	Dynamic

The combinatorial analysis of the three modes – plantation slavery, feudalism, and capitalism – allows us to highlight the distinctiveness of each of them (table 4). The feudal mode of production has three distinctive features: ownership of part of the tools of production by direct producers; their autonomy in organising work processes that are essentially individual and fragmented, and, finally, the fact that the lordly levy is disjointed from the work process itself. While it does not have any of the analysed characteristics in common with the capitalist mode of production, like slavery, it is defined by unfree labour and the absence of any dynamic of systematic increase in productivity. Unlike capitalism, then, feudalism is not productivist.

Here, the wager I am making is that this identification of the characteristics of feudalism will help us to better understand the mutations of contemporary capitalism. Can we identify paradoxical resurgences of feudal logics, even in societies where market production has become generalised?

The Logic of Techno-Feudalism

> To tax rather than to organize production, to rule on death rather than to administer life.
>
> Gilles Deleuze[47]

Das Digital is the promising title of Viktor Mayer-Schönberger and Thomas Ramge's book, translated in English as *Reinventing Capitalism in*

---

47 Gilles Deleuze, 'Postscript on the Societies of Control', *October* 59, Winter 1992, pp. 3–7, p. 4.

the Age of Big Data. Their thesis is that the combination of Big Data, algorithms, and artificial intelligence is radically altering the way that markets operate. On the one hand, data makes it possible to accompany transactions with much richer information than exists on traditional markets. On the other hand, algorithms support agents in their decision-making so that they can escape their cognitive biases and adopt more coherent behaviour.

Thanks to massive data on products and preferences, and thanks also to algorithms capable of examining potential transactions in multiple configurations, the matching process is becoming much nimbler. This is illustrated by personalised shopping recommendation systems, the matching of BlaBlaCar travellers based on their interest in chatting along the way, the automation of the initial recruitment phases in large firms, and the automatic ordering of intermediate goods in value chains.

Data and algorithms largely replace price signals in transactions: 'Data-rich markets finally deliver what markets, in theory, should always have been very good at – enabling optimal transactions – but because of informational constraints really weren't.'[48] Money has retained its role as a means of payment and store of value, but a multitude of indicators complement price signals to enrich economic information.

Mayer-Schönberger and Ramge's approach opens up interesting perspectives for the critique of the market system – and indirectly invites us to reopen the debate on economic calculation and the future of planning.[49] But it does not offer any convincing explanation of the issues raised earlier: the creation of impregnable monopolistic citadels, the widespread surveillance associated with the (useful) power of algorithms, or indeed the weakness of investment and growth . . . And these are the problems that we must try to shed light on.

---

48 Viktor Mayer-Schönberger and Thomas Ramge, *Reinventing Capitalism in the Age of Big Data*, New York: Basic Books, 2018, p. 7.

49 Cédric Durand and Razmig Keucheyan, 'Planifier à l'âge des algorithmes', *Actuel Marx* 1, no. 65, 2019, pp. 81–102; Evgeny Morozov, 'Digital Socialism? The Calculation Debate in the Age of Big Data', *New Left Review*, nos. 116–17, 2019, pp. 33–67.

One first approach is to assimilate these phenomena to the ordinary laws of capitalism. Centralisation, concentration, and devaluation of capital are all part of the play of accumulation. There is no need, then, to bring in new analytical frameworks to account for the changes in industrial structures brought about by innovation and competition.

The Marxist and Schumpeterian traditions surely have a robust theoretical apparatus for analysing these processes. The theory of 'real competition' developed by Anwar Shaikh, for example, seeks to explain how the profit objective leads to a confrontation between capitals, whose upheavals reveal recurrent patterns.[50] From another perspective, the long wave tradition is used to consider the rise of digital technology as a new techno-economic paradigm.[51] It thus succeeds other configurations of capital, variously arranged around oil and the car, steel and electricity, or yet earlier, railroads and the cotton industry. The current difficulties are explained by the fact that the institutions needed to establish a phase of prosperity are still lacking.

Evgeny Morozov warns us that, if we overestimate the radical nature of digital upheaval, we risk disarming the traditional forms of critique of capitalism.[52] On this reading, the issues of work and exploitation, contradictions and crises end up being sidelined in favour of questions of privacy and competition policy. Morozov's concern is legitimate, but we also need to avoid the opposite pitfall – the one that leads us, as

50 Anwar Shaikh, *Capitalism: Competition, Conflict, Crises*, Oxford: Oxford University Press, 2016.

51 Christopher Freeman and Francisco Louçã, *As Time Goes By: From the Industrial Revolutions to the Information Revolution*, Oxford: Oxford University Press, 2001; Carlota Perez, 'Technological Revolutions and Techno-economic Paradigms', *Cambridge Journal of Economics* 34, no. 1, 2009.

52 Evgeny Morozov, 'Critique of the Technofeudal Reason', *New Left Review* 134, April 2022, pp. 89–126. See also Sterenn Lebayle and Nicolas Pinsard, 'L'économie numérique: une involution du mode de production capitaliste?', *Revue de la régulation* 30, Spring 2021, and Jathan Sadowski, 'The Internet of Landlords: Digital Platforms and New Mechanisms of Rentier Capitalism', *Antipode* 52, no. 2, 2020, pp. 562–80. See also a response to these criticisms: Cédric Durand, 'Scouting Capital's Frontiers', *New Left Review* 136, August 2022, pp. 29–39; and a new round of argument: Cecilia Rikap, 'Capitalism as Usual? Implications of Digital Intellectual Monopolies', *New Left Review* 139, January 2023, pp. 145–60.

Nathalie Quintane writes, to relativise the 'changes underway by identi-fying and picking out in them only what we recognise, in order to associ-ate them with the already routine: which means, cutting off their claws'.[53]

Here, I have chosen to start from a pair of entirely classical concepts. One is what Marx called the *relations of production*. He explains, 'in the social production of their existence men inevitably enter into definite relations, which are independent of their will, namely relations of production appropriate to a given stage in the development of their material forces of production'.[54] The other is the *productive forces* with which they are associated – the resources, techniques, and knowledge mobilised in this production of social existence.

Yet I use these in the attempt to answer a new question, the question posed by the philosopher McKenzie Wark when she wonders 'whether what has emerged, in addition to and laminated on top of a capitalist mode of production, is something qualitatively different, but which generates new forms of class domination, new forms of the extraction of surplus, even new kinds of class formation'.[55] Wark's suggestion is very general. To the existing relations of production – linked to capital–labour relations and land ownership – she adds a new opposition between the hackers and the 'vectorialist class'. The hacker class produces informa-tion but cannot valorise it, while the vectorialist class possesses the vectors of information and thus concentrates in its hands the capacities for realising value.

Where I differ from Wark's thesis is that I doubt that information is on the way to becoming the main mode of value-production. As the hetero-dox economist Duncan Foley reminds us, this prospect is a mirage:

> Increasing-returns effects can create the illusion that information and knowledge-based commodity production can create value with effec-tively no inputs at all beside human creativity and ingenuity. But the

53 Nathalie Quintane, *Un œil en moins*, Paris: P.O.L., 2018, p. 373.

54 Karl Marx, 'Preface', *A Contribution to the Critique of Political Economy*, in *Selected Writings*, London: Hackett, 1994, p. 211.

55 McKenzie Wark, *Capital Is Dead*, London: Verso, 2019, p. 54.

creators of knowledge and information are human beings who need to eat, have somewhere to sleep, clothe themselves, and so forth.[56]

The use of the idea of refeudalisation also requires a degree of caution. Any isomorphism with medieval Europe and Japan is, of course, remote and incomplete. In particular, the 'hegemony of small-scale individual production' that Guy Bois placed at the heart of his definition of feudalism clearly no longer applies. In the twenty-first century, there is no involution of the division of labour or retraction of social cooperation in production. On the contrary, techno-feudalism is the result of what Ernest Mandel defined as the 'growing objective socialisation of labour', which has been 'the basic historical trend of capitalist development, from the Industrial Revolution onwards'.[57] Every minute of our lives is integrated into this taut network of productive interdependencies, enabling us to eat food grown and transported by others, to heat ourselves with power stations built and managed by others, to communicate via electronic networks or printed forms that we do not help to maintain, in all the sophisticated ways we know. The increasing proportion of our lives spent online only adds to the complexity of these social links.

In my view, the political economy of the digital age falls squarely within the realm of techno-feudal logic when the issue of rent is taken seriously. The idea of digital income is now widespread. It can even be found in the writings of the neoliberal economist Jean Tirole, who refers to a 'digital windfall' by analogy with the oil windfall, albeit without explaining its origins.[58]

While the exploitation of labour still plays a central role in the formation of a global pool of surplus value, the specificity of the current economy lies in the mechanisms that allow capital to feed its profits by drawing on this pool, even while limiting its direct involvement in

---

56 Duncan K. Foley, 'Rethinking Financial Capitalism and the "Information" Economy', *Review of Radical Political Economics* 45, no. 3, 2013, p. 165.

57 Ernest Mandel, 'In Defence of Socialist Planning', *New Left Review*, October 1986, 159, pp. 5–22.

58 Jean Tirole, *Économie du bien commun*, Paris: PUF, 2016, p. 526.

exploitation and disconnecting itself from the processes of production. This is the meaning given here to the idea of rent.[59]

At its heart, capitalism is driven by an investment imperative, linked to competition and the generalised dependence on the market. But the rise of intangibles is overturning this traditional logic. As digital assets and their users become inseparable, barriers are put up to the mobility of individuals and organisations. This attachment breaks down the competitive dynamic and gives those who control the intangibles an unparalleled ability to appropriate value without any real engagement in production. What then takes precedence is a relationship of capture. In this configuration, investment is no longer directed towards the development of the forces of production, but rather, towards the forces of predation. Let us look at this more closely.

The Structure of Digital Costs

Strategies for conquering cyberspace rely on the control of data flows: they need access to our telephones and computers, sensors in machine tools and vehicles, and even in our homes . . . There are not infinite points for capturing the data generated by individuals' and organisations' activities, any more than oil wells are infinite in number. The same is true when it comes to capturing our attention.[60] So, there is a kind of absolute scarcity of *original* data.

Of course, scarcity is also mediated by intellectual property rights that restrict the use of data and software. But these often consolidate pre-existing positions. The logic of intellectual monopolisation described in

---

59 Rent is a classic concept in economics, with links to different traditions. From a Marxist perspective, a theory of land rent was developed by David Harvey, *The Limits to Capital*, London: Verso, 2006, chapter 11. More recently, a systematic study of the notion of rent in Marx is presented by Deepankar Basu, 'Marx's Analysis of Ground-Rent: Theory, Examples and Applications', UMASS Amherst Economics Working Papers 241, 2018. From a quite different perspective, the Public Choice school has heavily drawn on this notion: Matthew D. Mitchell, 'Rent Seeking at 52: An Introduction to a Special Issue of Public Choice', *Public Choice* 181, no. 1, 2019, pp. 1–4.

60 Yves Citton, *Pour une écologie de l'attention*, Paris: Seuil, 2014.

chapter 3 operates outside of legal instruments alone: data extraction sites are strategic positions, and the data flows that emerge from them converge in places where their centralisation enables useful results to be produced. This is the Google model.

At the same time, the digital world is characterised by the near-zero cost of reproducing information. While original data is rare, it can be reproduced at very low cost, and the costs that do exist are mainly energy-related. At an aggregate level, these latter are hardly negligible, but they remain limited: in 2021, electricity consumption by data centres (excluding those used to produce cryptocurrencies) and data transmission networks represented between 2 and 2.7 per cent of global electricity consumption, a proportion that has grown only slightly since 2010.[61] At a disaggregated level, this cost is hardly noticeable, and this allows the spread of digital technologies to make information abundant.

The logic of increasing returns in industry is radicalised in the case of the digital economy, where there is a major difference between digital resources and natural resources. While the monopoly linked to the absolute scarcity of land is counterbalanced by diminishing returns, the monopoly on original digital data is redoubled by economies of scale and network complementarities.[62] Once the fixed costs of data collection and processing have already been met, the useful effects of digital services can be put to work at almost zero cost.

To help explain the turbulent logic of real competition, Anwar Shaikh has proposed the concept of 'regulatory capital'.[63] This notion refers to the capital that operates under the best reproducible production conditions for a given industry at a given time. This is the capital that benefits from the most advantageous unit costs and can continue its growth under these same favourable conditions.

---

61 IEA, 'Data Centres and Data Transmission Networks', iea.org, 11 July 2023.

62 The principle of diminishing returns refers to a situation in which the marginal return on a factor of production decreases. Conversely, economies of scale indicate a situation where an increase in the volume of activity leads to greater efficiency, generally due to the amortisation of fixed costs.

63 Shaikh, *Capitalism*, pp. 265–7.

In the case of mining or agriculture, which have decreasing returns, regulatory capital faces unit costs that are higher than average costs: the remaining investment opportunities are less attractive than the ones already in operation. For example, the cost of extracting oil from fields in Saudi Arabia is around $4 a barrel, while the more recent exploitation of oil from tar sands in Alberta is $40. Conversely, in the case of manufacturing industries such as the car industry, new plants incorporate more efficient technologies that enable them to operate at a lower unit cost than plants already in operation.

What is the situation in the digital sector? Neither of these dynamics gives a satisfactory account of the logic of additional investment. If we accept the premise that original data flows are scarce, then a new entrant can only operate at a higher cost, seeing as the new sources of data available operate at higher costs relative to the useful results produced. However, this opportunity for higher-cost entry is countered by the fact that incumbent firms fully benefit from network complementarities. For them, the higher extraction costs of an additional investment are counterbalanced by the fact that the addition of new data sources increases the useful results by more than if this new source were used in isolation.

Let us take the example of Siri. This virtual assistant, which uses natural language voice recognition, was developed in the 2000s at a research institute linked to Stanford University with funding from DARPA, the research-funding agency of the US Defense Department.[64] Called CALO, for Cognitive Assistant that Learns and Organizes, this project was the largest artificial intelligence programme ever to receive such finance. Briefly exploited by a start-up from this research institute in February 2010, and acquired a few months later by Apple, Siri was quickly incorporated into the Apple ecosystem, and thus fully valorised. So, the centralisation of capital at work in the absorption of start-ups by large digital firms is not just the result of a strategic rationale aimed at

---

64 Bianca Bosker, 'Siri Rising: The Inside Story of Siri's Origins – and Why She Could Overshadow the iPhone', *HuffPost*, 22 January 2013; Wade Roush, 'Xconomy: The Story of Siri, from Birth at SRI to Acquisition by Apple. Virtual Personal Assistants Go Mobile', xconomy.com, 14 June 2010.

preventing the emergence of potential competitors. For it also reflects an economic rationale whereby a process exploited by a start-up is better valorised within a larger entity, thanks to the complementarities of the various data sources and the combination of several algorithmic processes. Here, the organisation is superior to the market.

Table 5. Scarcity and returns for different means of production: land, industry, and digital

	Scarcity	Returns
Land	Absolute	Decreasing
Industry	Relative	Growing
Digital	Absolute	Growing and infinite

Here we clearly see that digital means of production clearly differ from others such as land and industrial capital. Their unique feature is that they combine the scarcity of strategic data-capture sites with infinitely increasing returns (table 5). And, as we shall see, this new configuration disrupts the process of real competition that drives capitalism.

A Relationship of Dependence

This particular cost structure is compounded by a dependency on Big Data and algorithms.

There are many original sources of data, such as the data on biodiversity collected by biologists, or the data produced by meteorological stations, or even official statistics on demography or taxation. But what characterises Zuboff's *Big Other* is the rise of data generated as the flip side of digital services. Individuals and organisations are willing to give up their data in exchange for the useful results provided by algorithms. As we saw earlier, this is how powerful feedback loops are formed, in which phenomena of increasing intrusion and increased algorithmic performance feed off each other. In Silicon Valley jargon, this is what is known as 'hyperscale', in reference to the problem of scalability in computing.[65]

---

65 André B. Bondi, 'Characteristics of Scalability and Their Impact on Performance', in Proceedings of the Second International Workshop on Software and Performance, Ottawa, Ontario, Canada, New York: ACM Press, 2000, p. 195.

The crucial element here is the existence of a network of interdependent users. What makes Google so powerful is less the non-rival use of algorithms than the synergies between services and the complementarities between users. Google chiefs Eric Schmidt and Jared Cohen speak of 'acceleration to scale' to describe this expansive loop that characterises modern technological platforms: 'What gives them their power is their ability to grow – specifically, the speed at which they scale. Almost nothing short of a biological virus can spread as quickly, efficiently or aggressively as these technological platforms.'[66]

This dynamic is responsible for all the great digital successes of the early twenty-first century. It has the consequence that, at the same time as services improve, each individual becomes more closely fastened to the world that the company controls. Vice versa, the growing involvement of each individual in turn augments the performance of digital services.

Economists seeking to account for this dynamic emphasise the role of cross-subsidisation, whereby a certain type of market actor is made to pay a high price in order to attract other participants at low or zero prices.[67] The case of free online content, such as recipes from Kitchen Stories, or the services offered by Google, Booking, or TheFork, illustrate this: consumers benefit from the service, but it is paid for by the advertisers. Through the site's both intensive and extensive reach, individuals converge on the largest platforms, which then become the

66 Eric Schmidt and Jared Cohen, *The New Digital Age: Reshaping the Future of People, Nations and Business*, London: Murray, 2014, pp. 9–10.

67 Economists call 'multi-sided markets' a type of market that requires the maintenance of two or more customer bases: credit cards, for example, require both consumers to use them and merchants to accept them. Companies operating in these markets must therefore implement pricing strategies that spread costs between the different types of user to increase the number of market participants and maximise their profits. The pioneering works on this subject are Jean-Charles Rochet and Jean Tirole, 'Platform Competition in Two-Sided Markets', *Journal of the European Economic Association* 1, no. 4, 2003, pp. 990–1029; Jean-Charles Rochet and Jean Tirole, 'Two-Sided Markets: A Progress Report', *RAND Journal of Economics* 37, no. 3, 2006, pp. 645–67; Mark Armstrong, 'Competition in Two-Sided Markets', *RAND Journal of Economics* 37, no. 3, 2006, pp. 668–91.

most efficient, concentrating supply, demand, and data to optimise their connections.

So, today's capitalist titans realise value through the nodes that distribute information and increase its quality. In other words, the services that these companies sell to us essentially consist of returning our collective power back to us, in the form of information that is adapted and relevant to each of us and thus attaches our existence to the services that they provide.

One of the keys to success in this operation is the mass of data available, which immediately introduces an issue of scale. In this regard, players based in China have a clear territorial advantage, for both demographic and political reasons. Firstly, in this billion-plus-consumer economy – the world's largest – data is potentially more abundant. Secondly, it is more accessible. As a result of China's belated capitalist development, the bourgeois ethos of privacy protection is not socially entrenched here, and the legal system that implements it remains one of the most rudimentary.[68] This allows companies and the government easily to appropriate, cross-compare and exploit individual data – as illustrated by the rise of the social credit system mentioned earlier. Finally, the restrictions imposed by the Chinese authorities on a number of leading US services – starting with Google, Facebook, and Twitter – have served to foster the development of Chinese alternatives. As a result, Chinese companies are positioning themselves at the forefront of most digital sectors. In the field of facial recognition, for example, Megvii, a start-up backed by Chinese and Russian public funds, technically outperforms competing products from Google, Facebook, and

---

68 In 'Privacy and Data Privacy Issues in Contemporary China', *Ethics and Information Technology* 7, no. 1, 2005, pp. 7–15, Lü Yao-Huai notes that, compared to Western countries, the right to privacy in China is extremely limited. He explains that, although the issue of privacy has become increasingly important, it remains in the background compared to 'social benefits and the national interest' (p. 11). Moreover, in his view, philosophical research on this subject remains too confined to specific subjects and does not address the ethical problem as a whole, which limits legal advances (p. 13). On his reading, the weakness of privacy protection in China compared with Western standards is ultimately due to the historical proximity of forms of collectivism.

Microsoft, thanks in particular to its access to an unrivalled government database of some 750 million identity photos.[69]

What is striking about this hyper-scale logic is the speed with which we are moving away from the principle of the supposed horizontality of the commercial exchange between agents freely able to enter into a transaction. The app invasion of everyday life is a sudden demonstration of the intense link being forged between human existence and cyber-territories. Social life is taking root in the digital glebe. The bedrock of the relations of digital production is now moulded by individuals' and organisations' dependence on structures that exercise monopolistic control over data and algorithms.

Of course, for consumers this constraint is not *absolute* – you can always decide to live in splendid isolation from Big Data. But this also implies considerable social marginalisation. All things considered, this kind of problem – a question of 'exit costs' – is not unlike that of the medieval peasants: to escape their servitude, they had to confront the dangers of fleeing their fiefdom and attempt an isolated existence on an *alleu*, a piece of land belonging only to them, on the borders of the known world.

Yet, for producers, the constraint is absolute. For any company or platform worker is part of a digital environment which necessarily receives a share of the data generated by their activity and, in return, fuels this same activity. Of course, there is always the possibility of taking one's custom elsewhere. But the network and learning effects are so powerful that, even when there is an alternative (which is not always the case) and it is possible to recover one's data (which is even less frequent)

---

69 Western media has widely reported on the rollout of facial recognition tech-nologies in China. The considerations reported here are taken from the following articles: Sijia Jiang, 'Backing Big Brother: Chinese Facial Recognition Firms Appeal to Funds', reuters.com, 13 November 2017; Yuan Yang, 'China Pours Millions into Facial Recognition Start-Up Face ++', *Financial Times*, 1 November 2017; Simon Leplâtre, 'En Chine, la reconnaissance faciale envahit le quotidien', *Le Monde*, 9 December 2017; 'Ever Better and Cheaper, Face-Recognition Technology Is Spreading', *Economist*, 9 September 2017; Simon Denyer, 'In China, Facial Recognition Is Sharp End of a Drive for Total Surveillance', *Washington Post*, 7 January 2018.

the high transaction costs constitute a lock-in situation, radically limiting any possibility of exit.

The big digital services are fiefdoms from which there is no escape. This situation whereby subordinate subjects depend on the digital glebe is essential, because it determines the ability of the dominant to capture the economic surplus. The theoretical model corresponding to this configuration, in which dependence and control of the surplus go hand in hand is – as introduced earlier – the model of predation. It is to this model that we must turn in order to understand the economic dynamics and the system of social conflict that characterise digital production relations.

The Possibility of Predatory Regulation

Marx reminds us that 'the battle of competition is fought by the cheapening of commodities'.[70] Competitiveness is the necessary condition for firms to make a profit. Firms that fail to abide by this imperative will see their activities suffer: the losses will mount and they will eventually disappear. At the aggregate level, the exploitation of labour and the realisation of value on the market are part of this process. But there is a certain form of irony in this game because – as Silicon Valley tycoon Peter Thiel explains – the goal of the individual entrepreneur in the competitive battle is precisely to escape the competition:

> Creating value isn't enough – you also need to capture some of the value you create . . . Americans mythologize competition and credit it with saving us from socialist bread lines . . . [But] capitalism and competition are opposites. Capitalism is premised on the accumulation of capital, but under perfect competition, all profits get competed away. The lesson for entrepreneurs is clear . . . competition is for losers.[71]

---

70 Marx, *Capital*, vol. 1, p. 777.
71 Cited in Adam Tooze, *Crashed: How a Decade of Financial Crises Changed the World*, New York: Viking, 2018, p. 462.

Duncan Foley highlights the paradoxical and contrasting effects of this desire to escape competition, the better to capture value:

> The global pool of surplus value emerges from the social relations of capitalism as an unintended by-product of the competition to appropriate surplus value. Its magnitude is an emergent and contingent phenomenon beyond the influence of any individual capitalist, responsive only to broad political, cultural, and social factors. The immediate competitive challenge for all capitals is the appropriation of a larger share of this pool of surplus value. Some modes of appropriation indirectly contribute to increasing the size of the pool of surplus value, but many, including a wide variety of methods of generating rents, do not.[72]

To put that in other words: in the real competition among dispersed capitals to corner the appropriation of value, some create surplus value while others settle for feeding their profits on transfer, at the expense of other agents.[73] So, from an analytical perspective, the profits of individual firms originate in the local process of labour exploitation *but also* in mechanisms of pure and simple appropriation. Appropriated profits are a levy on the total pool of surplus value which capitalists collectively obtain through the exploitation of labour. They are obtained as the outcome of an internal distributional conflict among the owners of capital. They can also result from a transfer drawn from the income of wage-earning households, such as interest on a consumer loan.

The issue of rent is directly linked to this logic of value appropriation disconnected from engagement in production. This is true of land ownership and natural resources, and it is also true of the financial sector. Marx spoke of 'industrial feudalism' – a phrase he borrowed from

---

72 Duncan K. Foley, 'Rethinking Financial Capitalism and the "Information" Economy', *Review of Radical Political Economics* 45, no. 3, September 2013, p. 261.

73 The concept of 'profits upon alienation', developed by Steuart and taken up by Marx, corresponds to these profits on transfer. See Costas Lapavitsas, *Profiting without Producing: How Finance Exploits Us All*, London: Verso, 2014, pp. 141–7; Shaikh, *Capitalism*, pp. 208–12.

Charles Fourier. He saw the emergence of the Crédit immobilier français, a joint-stock finance company set up under France's Second Empire,
as an attempt to monopolise control of the financing of industry. They do
this, he comments 'not with the view of productive investments, but
simply for the object of stockjobbing profits. The new idea they have
started is to render the industrial feudalism tributary to stockjobbing.'[74]

The reference to feudalism refers to the rentier, or non-productive,
nature of the mechanism for capturing value. This idea of rents prevailing over a properly productive logic can again be found in the case of
intangible-intensive firms, and particularly platforms.[75] The rise of
digital activities raises the question of the future existence of the
competitive process of profit generation. As long as capitals are effectively in competition, as long as consumers can call on different
producers, as long as assets can be transferred, the system will retain its
turbulent dynamic. In this case, appropriation strategies and areas of
surplus-value production will tend to balance each other out; and, if
appropriation activities monopolise too much capital, profit opportunities will appear in the productive sector, which will then attract new
investment. But must that necessarily remain the case? Would it be
possible for profit-generation strategies to be oriented mainly towards
the appropriation rather than the production of value? And, if so, what
would be the macroeconomic consequences? Ultimately, posed in
these terms, the problem is the emergence of predatory regulation in
the age of algorithms.

---

74 Karl Marx, 'The French Crédit Mobilier I', New York Daily Tribune, 21 June
1856, available at marxengels.public-archive.net; Charles Fourier, 'Théorie des quatre
mouvements et des destinées générales, partie 1', Dijon: Les presses du réel, 1998,
available at classiques.uqac.ca, p. 176.

75 This is what Mathieu Montalban and his co-authors note, for example, when
they write: 'The aim of any form of capital is to produce (exchange) value for profit,
not to provide use value, which is just a means for capital. Platforms are capturing
part of the rent from their position as intermediary or "market organiser". Very few
really create value for capital, so their activity resembles a redistribution of surplus
value rather than value creation', Matthieu Montalban, Vincent Frigant, and Bernard
Jullien, 'Platform Economy as a New Form of Capitalism: A Regulationist Research
Programme', Cambridge Journal of Economics 43, no. 4, 2019, p. 16.

Published in 1899, Thorstein Veblen's *The Theory of the Leisure Class* is the first of the few works economics devoted to the problem of preda- tion. His fundamental hypothesis is that predation persists also under capitalism – a reading he bases on a distinction between the system of production and strategies that seek profits through monopolisation, a phenomenon he constantly emphasised throughout his work.[76] From this perspective, the maximisation of returns on capital does not depend on the maximisation of production, but rather on the maximisation of control over collective life in general.[77] This control involves the control of strategic elements – intangible assets, reserved knowledge, or exclu- sive production goods – all of which are grouped together under the general term of good-will:

> Good-will taken in its wider meaning comprises such things as estab-
> lished customary business relations, reputation for upright dealing,
> franchises and privileges, trade-marks, brands, patent rights, copy-
> rights, exclusive use of special processes guarded by law or by secrecy,
> exclusive control of particular sources of materials. All these items
> give a differential advantage to their owners, but they are of no aggre-
> gate advantage to the community. They are wealth to the individuals
> concerned – differential wealth; but they make no part of the wealth of
> nations.[78]

In his technocratic vision, Veblen believed that, so long as the reins were handed over to engineers, the economy could provide for the entire population's prosperity. He, moreover, conceived an operational plan for an economy administered by a 'soviet of technicians' serving the

---

76 Thorstein Veblen, *The Theory of the Leisure Class*, Oxford: Oxford University Press, 1899; Marc-André Gagnon, 'Penser le capitalisme cognitif selon Thorstein Veblen: connaissance, pouvoir et capital', *Interventions économiques* 36, 2007, p. 569.

77 Ibid.

78 Thorstein Veblen, *The Theory of Business Enterprise*, Eastbourne: Gardners Books, 1904, p. 167.

material well-being of the greater number.[79] But he also lamented the subordination of the engineers to the particular interests of the owners of the means of production. While most of his contemporaries were bedazzled by the progress of industry, Veblen noted the obstacles that had been imposed on it. In his view, the main activity of business circles did not consist in organising production. Rather, their activity sabotaged the productive process, as each actor strove to hold the others to ransom more effectively:

> In the common run of cases the proximate aim of the business man is to upset or block the industrial process at some one or more points. His strategy is commonly directed against other business interests and his ends are commonly accomplished by the help of some form of pecuniary coercion.[80]

One of Veblen's strongest insights was his grasp of the modern character of the formation of a predatory class:

> Predation cannot become the habitual, conventional resource of any group or any class until industrial methods have been developed to such a degree of efficiency as to leave a margin worth fighting for, above the subsistence of those engaged in getting a living.[81]

So economic efficiency and innovation do not stand opposed to the rise of predatory standards. The opposite is true: the more economically developed a society is, the more it offers potential bases for predation. This is the premise on which the techno-feudal hypothesis is based.

Predation is an economic mechanism of allocation by appropriation. In the context of a predatory regulation of the economy, the aggregate result is at best a zero-sum game – if the appropriation corresponds to a

---

79 Thorstein Veblen, *The Engineers and the Price System*, London: Routledge, 1921, chapter 4.
80 Veblen, *The Theory of Business Enterprise*, p. 35.
81 Veblen, *The Theory of the Leisure Class*, p. 19.

simple transfer of value – and at worst a negative-sum game, if the process of predation itself entails costs and destruction. The historical contrast becomes clear when Perry Anderson compares the economic dynamics of conflict within the nobility with those of inter-capitalist competition:

> The normal medium of inter-capitalist competition is economic, and its structure is typically additive: rival parties may both expand and prosper – although unequally . . . because the production of manufactured commodities is inherently unlimited. The typical medium of inter-feudal rivalry, by contrast, was military and its structure was always potentially the zero-sum conflict of the battlefield, by which fixed quantities of ground were won or lost. For land is a natural monopoly: it cannot be indefinitely extended, only re-divided.[82]

Unlike parasitism, predation involves a relationship of domination between the predator and his victims.[83] So, according to this distinction, a pickpocket is not a predator, but a mafia godfather is. In the case of a classic military conflict, domination is established ex post by the victory of one party over another and the appropriation of the resources that this makes possible. But if the asymmetry is already present *ex ante*, we are, instead, dealing with the model of a predator hunting its prey.

This cynegetic (or 'hunting') model has two variants. In the first, the prey is exterminated or expelled, with the predator acting essentially as an aggressor. This is the case in ethnic cleansing operations where the land and property of the targeted population are appropriated by the aggressors. In the second, the predator may don the guise of a protector. For instance, in the case of ancient slavery, the predator adapted his behaviour to limit the relative gains that the prey could hope to make by fleeing, and this in turn allowed him to reduce the cost of surveillance.[84]

---

82 Anderson, *Lineages of the Absolutist State*, p. 31.
83 Vahabi, *The Political Economy of Predation*, chapter 1.
84 Moses I. Finley, *Economy and Society in Ancient Greece*, London: Penguin, 1983.

We can thus identify a form of continuity between the logic of subjugation and that of property.[85]

As Mehrdad Vahabi explains, what is decisive in the predatory relationship of the hunting type is the prior asymmetry between predator and prey: 'The presence of domination *ex ante* determines the party who is able to behave both as aggressor and protector in contrast to the party that can only act as its own protector without being able to reciprocate aggression.'[86]

Appropriation costs, domination, and exit costs are each apposite categories for thinking about the dynamics of the digital economy. In this context, appropriation costs refer to the initial investment needed to drive a dynamic of hyperscale growth. For a start-up, these will be fixed costs – for example, the design of an algorithm and the development of an interface. In the case of an acquisition, they concern the price a company pays to acquire a new strategic position in the digital realm. In both situations, these are sunk costs – the investment is essentially lost if the project being financed fails.

Secondly, domination is consubstantial with the mechanism of algorithmic governmentality and with its political dimension of surveilling, anticipating, and controlling behaviour. Whether we are talking about consumers, workers, or subaltern capitals in global value chains, the connections between information systems and practices serve to establish overlord positions – what we might call a spectral presence. These positions give those who control them a structural advantage, notably through the centralisation of data.

Finally, dependence on the digital glebe now conditions the social existence of both individuals and organisations. The flip side of this attachment is the prohibitive nature of the costs of escape and, as a result, the generalisation of situations of capture that fetter the competitive dynamic.

---

85 Just as there is a form of continuity between hunting and pastoralism. See Grégoire Chamayou, *Manhunts: A Philosophical History*, Princeton, NJ: Princeton University Press, 2012, chapter 3.

86 Vahabi, *The Political Economy of Predation*, p. 100.

Here, we have identified how predation prevails over production in the political economy of the digital. Yet this poses more questions than it solves. From the point of view of macro-economic dynamics, it suggests that investment in the protection and expansion of control over digital rents takes precedence over productive investment. This clearly shows the reactionary nature of the emerging mode of production.

Conclusion

Fortunes and Misfortunes
of Socialisation

Looking back with three decades' hindsight, we can see that the intuitions behind the Silicon Valley consensus have not *all* been proven wrong. One insight was correct: the transformations accompanying the rise of information technologies really are affecting the foundations of the mode of production, destabilising its basic principles. But, where techno-capitalist optimism promised a rejuvenating cure, the course of events instead points to degeneration. The rise of digital technology is overturning competitive relations in favour of relations of dependence, upsetting the overall mechanism and tending to give precedence to predation over production. It is this that gives rise to what I have called techno-feudalism.

Today, the question of overcoming capitalism is again being raised. This is not only because of effects of capitalism, such as the – politically explosive – increase in the concentration of property ownership, or the ecological doldrums into which this mode of development is driving us. Rather, it is also that a qualitative shift is taking place in the logic of this system. The tech giants' operations are essentially 'sabotage', in the sense that Veblen proposed, as they direct the powers of information towards creating mechanisms for capturing value. And yet, this socio-economic reordering also extends beyond the tech sector to encompass all fields of activity, as in the case of the monopolisation of intellectual property in value chains.

Over this shifting landscape hovers the spirit of the hackers of the 1980s: as the *Hacker Manifesto* author put it, 'This is our world now . . . the world of the electron and the switch.'[1] But even now, theoretical and political critique is still in its infancy. How can we map the circuits of rent extraction? How are they connected to the financial system and, in particular, to the mega-investment funds that organise its centralisation? How do they feed off the exploitation of click workers, the gig economy, or, indeed, older forms of wage labour?[2] Who are the prey, and under what conditions could their subjectivities come together in an alternative social power? Most of these questions remain to be explored.

Identifying the qualitative shift at work in contemporary capitalism is, then, only the beginning. But it is enough to provoke a powerful parallax effect, striking at both the liberal doxa and its only real adversary, the Marxist tradition.

From a liberal perspective, the digital economy is an ideological conundrum. For those who see competition as intrinsically virtuous, the digital citadels surely ought to be dismantled by regulators in order to restore healthy competition. The difficulty – rightly emphasised by the major firms in the sector – is that the force of feedback loops in the digital world produces centralisation. So, any effort at breaking them up implies a destruction of use-values, insofar as reduced data pools generate less agile algorithms and, ultimately, less user-friendly devices. In other words, the economic logic of consumer utility, which is the alpha and omega of the digital economy, stands against a renewal of antitrust measures, however much these latter are stimulated by real threats that the new mega-corporations pose to our societies.

---

1 The Mentor (Loyd Blankenship), 'The Conscience of a Hacker', *Phrack*, 8 January 1986.

2 The term 'gig economy' refers to the economy built on individualised work tasks. See Antonio A. Casilli, *En attendant les robots. Enquête sur le travail du clic*, Paris: Seuil, 2019; Janine Berg et al., *Digital Labour Platforms and the Future of Work: Towards Decent Work in the Online World*, Geneva: International Labour Organization, 2018.

We are facing a cumulative process that competition policy cannot stop. With the centralisation of this digital glebe, the scenario today taking form is reminiscent of that imagined by the economist John Stuart Mill in a situation where all the land in the country belonged to one man. In that case, 'he could fix the rent at his pleasure. The whole people would be dependent on his will for the necessaries of life, and he might make what conditions he chose.'[3] This generalised dependence on the owners of *das Digital* is the horizon of the digital economy – it means economic liberalism's becoming-cannibalistic in the age of algorithms.

Unlike the liberal viewpoint, the Marxist one is not so brutally invalidated by the techno-feudal mutation of the capitalist mode of production. Rather, it wins a kind of Pyrrhic victory. The historical trend towards socialisation is confirmed – but, at first sight, it takes on the hideous face of a generalised crushing of society.

In fact, market relations are constantly deepening their hold, so that our lives are increasingly dependent on the social division of labour. The concentration of financial resources in the hands of fund managers renders ownership more collective, irrevocably distancing control over the labour process from the right to an economic surplus. Above all, modes of production and consumption are becoming increasingly intelligible and, at the same time, malleable through the algorithmic processing of masses of data. The tendency is towards even the smallest fragments of life becoming incorporated into digital circuits and intertwined in the objectification of a grammar common to all social agents.

The long-awaited hour of full subsumption to capital has struck, leading human civilisation along a ridge between two alternatives. On one side, a steep, rocky slope, that of the catastrophic fall envisaged by Marx in the drafts of *Capital*:

> The *application* of science, that *general* product of social development, to the *direct production process*, has the appearance of a *productive power of capital*, not of labour, or it only appears as a productive power

---

3 John Stuart Mill, *Principles of Political Economy I*, book 2, chapter xvi, in *The Collected Works of John Stuart Mill*, vol. 2, London: Routledge, 1965 [1848], p. 416.

of labour ... and in any case it does not appear as the productive power either of the individual worker or of the workers combined together in the production process.[4]

Through the negation of autonomous, creative activity, individual and collective subjectivities are dislocated. Labour is caught up in this mystification: individuals are no longer anything, and capital is everything. The contemporary epidemics of work-related suffering are partly the result of such a dynamic of disaffection, which demotes human subjects and leaves them derealised.

This disaster extends beyond the sphere of production. Algorithmic governmentality's aspiration to control individuals without leaving any room for the formation of desires can only degenerate into a machine churning out 'sad passions'. The individual, in their work and in every phase of their life, increasingly finds that their existence has been expropriated. The philosopher Étienne Balibar calls the possibility of this definitive defeat a 'total subsumption'. It implies 'a complete loss of individuality ... in the sense of "individualization", or personal identity and autonomy'.[5]

As techno-feudalism gains momentum, this crushing logic is proceeding at great strides. Yet the more progress it makes, the less likely it seems to actually achieve this end-point. The sectors at the cutting edge of fusing the economic and algorithmic logics are running up against the wall of derealisation. Marketing researchers are already observing this with regard to plans to roll out autonomous shopping systems:

Autonomous shopping systems change the shopping process profoundly by reducing or even eliminating the need for human

---

4 Karl Marx, *Capital*, draft of chapter 6, 'Results of the Direct Production Process', in *Marx and Engels Complete Works*, vol. 34, London: Lawrence & Wishart, 1994, p. 472.

5 Étienne Balibar, 'Towards a New Critique of Political Economy: From Generalized Surplus-Value to Total Subsumption', in Peter Osborne, Éric Alliez, and Eric-John Russell, eds, *Capitalism: Concept, Idea, Image – Aspects of Marx's Capital Today*, Kingston, UK: CRMEP Books, 2019, available at eprints.kingston.ac.uk.

decision making, thereby challenging deep-rooted human–machine relationships. On the one hand, removing the decision-making process provides advantages such as the alleviation of cognitive trade-offs. On the other hand, consumers may be reluctant to forgo decision autonomy, their self-regulatory resources may be depleted, and feelings of decision satisfaction may not ensue.[6]

So, companies have been warned: faced with attempts to strip them of their substance, human beings are fleeing. If they do not themselves gain new forms of control, individuals will refuse to let machines take control of their choices for them.

But on the other side of the ridge is something quite different: a picture of radiant green valleys and streams brimming with promises of emancipation. For Marx, the historical law of accumulation favours individual development in certain respects. The fact is, 'large-scale industry . . . makes . . . the fitness of the worker for the maximum number of different kinds of labour into a question of life and death'.[7] It thus pushes for 'the partially developed individual, who is merely the bearer of one specialized social function [to] be replaced by the totally developed individual for whom the different social functions are different modes of activity he takes up in turn'.[8] The socialisation initiated under the auspices of capital thus creates the conditions of possibility for a process of liberation. The power emanating from the interconnection and interweaving of productive activities allows each individual to infinitely expand the range of their own activities.

We already have an evocative representation of the emancipation this could bring: the one offered by Alexander Bogdanov in his utopian book, *Red Star*. In this science fiction novel from 1905, the alien visitor has one of his hosts tell him about the principle of work organisation in this advanced extraterrestrial society:

6 Emanuel de Bellis and Gita Johar, 'Autonomous Shopping Systems: Identifying and Overcoming Barriers to Consumer Adoption', *Journal of Retailing* 96, no. 1, 2020, pp. 74–87.

7 Karl Marx, *Capital*, vol. 1, London: Penguin, 1990, p. 618.

8 Ibid.

The tables are meant to affect the distribution of labor. If they are to do that, everyone must be able to see where there is a labor shortage and just how big it is. Assuming that an individual has the same or an approximately equal aptitude for two vocations, he can then choose the one with the greater shortage.

The system thus allows for real-time adjustments which match the labour supply to the production process and the constant changes in individuals' desires:

The Institute of Statistics has agencies everywhere which keep track of the flow of goods into and out of the stockpiles and monitor the productivity of all enterprises and the changes in their work forces. In that way it can be calculated what and how much must be produced for any given period and the number of man-hours required for the task. The Institute then computes the difference between the existing and the desired situation for each vocational area and communicates the result to all places of employment. Equilibrium is soon established by a stream of volunteers.[9]

This science fiction, with its cybernetics of use value, is in fact already within reach. We learn as much from the McKinsey Institute – though their study explains it rather grudgingly, and without mentioning the question of work:

Leading companies are developing highly integrated planning systems that already use the most advanced analytics and machine-learning solutions available today. These high-tech methods, also referred to as 'advanced planning', will, in the future, take control of steering [economic activity] . . . Like an invisible hand, the system works autonomously, effectively, and efficiently. Planners only have to intervene in exceptional cases to check and make corrections. More than that, the system improves forecasting accuracy, as not only does it

---

9 Alexander Bogdanov, *Red Star*, Bloomington: Indiana University Press, 1984, p. 66.

draw on multiple data sources, it also interconnects them using artificial intelligence and machine learning. At the same time, advanced planning enables an ever-tighter integration of stock management, procurement, logistics, marketing, and sales, leading to greater efficiency improvements.[10]

The future belongs to the invisible hand of algorithms. Thanks to digital feedback loops, the division of labour has ever less need for a chaotic and impoverishing detour via the commodity. But at the dawn of the hegemony of this new kind of economic calculation, a question arises: Who are its operators going to be? The chiefs of the techno-feudal citadels seek to monopolise the intellectual control of the socio-economic processes of production and consumption. But resistance against individual derealisation presents a serious obstacle to this project.

The advent of the 'totally developed individual' requires that the farewell to the market go hand in hand with a reinvestment in subjectivity. This must especially take the form of a genuine economic democracy. Only then will the freely chosen limits of individual autonomy be compatible with a collective and conscious mastery of the economic question – and of its place in the biosphere.

---

10 Nikolaus Föbus, Tim Lange, Markus Leopoldseder, and Karl-Hendrik Magnus, 'The Invisible Hand: On the Path to Autonomous Planning in Food Retail', McKinsey Institute, August 2019.

Appendix I
Productivity and Price Indexes: Truly Political Questions

The period since the 1950s has seen recurrent controversies about the supposed underestimation of productivity, and its corollary in the overestimation of price levels. Such polemics have, by and large, been raised by conservative economists who seek to cut social benefits. Since the price level indicator is used to determine the size of various kinds of welfare payments, any change to it is bound to affect the scale of state-led income redistribution.[1] These economists prefer to conceive of the price index as an 'index for analysing the cost of living at constant utility'. They therefore insist on also taking into account improvements to existing products and new goods and services that are supposed to increase consumer utility: the switch from fixed-line telephones to mobile phones, from Michelin maps to Google Maps, from the local film club to Prime Video, etc. This approach leads to a downward revision of inflation and the social incomes that are linked to it by legal norms. Conversely, when trade unions were more

---

1 There was a major debate on this subject in the United States in the 1950s and then another in the 1990s. See Michael J. Boskin et al., 'Consumer Prices, the Consumer Price Index, and the Cost of Living', *Journal of Economic Perspectives* 12, no. 1, 1998, pp. 3–26.

powerful, they stood for an index based on household spending. This approach instead points to the idea of an increase in the cost of living, which also includes changes in the number and type of necessary goods over time. Looking at 'inflation as perceived and experienced by households in their role as consumer' has been recently again a matter of interest for statisticians.[2]

Beyond this question of distribution, conceptions of price indexes and their uses are a focus of deep dispute in society – in which problems specifically regarding quality cannot be reduced to an underestimation of the importance of technological improvements.[3] A consideration of the relational dimension of services and the issues around planned obsolescence allows us instead to see tendencies pointing to an underestimation of the rise in prices. For example, the blinds installed on the windows of a French home, or the furniture bought from a big retailer to fit out a kitchen, will have a much shorter lifespan than the cherry-wood cupboards that adorn the living room of an old farmhouse in the Auvergne, or the wooden shutters that have been repainted many times to protect the windows for many decades. Adjusted for the quality effect, the price of modern blinds and furniture, destined to be replaced after no more than fifteen years, tends to be undervalued compared with that of products designed to last for generations. From this point of view, productivity and growth are therefore overestimated and inflation underestimated. Furthermore, the shift to online shopping radically alters the social experience of shopping and the relationships in which it is embedded – a fact which is difficult to capture in price indexes.

---

2 J. Astin and J. Leyland, 'Measuring Inflation as Households See It: Next Steps for the Household Costs Indices', ONS paper, 2023.

3 On the debates concerning the construction of the price index and its uses in the French context, see Florence Jany-Catrice, 'Conflicts in the Calculation and Use of the Price Index: The Case of France', *Cambridge Journal of Economics* 42, no. 4, 2018, pp. 963–86; Florence Jany-Catrice, *L'Indice des prix à la consommation*, Paris: La Découverte, 2019. For the US see T. A. Stapleford, *The Cost of Living in America: A Political History of Economic Statistics, 1880–2000*, Cambridge: Cambridge University Press, 2009.

The construction of inflation figures, and thus of growth and productivity numbers, is the result of political and social *choices*, which bear considerable influence on the way our societies talk about themselves and organise themselves. It expresses judgements about legitimate needs that deserve to be better explained and publicised, as do their connection with the rise of new indicators of wealth.[4]

---

4 On the thorny question of needs and the political issues involved therein, see Razmig Keucheyan, *Les Besoins artificiels. Comment sortir du consumérisme*, Paris: Zones, 2019.

Appendix II

Hipster Antitrust against the Chicago School

At the end of 2018, the journal *Competition Policy International* devoted a special issue to what one of its editors, Konstantin Medvedovsky, calls 'hipster antitrust'. He used this term to refer to the renewed appeal, in the competition policy field, of ideas hostile to big firms:

> The consumer welfare standard in antitrust is an important part of antitrust law and practice in the United States, but an increasing number of policy thinkers are starting to question whether it should maintain its primacy. Should courts and antitrust enforcers balance factors such as employment, wages, small businesses against consumer welfare effects in evaluating mergers and conduct? Do we need special rules for technology platforms in particular? Should we just bar large firms from making any further acquisitions or even consider just breaking them up? And if we should reconsider the consumer welfare paradigm, what would an alternate regime actually look like?[1]

---

1 Konstantin Medvedovsky, 'Letter from the Editor', in 'Hipster Antitrust', special issue, *Antitrust Chronicle* 1, no. 1, April 2018, competitionpolicyinternational.com.

Since the 1980s, competition policy in the United States has been dominated by Chicago School doctrine. This is a position very much in favour of big business, which believes that government intervention in the field of competition has often been harmful and should therefore be strictly limited to cases where the harm to consumers has been clearly established. Richard Posner, one of the leading figures in this current, sums up their argument as follows:

> Firms cannot in general obtain or enhance monopoly power by unilateral action – unless, of course, they are irrationally willing to trade profits for position. Consequently, the focus of the antitrust laws should not be on unilateral action; it should instead be on: (1) cartels and (2) horizontal mergers large enough either to create monopoly directly . . . or to facilitate cartelization.[2]

Clearly, Posner's main concern is the formation of illicit cartels. But beyond that, he proposes that we put our faith in the forces of competition – whether actual or potential. In particular, public authorities should not concern themselves with 'unilateral actions', which mainly means two things: predatory pricing and vertical integration.

Predatory pricing is a tactic whereby a dominant company tries to squeeze out its competitors by charging prices below its production costs. For Posner, this strategy is doomed to failure:

> The predator loses money during the period of predation and, if he tries to recoup it later by raising his price, new entrants will be attracted, the price will be bid down to the competitive level, and the attempt at recoupment will fail.[3]

In short, the game is not worth the candle, since the aspirant predator will lose out every time.

---

2 Richard A. Posner, 'The Chicago School of Antitrust Analysis', *University of Pennsylvania Law Review* 127, 1979, p. 928.

3 Ibid., p. 927.

Posner likewise claims that vertical integration is another unilateral action that does not risk distorting the market. For him,

> it makes no sense for a monopoly producer to take over distribution in order to earn monopoly profits at the distribution as well as the manufacturing level. The product and its distribution are complements, and an increase in the price of distribution will reduce the demand for the product.

This would hurt the company's sales and therefore ruin any hope of surplus profits. In conclusion, vertical integration will only take place if it is 'motivated by a desire for efficiency rather than for monopoly'.[4]

Without going further into the details of this analysis, we can indicate what its main upshot is. Public intervention does not need to concern itself with the problem of industrial concentration:

> Persistent concentration implies either that the market in question simply does not have room for many firms (economies of scale) or that some firms are able persistently to obtain abnormal profits by cost reductions or product improvements that competitors and new entrants are unable to duplicate. Neither case is an attractive one for public intervention designed to change the market structure.[5]

A monopolistic position is not in itself contrary to the common good. It is harmful only if it is based on the existence of barriers to entry that prevent competition. Otherwise, the possibility of a new competitor entering the market will be enough to discipline existing firms. From the Chicago School's perspective, these barriers to entry are few in number and non-determining.[6] In practice, there are only two important scenarios. The first is one in which new entrants have to pay an

---

4 Ibid.

5 Ibid., p. 945.

6 The classic definition was given by Georges J. Stigler, *The Organization of Industry*, Homewood, IL: Richard D. Irwin, 1968, pp. 67–70.

excessively high-risk premium to their capital provider, because of their inexperience in this new field of activity. However, according to the Chicago School doctrine, this additional cost of financing new entrants is insufficient to fundamentally alter the market's competitive nature. In the second case, considered as an exceptional situation, the monopoly is based on the control of an exclusive resource. As a general rule, markets are deemed contestable and therefore competitive.[7]

The Amazon Paradox

Chicago-style antitrust ideas stem from the anarcho-capitalist tendencies which Michel Foucault analysed in his *The Birth of Biopolitics*.[8] This antitrust approach takes an extremely cautious approach to state intervention and looks kindly on big businesses' strategies. Even if it is not literally implemented by US political authorities, it has exerted a dominant influence on competition policies since the 1980s.[9]

However, since the turn of the millennium, and during the 2010s more particularly, industrial concentration has accelerated spectacularly in the United States, especially in the digital sector (see chapter 1). In response to this new situation, the anti-monopoly movement has grown considerably stronger. It is now a rallying cry of the Democratic Party. Back in 2016, the party's election platform stated that it wanted to 'promote competition by stopping corporate concentration'. It explains:

> We will make competition policy and antitrust stronger and more
> responsive to our economy today . . . We support the historic purpose
> of the antitrust laws to protect competition and prevent excessively

---

7 William J. Baumol, John C. Panzar and Robert D. Willig, *Contestable Markets and the Theory of Industry Structure*, New York: Harcourt Brace Jovanovich, 1982.

8 See below, p. 212.

9 Jonathan B. Baker, 'Policy Watch: Developments in Antitrust Economics', *Journal of Economic Perspectives* 13, no. 1, 1999, pp. 181–94; Jonathan B. Baker, 'The Case for Antitrust Enforcement', *Journal of Economic Perspectives* 17, no. 4, 2003, pp. 27–50.

consolidated economic and political power, which can be corrosive to a healthy democracy. We support reinvigorating DOJ and FTC enforcement of antitrust laws to prevent abusive behavior by dominant companies, and protecting the public interest against abusive, discriminatory, and unfair methods of commerce.[10]

This position breaks sharply with the reductionism of the Chicago approach, which focuses on consumer welfare alone. It is concerned with the dangers that an excessive concentration of economic power entails for the mechanism of competition and even for democratic politics. Rooted in US society since the nineteenth century, this position was marginalised from the Reagan era onwards. Yet today, it is making a strong comeback thanks to a series of studies documenting the increase in concentration in the US economy, the decline in entrepreneurship, and, above all, the link between these phenomena and rising inequalities.[11]

Among these studies, Lina Khan's piece published in the *Yale Law Journal* in 2017 is now a point of reference. Khan is a lawyer who worked with Barry Lynn's team at the New America Foundation and then at the Open Market Institute before studying at Yale. She was nominated by President Joe Biden as chairwoman of the Federal Trade Commission in 2021. Her 2017 article is entitled 'Amazon's Antitrust Paradox', in reference to Robert Bork's 1978 book, *The Antitrust Paradox: A Policy at War with Itself*.[12]

The paradox that Bork tackled can be summarised as follows: by pursuing multiple simultaneous objectives, and targeting a vague idea of domination, antitrust policies in the United States end up undermining what should be their main objective: market efficiency. He thus issues a plea for a prudent antitrust policy that refuses to make the issue of

---

10 '2016 Democratic Party Platform', American Presidency Project, 21 July 2016, presidency.ucsb.edu.

11 David Autor et al., 'Concentrating on the Fall of the Labor Share', *American Economic Review* 107, no. 5, 2017, pp. 180–5.

12 Robert H. Bork, *The Antitrust Paradox: A Policy at War with Itself*, New York: Free Press, 1993.

dominance a problem, so long as the forces of competition remain at work, however latently.

For Khan, the paradox is quite a different one. Her case study of Amazon reveals both the limits of Bork's doctrine and those of the Chicago School:

> Due to a change in legal thinking and practice in the 1970s and 1980s, antitrust law now assesses competition largely with an eye to the short-term interests of consumers, not producers or the health of the market as a whole; antitrust doctrine views low consumer prices, alone, to be evidence of sound competition. By this measure, Amazon has excelled; it has evaded government scrutiny in part through fervently devoting its business strategy and rhetoric to reducing prices for consumers. Amazon's closest encounter with antitrust authorities was when the Justice Department sued other companies for teaming up against Amazon. It is as if Bezos charted the company's growth by first drawing a map of antitrust laws, and then devising routes to smoothly bypass them. With its missionary zeal for consumers, Amazon has marched toward monopoly by singing the tune of contemporary antitrust.[13]

Khan's contribution sheds a great deal of light. On the one hand, she closely engages with the Chicago doctrine – and the arguments against it from the theoretical and practical tradition of US antitrust the past two centuries. On the other hand, she conducts an in-depth examination of Amazon's anti-competitive practices. Her conclusion is unequivocal: Amazon is a tentacular firm, with multiple anti-competitive practices, yet it manages to avoid being reeled in by the law.

Khan describes numerous situations where Amazon's conduct ought to have prompted a reaction from the authorities: for example, the fact that Amazon sells bestselling books, the Kindle e-reader, or its Amazon Prime service at below cost, enabling the company to establish a

---

13 Lina M. Khan, 'Amazon's Antitrust Paradox', *Yale Law Journal* 126, no. 3, 2016, p. 716.

dominant position in various fields and play on their complementarities to reinforce network effects. The antitrust doctrine currently in force is unable to see where and how Amazon manages to offset its losses – though this is characteristic of its abuse of a dominant position. In the books sector, its building of a hegemonic position raises the risk of reducing the diversity of products available to consumers. This is also a political risk, since the organisation of the book sector is directly linked to that of the circulation of ideas.[14]

Another illustration of this argument is the fact that Amazon is a sales platform for various producers, which gives it a privileged position as an observer. After all, if it sees that a manufacturer's product is a great success, it will soon market a version under its own brand, which is sold at a lower price or better promoted, and which will inevitably corner the lion's share of the market. For example, when Amazon saw how popular stuffed animal pillows modelled on National Football League mascots were with consumers, it was quick to release these products under its own brand name, sidelining the original producer.

Amazon is also one of the most powerful IT services companies, not least because of the cloud storage space it offers to businesses. Here again, the combination of different businesses enables the company to increase its advantage. For example, it has been shown that Amazon has used server usage data to identify, via traffic volumes, start-ups whose business is taking off and thus guide its venture capital operations.

Limits to Competition

Through her study of the Amazon case, Khan diagnoses the failure of the Chicago approach and the policies inspired by it. Firstly, even if the sole criterion is consumer welfare, price does not provide sufficient grounds for judgement: antitrust policy must also integrate a concern for quality, diversity, and innovation over the long term. By this yardstick, industrial

---

14 Ibid., p. 767.

concentration is a threat that must be taken seriously. But such a broad-
ening of criteria is not enough, either:

> The undue focus on consumer welfare is misguided. It betrays legisla-
> tive history, which reveals that Congress passed antitrust laws to
> promote a host of political economic ends – including our interests as
> workers, producers, entrepreneurs, and citizens. It also mistakenly
> supplants a concern about process and structure (i.e., whether power is
> sufficiently distributed to keep markets competitive) with a calculation
> regarding outcome (i.e., whether consumers are materially better off).[15]

Here, Khan is reasserting the traditional approach to US antitrust,
which prevailed up until the 1970s. Often described as structuralist, it
emphasises market structures and makes the degree of concentration a
criterion of judgement in its own right. She argues that, in matters of
competition, the authorities must take multiple interests into account:
producers, consumers, workers, and citizens must all be protected
against monopoly abuse.

The damaging effects of excessive concentration of economic power
can take many forms: undue pressure on suppliers, consumer capture,
control of the political system through the media, etc. Or it may produce
situations where firms are so large that they are able to obtain multiple
advantages and support from the public authorities. They become 'too
big to fail', for their collapse would present a systemic threat.

All these arguments about the economic, social, and political dangers
of concentration of economic power are perfectly valid. But Khan's argument, and the 'hipster antitrust' thesis, go further: they do not just point
out the dangers of private monopolies, but also value competition for its
own sake. Ultimately, Khan shares with the authors of Magna Carta the
aspiration for a decentralised and harmonious competitive order. They
share the same normative ideal of an economy of private entrepreneurs.
From this perspective, competition is not a means but an end, a desirable
objective in itself.

---

15 Ibid., p. 737.

Antitrust policy must prevent too much industrial concentration, because it constitutes a threat to competition. In this respect, Khan is very clear: 'Antitrust law and competition policy should promote not welfare but competitive markets.' The aim is to preserve 'the neutrality of the competitive process and the openness of market structures'.[16] On this point, it is worth emphasising the affinity between the hipster antitrust approach in the US, the European Union's competition policy, and the ordoliberal doctrine on which it is based.

The proceedings brought in the EU against the US digital giants cost Google two record fines in 2017 and 2018, totalling €6.7 billion. In the first case, Google was fined for favouring the visibility of its shopping comparison tool in its search engine. In the other, it was penalised for forcing manufacturers of Android phones to pre-install a package of Google services, thereby centralising user data on the majority of all smartphones. Barry Lynn was ousted from the New America Foundation following a press release which welcomed the ruling against Google in Europe.

Conversely, it was Lina Khan's work that prompted the European Commission to open an investigation into Amazon. Margrethe Vestager, the commissioner responsible for competition, echoed Khan's analysis when she said that what was at issue was Amazon's dual role, as both a distribution platform for other companies' products and a sales site for its own. This integrated structure gives Amazon exclusive access to its customers' and suppliers' data, on which it bases its supremacy.[17]

With the battle over hipster antitrust, we are seeing a new phase in an internal struggle within neoliberalism. On the one hand, the heirs of the Chicago approach are siding with what Michel Foucault calls anarcho-capitalism, which is hostile in principle to any form of state intervention in the economic and social sphere. On the other hand, the advocates of traditional antitrust are re-enacting a rapprochement between different currents that took place in the United States from 1938 onwards.

---

16 Ibid., pp. 737, 744.
17 Natalia Drozdiak and David McLaughlin, 'With Amazon Probe, EU Takes Cue from "Hipster" Antitrust', bloomberg.com, 19 September 2018.

In that moment, institutionalist and neoliberal economists were converging, as the former abandoned their preference for public regulation and cooperation, and the latter moved away from the precepts of laissez-faire. Public intervention against monopolies was seen as necessary. For the former, the aim was to prevent an excessive concentration of economic power from threatening political freedoms. The latter wished to preserve the quality of the process of allocating resources through prices.[18]

This desire to give structure to competition was exactly what marked the ordoliberal approach. Ordoliberalism was central to the doctrine that guided the economic policy of the Federal Republic of Germany after 1945, and subsequently European integration. Wilhelm Röpke, one of the most eminent representatives of this movement, whom Foucault cites, wrote in the 1930s: 'The free market requires an active and extremely vigilant policy.'[19] By advocating active state intervention to protect competition, in the name of its own intrinsic virtues, Lina Khan and the hipster anti-monopolists are following in the ordoliberals' footsteps.

Ultimately, despite the differences between hipster antitrust and the Chicago anarcho-capitalist approach, these two currents share the same confidence in private enterprise and the virtues of market coordination. They diverge in their analysis of the quality of the economic process resulting from the development of information technologies.

Hipster anti-monopolists can, however, be credited for pointing out the threats associated with the titanic accumulation of economic and political power resulting from the exponential growth of digital platforms. The danger is there: the big web firms have become impregnable citadels, capable of repelling their competitors' assaults, buying up start-ups or placing them under their thumb, and influencing the political agenda and the terms of public debate. But the question that these

---

18 Thierry Kirat and Frédéric Marty, *The Late Emerging Consensus among American Economists on Antitrust Laws in the Second New Deal*, Montreal: Centre interuniversitaire de recherche en analyse des organisations, 2019.

19 Michel Foucault, *The Birth of Biopolitics: Lectures at the Collège de France, 1978–79*, London: Routledge, 2008.

writers avoid is that of the sources of this power, the efficiency gains associated with concentration.

In the age of Big Data, the question is whether the dynamics of monopolisation are appropriate to grasping the type of economic process which is today under way. The heirs of the Chicago School have an easy time of pointing to the body of evidence which suggests that increased concentration is the result of technical changes in economies of scale and corresponding productivity improvements.[20] In other words, reintroducing competition, for example by breaking up Google or Amazon, would weaken the services actually on offer. By focusing solely on the question of firms' market power, hipster anti-monopolists miss an essential issue: the change in the quality of the economic process which is associated with the development of information technologies.

---

20 Joshua D. Wright et al., 'Requiem for a Paradox: The Dubious Rise and Inevitable Fall of Hipster Antitrust', George Mason Law and Economics Research Paper no. 18-29, 2018, p. 27.

Acknowledgements

I would like to thank Razmig Keucheyan, Hannah Bensussan, Raphaël Porcherot, Cecilia Rikap, and participants in the Planifier les communs seminar; Bernard Chavance, Thierry Kirat, Mehrdad Vahabi, and the participants in the État prédateur seminar; Bruno Amable, Mary O'Sullivan, and participants in the UNIGE Political Economy seminar; Tristan Auvray, Riccardo Bellofiore, McKenzie Wark, William Milberg, Arthur Jatteau, Florence Jany-Catrice, Stefano Palombarini, Duncan Foley, Anwar Shaikh, Marc-André Gagnon, Mathieu Montalban, François Moreau, Nathan Sperber, Olivier Weinstein (†), Benjamin Coriat, Thierry Labica, Sterenn Lebayle, Luis Miotti, Agnès Labrousse, Céline Baud, Sébastien Villemot, Stathis Kouvelakis, David Flacher, Philippe Askenazy, Audrey Cerdan, Nabil Wakim, Mélanie Tanous, and, of course, Jeanne, Loul, Isidore, La Rocaille, Valcivières, and the cheerful company of 108.

I carried out this research under the auspices of the CEPN (CNRS, Sorbonne Paris Nord University), whose team I would like to thank. In the preparatory phase, IFRIS supported my spell at the economics department of the New School (New York).

Index